Culture and Revolution

CULTURE AND REVOLUTION

*Edited by Paul Dukes
and John Dunkley*

Pinter Publishers
London and New York

First published in Great Britain in 1990 by
Pinter Publishers Limited
25 Floral Street, London WC2E 9DS

British Library Cataloguing in Publication Data

A CIP catalogue record for this book is available from the
British Library

ISBN 0 86187 788 8

Library of Congress Cataloging-in-Publication Data

Culture and revolution / edited by Paul Dukes and John Dunkley.
    p. cm.
    "Most of the papers in this volume were delivered at the Third Annual Cultural History
Conference, held in the University of Aberdeen in July 1888"—Foreword.
    Conference sponsored by the Aberdeen University Cultural History Group.
    Includes bibliographical references.
    ISBN 0-86187-788-8
    1. Civilization, Modern—18th century—History—Congresses.
    2. Great Britain—History—Revolution of 1688—Influence—Congresses.
    3. France—History—Revolution, 1789–1799—Congresses.
    4. Revolutions—Europe—History—Congresses. I. Dukes, Paul, 1934–.
II. Dunkley, John, III. Cultural History Conference (3rd: 1988
University of Aberdeen)
IV. Aberdeen University Cultural History Group.
CB411.C85   1989   89-25567
909.7—dc20   CIP

Typeset by Selectmove Ltd, London
Printed and bound in Great Britain by
Biddles Ltd of Guildford and Kings Lynn

322910

CONTENTS

THE CONTRIBUTORS

Jeremy Black is Lecturer in History at the University of Durham. His output includes, among other books, *The English Press in the Eighteenth Century* (London, 1987). His *Eighteenth-Century Europe, 1700–1789*, is due for publication in 1989.

Terry Brotherstone is Lecturer in History at the University of Aberdeen. He is the editor of *Covenant, Charter and Party*, a collection of essays to be published in 1989, and has contributed articles to the *Journal of the Scottish Labour History Society*, and the *New Edinburgh Review*.

Jennifer Carter is Senior Lecturer in History at the University of Aberdeen. She is co-editor (along with Joan Pittock-Wesson) of *Aberdeen and the Enlightenment* (Aberdeen, 1987) and General Editor of the Aberdeen University Quincentenary History Project. She has also produced several articles and essays on late seventeenth- and eighteenth-century English history.

Micheline Cuénin was formerly Professor of French Literature at Paris III University. Her major works include *Roman et société sous Louis XIV: l'oeuvre de Mme de Villedieu* (Paris, 1979), *Le Duel sous L'Ancien Régime* (Paris, 1982) and critical editions of works by Madame de Lafayette, Madame de Villedieu and Molière.

Paul Dukes is Professor of History at the University of Aberdeen. His most recent book is *The Last Great Game: USA versus USSR: Events, Conjunctures, Structures* (London, 1989). His earlier works are on Russian, European and comparative history.

John Dunkley is Senior Lecturer in French at the University of Aberdeen. His major publications include *Gambling: A social and moral problem in France, 1685–1792* (Oxford, 1985), a study of Beaumarchais's *Barbier de Séville* (forthcoming), and critical editions of works by Dufresny, Regnard and Crébillon père.

Robert Lawson-Peebles is Lecturer in American and Commonwealth Arts at the University of Exeter. He formerly taught at Oxford, Princeton and Aberdeen. He is the author of *Landscape and Written Expression in Revolutionary America* (Cambridge, 1988) and is co-editor (along with Mike Gidley) of *Views of American Landscapes* (Cambridge, 1989).

David Lovejoy, formerly Professor of History at the University of Wisconsin and now resident in England, is the author of several works on American colonial history, including *The Glorious Revolution in America* (New York, 1972) and *Religious Enthusiasm in the New World: Heresy to Revolution* (Cambridge, Mass., 1985).

John Pappas, formerly Professor of French at Fordham University and now resident in France, is the author of *Berthier's Journal de Trévoux and the Philosophes* (Geneva, 1957), *Voltaire and d'Alembert* (Bloomington, 1962) and a range of other articles and essays on eighteenth-century French intellectual history.

Noel Parker has worked in Manchester as a regional academic member of the Open University for over a decade, teaching on political, philosophical and historical topics, and administering. He is the author of *Portrayals of Revolution: Images, Debates and Patterns of Thought on the French Revolution* (London, 1989). He is a regular contributor to *Radical Philosophy*.

Murray Pittock, formerly British Academy Research Fellow at the University of Aberdeen, is Lecturer in English at the University of Edinburgh. He is the author of *New Jacobite Songs of the Forty-Five* (forthcoming) and is currently completing *The Invention of Scotland: The Stuart Myth and the Scottish Identity*.

Richard Sher is Professor in the Department of Humanities at the New Jersey Institute of Technology and Secretary of the Eighteenth-Century Scottish Studies Society. He is the author of *Church and University in the Scottish Enlightenment* (Edinburgh, 1985) and a number of other pieces on aspects of eighteenth-century Scottish intellectual history.

Richard Stites, Professor of History at Georgetown University, is the author of several works on the cultural history of revolutionary Russia and the women's emancipation movement. His most recent book is *Revolutionary Dreams: Utopian Vision and Experimental Life in the Russian Revolution* (New York, 1989).

FOREWORD

Most of the chapters in this volume were papers delivered at the Third Annual Cultural History Conference, held in the University of Aberdeen in July 1988. The conference was organised by Joan Pittock-Wesson, convener of the Aberdeen University Cultural History Group, with the collaboration of John Dunkley. The support of British Petroleum, Gillanders Motors (Dyce) Ltd, Grampian Regional Council, Waterstone's Booksellers and the University of Aberdeen is gratefully acknowledged.

The editors would like to record their thanks to William Scott, of the Aberdeen University History Department, for the expert advice he offered on some of the papers.

The book is dedicated to the memory of Donal Byrne, Richard Hallett and Nicola Mackie.

Paul Dukes
John Dunkley

INTRODUCTION

Paul Dukes

At first glance, the two terms contradict each other. 'Culture', suggests, slow movement; 'revolution' is swift and sudden. Possibly, they can be reconciled if we accept the concept of a 'long revolution', but that seems to describe a process more akin to evolution.

Certainly, the culminating moments of the major political revolutions of the Western world from the seventeenth century onwards have been short and sharp, literally in the case of the executions of Charles I and Louis XVI, more figuratively with the Declaration of Independence and the storming of the Winter Palace. Yet explanations of such events cannot be satisfactory without longer perspectives, without the consideration of conjunctures and structures.

The adoption of these terms leads us back to the idea of culture, the *longue durée* comprising the deeper currents which govern the basic direction of the quicker movements at the top – 'surface disturbances, crests of foam that the tides of history carry on their strong backs'. The quotation is of course from Fernand Braudel, for so long doyen of the *Annales* school of interpretation which was formed before the Second World War and developed after it, and we are thereby reminded of the basic circumstances that our view of earlier revolutions is through a twentieth-century lens. Hence, the decision to include two essays on the impact of the Russian Revolution along with ten others on the period from the 'Glorious and Bloodless' Revolution of 1688 to the French Revolution of 1789. Only in such a manner will it be possible to advance some tentative propositions about the relationship between culture and revolution.

We will return to that problem after a brief introduction to the essays themselves, which may be divided into four groups: 1688 and after; before 1788; 1788 before and after; 1917 and after. First, Jennifer Carter considers the impact on British ivory towers of the ejection of James VII and II and the arrival of William and Mary. Oxford and Cambridge and the five Scottish universities – St Andrews, Glasgow, Edinburgh and the two in Aberdeen – King's and Marischal Colleges – were shaken, if not quite to their very foundations, but there were variations in this process from institution to institution, and from country to country. Jennifer Carter concludes that 'the experiences of England and Scotland were no less different in the field of academic life than they were in so many other ways in the thirty years after 1688'. The reasons for the difference were also more widely applicable: they included the circumstance that arguments about property rights, both private and corporate, carried somewhat less weight in Scotland than in England, and the overriding concern for closely interconnected religious orthodoxy and political loyalty. Because of their remoteness from London, the Scottish universities were more closely watched for the seditious threat of Jacobitism, even if this old loyalty was to be found in the English universities, too.

So remote that central government anxiety about them was far less keen, the American colonies nevertheless felt the shock waves of 1688 crossing the Atlantic. As David Lovejoy points out, the Glorious Revolution was certainly shared by the colonists, although that was only half the story, for groups of them in each colony seized the opportunity for an attempt at supremacy. If the consequences of this attempt varied considerably, they tended towards failure rather than success. David Lovejoy asserts: 'In the short run the Glorious Revolution in America, contrary to the tenor of political changes in the realm, taught colonies that they were dominions of the Crown, dependent and subordinate and subject to the royal grace and favour of the king.' However, as he goes on to point out: 'what colonists did not win in 1689, by attempting to make the Revolution theirs, too, they tended to assume over the long pull of the eighteenth century'.

Back across the ocean, another smaller stretch of water retained enormous significance throughout the same long pull. Having made a last ditch stand for his throne in Ireland, James VII and II found refuge in France, from which his descendants crossed the Channel in the attempt to regain their inheritance. The Jacobite cause found expression in several media, not least the literature celebrated by Murray Pittock. As well as ringing the changes on the age-old themes of love, death and violence, this literature embodied what he calls the 'naked, frontiersman side of the Augustan struggle'. Close at first to the analytic dimensions of the Tory world-view, as may be seen in aspects of the work of Pope and Swift, Jacobite literature soon developed a strong Scottish element. Indeed, it gave expression to the only serious nationalist force in Scotland from 1715 onwards. For forty years and more, it gave a stirring voice to the cause of James and Charles. However, almost immediately after the last attempt of 1759, mawkish sentiment began to creep in, to such an extent by 1789 that the Hanoverian Prince George could appear at a masquerade ball in Highland dress. The threat from the king over the water was about to be replaced by a more terrifying republican danger: Jacobitism gave way to Jacobinism.

But, before the French Revolution, another attempt to turn the world upside down had begun with the American Declaration of Independence in 1776. Robert Lawson-Peebles takes up the story as told by Jennifer Carter, David Lovejoy and Murray Pittock in an examination of aspects of the academic career of William Smith, who encountered the Jacobite movement in Aberdeen in 1745, and a key moment in the American Revolution in Philadelphia in 1778. Smith expressed his attitude to the '45 in a work published ten years later. If clergymen had not uttered appropriate warnings from time to time, 'most certainly Popish Error and Popish Slavery (perhaps

Heathen Error and Heathen Slavery) had long ere now overwhelmed us! Where then would have been the Blessings purchased by our Reformation and glorious Revolution?' Generally speaking, Smith was adopting the ideology of 'familialism', which was rooted in a correspondence between the human body, the family and the body politic, in a constellation of concepts revolving around the word 'union'. In his commonplace book, for example, references to a play about Sir Walter Ralegh eulogise the English family as it was believed to exist in the 'Merrie England' of Good Queen Bess. With the arrival of the American Revolution, however, Smith was able to preach a sermon in 1778 excluding Britain from its place in the family circle. The parentage of King George was disclaimed, and the headship of the family transferred to George Washington, soon to be known as the Father of his Country.

The first group of essays has taken us from 1688 to 1789, for the most part in Britain and America. We have seen how the legacy of the Glorious Revolution and of the Jacobite antithesis to it was adapted and evolved through the succeeding century. The second group, on the other hand, is a preface rather than a postscript. That is, rather than considering the manner in which a revolution lived on and mutated in the memory, it looks at ways in which another revolution was prepared and formulated in the mind. One of the most interesting and significant questions about the events unfolding from 1789 onwards is, to what extent were they the result of that variegated movement of intellectual agitation known as the Enlightenment? It is to aspects of his question that the next three essays address themselves. In particular, the first of them examines the problem of the pursuit of happiness, much beloved by the *philosophes* and later included as a basic right along with life and liberty by Thomas Jefferson and his associates in the American Declaration of Independence. Micheline Cuénin argues that in and around the year 1688, 'happiness' in French was taken to mean social success, luck and favour. This necessarily leaves aside the vast majority of the people, although Madame Cuénin suggests that their simple faith in God and the King gave many of the peasants a kind of happiness. But for those accepting the current definition at the turn of the century, residence in a town, preferably Paris, was necessary for its realisation. And each individual would carry on the pursuit according to the dispositions of his 'machine', that is, his body and soul. But while Maupertius included in his calculations 'only pleasures and pain', Montesquieu towards the end of his life was prepared to assert: 'Despite what I may have said concerning happiness founded in my machine, I do not maintain for all that that our soul cannot contribute to our happiness by the direction it takes.' Certainly, the pursuit of happiness once on the agenda remained there as the century wore on, and then was to constitute a question of central importance for the revolutionaries in America and France alike.

Another necessary, although by no means sufficient, precursor to the convulsions towards the end of the eighteenth century was the revolt of the *philosophes* against aristocratic tastes. John Pappas describes the manner in which, in theatre, poetry, art and music, Diderot and his associates attacked as stilted, unrealistic and unrelated to everyday life the traditional genres and aesthetic values upheld by the aristocracy. As replacements, they proposed a mode of expression which would more accurately reflect bourgeois life and values, more realistic and more emotional. As John Pappas sees it, this was not just a theoretical quarrel about aesthetics: 'it was a power struggle in which the *philosophes* sought to wrest from the nobility the right to dictate literary and artistic rules to the nation.' The measure of the victory of the *philosophes* was such that the Marquis de Ségur would come to describe the enthusiasm of young noblemen in the following manner: 'We criticized the powers at Versailles, and we paid court to those of the Encyclopedia. We preferred a word of praise from D'Alembert, from Diderot, to the most brilliant favour of a prince.'

With a comparable but more concentrated approach, John Dunkley describes the appearance on and off the stage of the eighteenth-century French financier and merchant. After reminding us that neither the social nor the ethical norm was set by the bourgeois in the theatre of Molière, he goes on to chart the assertion of bourgeois values in some representative dramas written by Molière's less well-known successors, and then by the renowned Beaumarchais. Fortunes were mixed for different groups within the bourgeoisie. While the merchant was singled out by playwrights and *philosophes* alike as 'the ideal modern man, productive and patriotic', the financier was vilified for 'ferocious extortion and shameless peculation'. The latter stereotype was so powerful that, during the Terror, twenty-eight general farmers of the taxes were guillotined, considered guilty of milking the State, whereas in fact the Council declared in 1806 that the State had actually owed vast sums of money to the farmers. Here, as elsewhere, we are reminded that history, not just of revolutions but perhaps especially of them, is not just a matter 'facts' but also of subjective perceptions, beliefs and loyalties, of 'culture' in general.

While concentrating on the French Revolution itself, the third group of essays also looks backwards towards 1688 and forwards – if less surely – towards 1917. A self-proclaimed 'Revolution Whig' and man of the Enlightenment, William Robertson firmly believed that, as far as the beneficial effects of 1688 were concerned, 'A view more enlarged and more noble opens to us. All the civilised nations of Europe may be considered as forming one extensive community'. Thus, as Richard Sher points out, Robertson interpreted the events in France from 1789 to 1790 in terms of the Whig view of 1688 and the French rhetoric of 1788 – 'as a blow against despotic tyranny in the name of ordered liberty and constitutional monarchy'. If Robertson was not happy with the manner in which the French Revolution threatened to develop, this was not only because of departure from its former principles, but also because he saw the Revolution of 1688 and its glorious consequences as 'the work of God and not of man', of 'that superintending providence, in whose hand it is to lift up nations and to cast them down'.

As Jeremy Black tells us in the next contribution, the centenary of the Glorious Revolution in 1788 provided the British press with an opportunity for a restatement of the significance of that episode, which then provided a yardstick against which the events unfolding in France would be measured. Thus *The Times* could observe on 3 August 1789 that 'France and England looking up to the same standard for happiness will probably prevent all national hostilities.' Earlier, on 22 July 1789, *The Times* had suggested that the French experience of supporting the cause of liberty in America was also of importance: 'A people who have once fought for the emancipation of another nation can afterwards but ill relish the slavery in their own.' However, as with William Robertson, most of the British press was happy with the French Revolution only as long as it could be celebrated within accepted norms. For example, reporting a commemorative dinner on 14 July 1791 at the appropriately named George Inn, the *Derby Mercury* stated: 'The day was spent in great harmony and decorum, and the following loyal and constitutional toasts were drunk . . .' When the head of Louis fell, and the violence of the mob appeared to get out of hand, such balance could not easily be maintained.

It is to the question of the mob or the crowd, the people or the public, that Noel Parker turns in his analysis of the early historiography of the French Revolution. Was its behaviour romantic or rationalist? He traces developments from de Staël and Thiers, through Thierry and Guizot, to Michelet, before concluding that 'The injection of idealism into their view of social reality and romantic taste into their interests enabled them to pay attention to the people in a new way, portraying anonymous, "irrational" masses as historical actors'. To quote Noel Parker's final words:

> They did this by identifying the historical actors *through* ideal entities of which they or their actions were instances: race, legal or institutional forms, social organisation and *mores* peculiar to their culture, shared emotions, higher principles motivating their deeds. These elements extended the range of the historians' chronology, and broadened their subject matter with a larger range of historical actors. Hence, they moved progressively away from the juxtaposition that opposed reason to the people-public, which had characterised the earlier histories. Reason, passion and the people came to be conceived of together in a historical movement such as the Revolution.

With such an approach, these early 'republican' historians pointed the way forward in the longer run towards the formation of the *Annales* school, in the shorter – towards that of Marxism. Marx himself of course acknowledged the importance of such predecessors, as well as refining the method announced in the *Communist Manifesto* through analysis of the 1848 Revolution and its Bonapartist sequel, then of the Paris Commune of 1871. Towards the end of his life, Marx switched his attention towards developments in Russia, but died before he could clearly spell out general conclusions from detailed researches.

Lenin and the Bolsheviks were very conscious of French precedents in addition to the Marxist inheritance as the events of the Russian Revolution unfolded from 1917 outwards. In his contribution, Richard Stites points out how these events followed more than a century of self-conscious revolutionary tradition, much of it influenced by French radical forms, both real and imagined. Moreover, through psychological affiliation or physical presence or both, many of the Bolsheviks considered themselves members of a European elite, again often, although by no means always, with a French emphasis.

The tradition percolated through to the general public in several ways. For example, in a Petrograd pageant, there were representations of both the *sans culottes* of 1789 and the *communards* of 1871. Among the new, secular names given to children were not only Marat and Robespierre but also Bastille and Guillotine. Of course, the Revolution looked forward as well as backward: to take the names again, there were harbingers of the future such as Industry and Electrification.

As the process of industrialisation and electrification moved forwards in the Soviet Union in the mid-1920s, the question of 'culture and socialism' was addressed by L.D. Trotsky. About thirty years later, the subject of 'cultural history as a synthesis' was discussed by Jacques Barzun in the USA, where that process was much further advanced. In a concluding essay, Terry Brotherstone presents an exposition and a comparison of these two approaches, and of the historical situations in which they were produced. Thus, Trotsky could argue that 'a machine which automatically manufactures bottles is at the present time a first-rate factor in the cultural revolution, while a heroic poem is only a tenth-rate factor', and Barzun would attempt in various ways to overcome a different kind of 'materialism' in the conditions of mature industrial capitalism existing in the post-Second World War USA. Terry Brotherstone asserts that the arguments of both Trotsky and Barzun have a relevance in the late 1980s to the task of defining cultural history and its place within society at large.

In the light of our brief summary of the contributions, let us advance a few conclusions about the implications of the collection as a whole. Three centuries after our principal point of departure, where have we arrived?

First of all, perhaps, we need to recognise the agitation (revolution would be too strong a word) among academic disciplines: earlier confidence concerning their internal characteristics and their frontiers has to a considerable extent disappeared, and they are now seeking ways of redefining and regrouping themselves. If, for example, historical research can be pursued only on the basis of 'regulative fictions', does it any longer possess an existence apart from serious historical novels, works of 'faction'? Indeed, might it be argued that an imaginative writer can approach closer to the truth than a prosaic academic?

Secondly, within today's intellectual framework, can there be any reconciliation between two fundamentally different approaches to enquiry, one bound by chronology, the other removed from it? On the one hand, there is a fresh emphasis on context, on the circumstances in which the writer or artist worked, in the 'new historicism'. On the other hand, pursuit of 'eternal verities', of philosophical or literary appraisal, does not want to be restricted by time or indeed place. In a latter-day version, deconstructionism, analysis is concerned with the thing itself, poem or painting, without regard for its mundane setting.

In *Culture and Revolution*, we have not resolved such problems, but we do believe that we have thrown light on them by attempting to reconcile the moment with the situation, the revolutionary event with the cultural *longue durée*. We have at least illustrated the manner in which 1688, 1776, 1789 and 1917 were adumbrated and/or made their impact in the longer as well as the shorter run, and across national boundaries. In other words, we would claim to have approached our basic theme both synchronically and diachronically, and thus to have contributed to its deeper appreciation, to have shown at least something of the inherent change and continuity.

Returning to the first question, concerned with the boundaries between academic disciplines, we should perhaps note that it was during the century of major concern to us in this volume, from 1688 to 1789, that those boundaries were first set up. Regarding the second question, confronting the chronological approach with the 'timeless', here again that same period bore considerable significance.

The light thrown by the various contributors on these and other questions will differ according to the outlook of different readers. Equally, the authorial 'we', already subject to some strain, collapses completely in the face of the more general questions, what is cultural history, and what is its significance today? By no means all the contributors would want to respond to the challenge posed by Terry Brotherstone, and there would be no unanimous answer even from those willing to take up the challenge. Some, no doubt, would want to argue that 'bottle manufacture' has lost its former importance, even perhaps in the Soviet Union, as scientific-technological priorities have superseded industrial, and as green imperatives have overtaken red. Others might well accept the insistence on the lasting importance of the class struggle and the necessity for its resolution.

All the contributors, apparently, and the majority of the readers, let us hope, will agree that understanding of revolution requires more than examination of the events themselves, that it can be approached only by the consideration of the superficially contradictory term – culture. Equally, perhaps, we move closer to an understanding of the term 'culture' if we evaluate the impact made upon its various manifestations by the controversial events of revolution.

1

BRITISH UNIVERSITIES AND REVOLUTION, 1688–1718

Jennifer Carter

The Glorious Revolution was experienced very differently in England, in Scotland and in Ireland. It was almost bloodless in England, but it was not so in Scotland, and it was bloody indeed in Ireland. In England the Revolution Settlement was a pragmatic political compromise, with the Declaration of Rights blending Whig and Tory versions of what had occurred, whereas in Scotland the Claim of Right was more openly contractualist, asserting that King James had altered the constitution 'from a legal limited monarchy, to an arbitrary despotic power' and had thus forfeited the right to the crown. In England, one result of the Revolution was a strictly limited religious toleration, while in Scotland the Church establishment was less accommodating, and in Ireland persecution became the rule. These differences find echoes in the relationship of universities and governments, and this paper explores the different experiences of the English and the Scottish universities in the thirty years after 1688.

The English universities were involved in the Revolution not least because of the affair of Magdalen College, Oxford. The rights of the Magdalen Fellows were specifically mentioned in William of Orange's invasion manifesto, which, among its indictments of the Ecclesiastical Commissioners, claimed:

> The said Commissioners . . . have turned out a President chosen by the Fellows of Magdalen College, and afterwards all the fellows of that College, without so much as citing them before any court that could take legal cognisance of that affair, or obtaining any Sentence against them by a competent judge . . . and now those evil Counsellors have put the said College wholly into the hands of the Papists; though they are incapable of all such employments, both by the law of the land, and the statutes of the college.

Despite this forthright pronouncement, there was no subsequent word about the universities, nor indeed about any other educational matter in the Bill of Rights.[1] In contrast to the English Bill of Rights, the Scottish Claim of Rights devoted to educational matters the first three of the fourteen clauses in which it accused King James of wrongdoing. In the 1690s, while the English government was tending to draw back from direct intervention of James II's kind in university affairs, the Scottish Parliament launched a commission which embarked on a major overhaul of the Scottish universities, and to a lesser extent the schools, attempting not merely to secure loyalist teachers, but also to regulate the administration and curriculum of the universities. Again, after 1715, four of the Scottish universities were revisited, and in Aberdeen almost the whole staff at both King's College and Marischal College was replaced. While it would be easy to exaggerate the extent to which the English government withdrew from involvement in university affairs after 1688, in Scotland there was certainly no lessening of intervention after the Revolution, not least because in Scotland Jacobitism in politics and episcopalianism in religion seemed greater threats than did their equivalents in England.

Before the Revolution, both Oxford and Cambridge had long been used to political pressures of various kinds, including those on appointments: 'academic freedom had little or no status as an ideal in Elizabethan and early Stuart times.[2] The Civil Wars and Interregnum brought many upheavals. For instance, in 1647 a parliamentary visitation made 'almost a clean sweep' of Oxford college heads, as well as deposing the Vice-Chancellor and various professors, and installing others in their places.[3] The Restoration saw further, if more moderate changes, including the deprivation of those who would not take the oaths prescribed by the 1662 Act of Uniformity. On 21 August 1660 Henry Hickman, an Oxford acquaintance of Pepys, 'spoke very much against the height of the new old-clergy, for putting out many of the religious fellows of colleges and enveighing against them for their being drunk' – 'which if true I am sorry to hear', adds Pepys sententiously. Anthony Wood, on the other hand, thought that: 'whereas great cruelty was acted in the Presbyterian visitation 12 years before, now nothing but moderation'.[4] Similarly, at Cambridge there were great turnings-out from 1644 onwards, six colleges losing virtually all their fellows. As at Oxford, most of the survivors came back at the Restoration, though again there were some who had to leave after the Act of Uniformity. Like Oxford, Cambridge was strongly loyalist, demonstrating this, for example, by conferring 160 degrees on royal request within a year of Charles II's accession. The King demanded not only the conferring of degrees, but also the nomination of the fellowships (though he declared in 1674 that compliance with his recommendations was not expected if the candidates were not properly qualified), and the Crown also interfered in the election of college heads.[5] All this was accepted as normal behaviour in Charles II's reign, but similar interventions by James II were resented because of their religious and political implications.

A confrontation at Cambridge arose when, in February 1687, a royal mandate ordered the admission as an MA of Father Alban Francis, a Benedictine monk. Burnet makes the point that mandated degrees were frequently given, for example to visiting ambassadors (indeed one had been conferred on the Moroccan Ambassador's secretary, who was a Mohammedan) but 'a great distinction was made between honorary degrees given to strangers . . . and those given to such as intended to settle among them'.[6] The Senate decided that Francis should not be admitted to the degree of MA without taking the oaths, and advised the Vice-Chancellor, John Peachell, Master of Magdalen

College, to petition the King to withdraw the royal mandate. Petitions were ignored, and the Vice-Chancellor and a delegation from the university appeared before the Ecclesiastical Commission and were given rough treatment. Isaac Newton, Lucasian Professor of Mathematics, was the strong man of the delegation, persuading his colleagues not to accept the compromise that Francis be admitted on a no-precedent basis. Partly because of the stand he took at this time, Newton was in 1689 elected as one of Cambridge University's members of the Convention Parliament, and he helped to smooth the way towards the acceptance of the Revolution Settlement in Cambridge. In 1687 Newton stressed the significance of the university's electoral rights in the Francis case: 'if a priest be Master, you may have a hundred and they must choose burgesses to Parliament', adding: 'those that counselled his Majesty to disoblige the University cannot be his true friends for 'tis notorious that no body of men in England have been so loyal'. The Ecclesiastical Commission deprived Peachell of his vice-chancellorship and suspended him from the mastership of his college, while warning the other university representatives to give readier obedience to royal commands in future, but it did not insist on the admission of Francis. Thus the attack on Cambridge was not pressed home, though later in 1687 the Ecclesiastical Commission did alter parts of the college statutes of Sidney Sussex because they were held to reflect on Roman Catholicism.[7]

At Oxford more determined action was taken by James II. His first step was a small one. The Master of University College, Obadiah Walker, obtained a royal dispensation to withdraw from Anglican worship and have mass said at his lodgings. This did not greatly trouble the university, because though proclaiming himself a Catholic now, Walker had been an Anglican when appointed to office, and his masses were originally to be private. However, his chapel was soon used '"for public mass, where some scholars, and many troopers were present". The rabble shouted "Obadiah and Ave-Maria" and had to be driven away by the soldiery'.[8] In this incident it is interesting that the public and the student reaction to open Catholicism was stronger than the official university reaction, and that troops played a part in the affair. Next came a somewhat similar episode at Christ Church. Following the death of the Dean, who was also Bishop of Oxford, in July 1686 the Chapter was persuaded to install as dean John Massey, Fellow of Merton, who was one of Walker's followers. Massey was a known Catholic, and as a mere MA was not qualified for office in what was technically an Anglican cathedral as well as a college. Once installed, Massey set up a Catholic chapel, and college discipline collapsed, with the undergraduates crowding into his masses to jeer.[9]

Then came the Magdalen College affair. Following the death of their President on 24 March 1687, the Fellows ignored a royal *mandamus* in favour of Anthony Farmer, a Cambridge graduate recommended by Walker, who was disqualified for office in every respect, including that of moral character. On 15 April the Fellows chose as president one of their own number, John Hough. This was a legal election, though it had been preceded by a hot debate from which two Roman Catholic Fellows withdrew before the vote was taken. The Ecclesiastical Commission promptly declared the election invalid. The King now appointed as president Samuel Parker, the new Bishop of Oxford, a man who in normal circumstances would have been a perfectly acceptable candidate, though at the time he was mortally ill. The Fellows, however, stuck to their choice of John Hough, maintaining this even in the face of the King himself, and at the price of their own deprivation from office. In September 1687 James came down to Oxford and at a conference with the Fellows was so angry that for a time he could not speak; but regardless of royal rage, spoken and unspoken, the Fellows remained firm, and the Vice-Chancellor declared: 'We must observe our statutes, and no power under heaven can dispense with these oaths'.[10] In November 1687 twenty-five Fellows were expelled, and by March next year Parker had been succeeded as president by Bonadventura Gifford, and masses were being said in Magdalen Chapel. In the words of G.V. Bennett: 'It is difficult to overestimate the shock and anger which these events caused, not least among those bishops and clergy who had been educated at Oxford'.[11] Thus did Magdalen become a *cause célèbre*, and its Fellows win such unusual fame for academics that they even figured on a set of political playing cards issued immediately after the Revolution.[12] As Burnet put it rather smugly: 'The Nation, as well as the university, looked on all this proceeding with a just indignation. It was thought an open piece of robbery and burglary, when men, authorized by no legal commission, came and forcibly turned men out of their possessions and freehold'.[13] Following the Magdalen affair, *quo warranto* proceedings were commenced against the Charter of Oxford University in June 1688; but within four months James was frantically reversing his policies, to try to recover what had once seemed almost automatic loyalist support from the universities and the Church of England. The Ecclesiastical Commission was disbanded, and the displaced Fellows of Magdalen returned to their college, while the Catholic incumbents there and elsewhere crept away. The Prince of Orange, on his march to London, was met at Abingdon by the Vice-Chancellor, who offered to put all the university's plate at his disposal.[14]

Yet when the Revolution Settlement was made in 1689, it was accepted only with great difficulty at the English universities. All officials, heads of colleges, and Fellows, were required to swear allegiance to King William and Queen Mary, and there were many torments of conscience before most of them did in fact do so. Oxford eventually had only eight nonjurors, and Cambridge perhaps forty-two. The larger number at Cambridge doubtless reflects the influence Archbishop William Sancroft, a Cambridge man and the leading nonjuror; and twenty-eight of them were concentrated in one college, St John's, which was notably High Church, Tory, and even Jacobite.[15] At St John's a Jacobite group continued in the 1690s to hold its own prayer meetings: 'the service they used was the Common Prayer, and always pray'd heartily for King James naming him most commonly; but in some meetings they only prayed for the King, not naming who'.[16] Praying for the king alone, or for the king and queen but not naming them, was an expedient at Oxford too, and had Scottish parallels.

It is hardly surprising that the English universities were the object of so much government attention from the 1640s to 1688, considering the place they held in national life, their many political connections, and above all their interrelations with the Church of England. The two English universities each elected two MPs, and Millicent Rex observes them in the period 1660 to 1690 exercising that right vigorously, with few uncontested elections, even if the results did not run seriously counter to the normal seventeenth-century trend whereby university seats accommodated courtiers.[17] In James II's reign the universities had 'an important part to play'[18] in the King's plans, but James's policies, and the people he chose to implement them, lost him the loyalty of the universities and made Magdalen College a symbol of national resistance. As Burnet summed up:

> For whereas in all countries the rights of colleges are such sacred things that these are never disturbed even when other things are broke in upon, and Oxford and Cambridge are two such vast bodies, in which the whole nation is so much concerned that one would have thought these should have been the last of all to whom this new commission should have given any trouble, yet they have just begun where they should have ended.[19]

After the Revolution the two English universities enjoyed a greater immunity from direct government interference in their affairs than previously, the more remarkably so considering that Oxford became a centre of opposition to post-Revolution governments. The extent of this change should not be exaggerated, and certainly the politics of the universities remained a matter of great concern to successive governments after the Revolution. The pursuit of preferment, as well as their right to elect their own MPs, drew academics into constant contact with politicians. But there does seem to have been a change of atmosphere: after the Revolution normal political bargaining resumed, but not that more brutal treatment of the universities by governments which had characterised earlier periods, culminating in what could be seen as James II's illegal attack on property rights.

At Cambridge after the Revolution the conventions governing mandated degrees were changed so that in future they could be conferred only on the advice of the heads of houses, conveyed through the university's Chancellor; while 'royal attempts to nominate to college headships were decisively checked by the free election of Provost Roderick of King's in 1689 in defiance of a royal mandate'.[20] Notwithstanding the new arrangements about mandated degrees, many continued to be conferred, notably in the 1720s, in order to influence the voting in parliamentary elections at the university.[21] With the Duke of Newcastle as High Steward of the university from 1737 to 1748, and as its Chancellor from 1748 to 1769, Cambridge became 'the Whig University, and as far as its parliamentary representation was concerned little better than one of Newcastle's boroughs'.[22] As for election to college headships, if the King's College election of 1689 set a new precedent, it did so by excluding a highly distinguished royal nominee. When Provost John Coplestone died on 24 August 1689, William III nominated Isaac Newton, but the Fellows were determined to elect the men of their own choice, Charles Roderick, Headmaster of Eton. 'According to College tradition there were stormy debates at Hampton Court, between the law officers of the Crown and the representatives of the Colleges . . . the voice of a deaf and indignant fellow, sounding through the galleries . . . "Mr Attorney General, if we must bear the grievances of former reigns, then is the King in vain come in"'.[23] By October 1689 the King had been persuaded to accept the College's choice gracefully. 'After 1689 the University moved into quieter days.'[24] It was easier for Cambridge than for Oxford to settle down after the Revolution, since Cambridge churchmen were to win all the glittering prizes of preferment in William's reign.[25] However, there was some reversals ahead, with Oxford more popular at Whitehall during parts of Anne's reign, and Cambridge not without some lingering Jacobite sympathisers. The biographer of Richard Bentley, Master of Trinity from 1700 and one of the most learned, if also most difficult academic of his time, comments that:

A vulgar error has represented this University as the headquarters of Whig politics. At the General Election in 1715, the Tory Representatives were re-elected . . . It is however equally certain that only a small proportion of the High Church party at Cambridge were Jacobites . . . the Nonjurors were not numerous . . . But on the night of the Pretender's birthday, and again on that of King George, disturbances did take place through some young men, who had either imbibed Jacobite principles, or thoughtlessly availed themselves of these occasions for juvenile licence; some windows were broken, and come cries were heard of 'No Hanover'. But the excesses, being few and trivial, were censured by the Vice Chancellor as ordinary breaches of discipline, without reference to their political tendency.[26]

Undergraduate pranks might be passed off as ordinary breaches of university discipline at loyalist Cambridge, but they were taken more seriously by the government when they happened at Oxford.

At Oxford, after 1689, enthusiasm for the new regime was restrained less by the change of king (as the very small number of nonjurors shows) than by William's intended Church settlement. Oxford took the lead in defeating the King's hoped-for comprehension and thus became: 'Like the Tory party itself . . . an opposition interest . . . a major centre of opposition to the government'.[27] Just how uncomfortable that position could be was shown in many ways – by the disappointing lack of Church preferments for the heroes of Magdalen; by the unsuccessful attempt of Oxford's MPs (aided by those of Cambridge) to get through Parliament a bill reasserting the university's privileges, brought into question by James's *Quo Warranto;* and by the vindictive requirement of 1694 that members of the university must take a special oath of loyalty imposed on no one else.[28] Oxford's role as a centre of opposition was reinforced in the minds of politicians by the Sacheverell affair in Anne's reign: 'A fellow of an Oxford college had actually precipitated the collapse of an administration which had fought and virtually won the greatest war in the nation's history. It was an event long to be remembered by the politicians'.[29] Oxford's unpopularity continued under the Hanoverian regime. 'The Jacobites looked on Oxford University as one of their strongholds', an attitude to which the university gave credibility in 1715, following the attainder of its Chancellor, the Duke of Ormonde, when it immediately elected his brother, Lord Arran, to succeed him. Lord Arran held office until 1758.[30] 'For many contemporaries Oxford's position under the first two Hanoverians was a simple and straightforward one, that of committed and even traitorous opposition to the established regime.' The reality was more complex.[31] But Oxford's reputation with the government and the public meant, for instance, that undergraduate riots looked political and Jacobite, even when, as in 1715 to 1717, they were more complicated in their causation, being in part town-gown, or soldiers versus scholars affairs, and even in part caused by Whiggish troublemakers.[32] Government worries and public reaction fed a pamphlet war against the university. One pamphleteer demanded a royal visitation, so that:

> The universities, those Nests, or Cages of unclean Birds, would be effectually cleansed, the Church be honour'd with a learned, sober, pious and labourous Clergy, Religion would flourish, Virtue be encouraged, Wickedness fly, and be asham'd to show its Face, a Protestant government be secured and established, and God would delight to dwell among us.[33]

The Earl of Sunderland drew up a universities' reform bill on draconian lines, proposing to vest all university and college appointments in a body of royal commissioners. The bill was dropped after the defeat of the Peerage Bill in 1719.[34] The comments of William Stratford are interesting: in 1717 he wrote: 'I never was in much pain for the bill about the universities, it would have been so flagrant a breach of property, and so many private interests, besides that of those who are resident here, would have been concerned in it, that I can never think it would pass', and again, before the threat had died in 1719, he wrote: 'I believe they would have found it difficult to have framed any bill against us so as to have answered their end and not to have made all the property in England precarious'.[35] Government annoyance with Oxford ran high once more, following an undergraduate Jacobite riot in February 1748, and further demonstrations at the opening of the Radcliffe Camera in April 1749. A commission of inquiry was contemplated, but was not carried through, partly because Newcastle, as Chancellor of Cambridge University, did not want to see the two universities lumped together.

> Any general academical Rules may possibly comprehend both Universities; but I can never admit, That if the late and notorious Conduct of the University of Oxford, should make any visitation or Enquiry there advisable, That will be any Reason for the same at Cambridge whose Behaviour is as meritorious, as the other is justly censured.[36]

Thus, despite what many post-Revolution governments felt to be provocative political behaviour in the English universities, especially Oxford, no substantial action was taken against them. Normal political and patronage connections indeed operated, especially in the matter of university election of MPs, but it is notable that the two English universities exercised their 'right to send even nonentities to the House of Commons . . . at a time when the electoral system of the country was coming more and more under the influence of the pocket borough', and in the post-Revolution period Oxford established and long maintained a tradition of electing that good old sort . . . an independent country gentleman, a true friend to Church and King', Oxford's record being judged 'one of the most dignified and genuinely independent constituencies in this period'.[37] There was no direct intervention of the pre-Revolution type in the internal affairs of the English universities between 1688 and the reforms of the nineteenth century.

To all of this, the situation of the Scottish universities presents a contrast. Like England's two, Scotland's five universities were already long-established, and well accustomed to government interference before 1688. Thus, for instance, at the time of the Popish Plot, the Scottish Privy Council suspended classes of Edinburgh because of anti-popery demonstrations by the students; and staff were removed and replaced at the universities, especially in the 1630s and in 1660.[38] The Revolution of 1688 was followed by parliamentary action which affected each of the five Scottish universities to a different extent. This purge was designed mainly to secure the loyalty of teachers to the new order in Church and State, but it also had administrative and curricular aspects.[39]

At Edinburgh, the parliamentary commission, nicknamed by a pamphleteer the 'Presbyterian inquisition' is said to have 'transformed Edinburgh from an Episcopal college . . . into a Presbyterian seminary' and to have made it 'pre-eminently the Whig University of Scotland'.[40] The university's Principal (Alexander Monro) and its Professor of Divinity (John Strachan) were deposed in 1630, and Edinburgh became so Whiggish that Jacobitism found no sympathisers there. Indeed during the '45 classes were suspended so that staff and students could take an active part on the Hanoverian side. 'Charles Mackie, professor of History and a stout Whig, went around spreading atrocity stories about the Jacobites and, when challenged, replied he did not give his own stories much credit, but thought "telling them may have a good effect".'[41] Loyalty paid off financially for the university. At the Hanoverian accession an act of parliament allowed the town council of Edinburgh to collect local excise duties and apply the proceeds to paying university salaries.[42] The bulk of Edinburgh's chairs were in the gift of the town council, which could add an extra layer of complication to university affairs (as was also the case, though to a lesser extent, with Marischal College, Aberdeen) but essentially academic appointments at Edinburgh were part of the normal process of political management in the 'client society' of eighteenth-century Scotland.[43] For instance, when William Robertson was canvassing for the principalship of Edinburgh in 1762 he wrote to an ally: 'The office is in the gift of the Town Council, but that you know alters the matter only one remove', and again: 'I need not say to you, that a letter from Ld Bute to Baron Mure or Ld Milton fixes the Election infallibly'.[44] Given the right political stance, some financial help through government, and the advantages of a growing local prosperity and increasing student numbers to draw upon, Edinburgh (like Glasgow) went from strength to strength in the eighteenth century, and (again like Glasgow) was able to attract some of the ablest teachers of the time from other Scottish universities.[45]

The much older university foundation of Glasgow followed a similar pattern to Edinburgh in this period. In 1630 the Principal (James Fell), the Professor of Divinity (James Wemyss) and two Regents (William Blair and Thomas Gordon) were put out, though on demitting office Principal Fell received formal thanks for his services, and half a year's salary. As J.D. Mackie says: 'In the University . . . the "Revolution Settlement" was very gently effected'.[46] Glasgow was conspicuously loyal to post-Revolution governments, the faculty offering to fund a company of foot at the time of the Jacobite threats in 1708, 1715 and 1745. They were rewarded by royal favour and official financial help, so that the university's finances were in a thriving way' by the 1720s. A royal commission of 1727 came in only to sort out some internal difficulties, and student indiscipline, and no further government intervention was seen until the nineteenth century.[47] Thus Glasgow, like Edinburgh, slid fairly painlessly though the post-revolutionary period. Some staff had been replaced, and academic appointments remained highly politicised, but some advantages had been gained. The two major Scottish universities may not have had the same degree of 'independence' as Oxford and Cambridge, but they both enjoyed very considerable success in the eighteenth century.

Further north, events were stormier. At St Andrews the Revolution was a turning point towards the eighteenth-century decay of the university, though it was not wholly responsible for that outcome. As R.G. Cant explains, the abolition of episcopacy reduced the importance of St Andrews as a centre of the Episcopal Church, and this and other factors meant a long-term decline for the town and district, while town-gown quarrels became so acute that in 1697 the university nearly moved to Perth. The financial problems of the university were compounded by declining student numbers and by the government's not granting it financial favours.[48] The commission of the 1690s was bound to deal hardly with St Andrews, since most of the masters had joined the Scottish bishops in a laudatory *Address to the King* just before William of Orange's invasion.[49] The Rector, Alexander Skene, put in a dignified refusal to conform on behalf of himself and all but one of his staff:

> We find that in the present juncture no man can possesse or enjoy any station or profession in this University without takeing those solemne ingadgements required and particularly mentioned in the aforesaid Act of Parliament; and though we are not ashamed nor weary of the honour we have had in serving God in these our stations, yet seeing we hope never to exchange the peace and integrity of our consciences . . . with any worldly enjoyments, we take this occasion to declare here, and are ready to doe to all the world, that as yet we are not in conscience cleare to take these ingagements.[50]

Dr Skene was questioned about his public prayers for 'the king': had he also prayed for 'the queen'? Obviously he had not, nor had he named the new monarchs in his prayers.[51] The Rector and all but one of the sixteen staff were deprived of their offices. The visitorial committee then went on to hear grievances against the university voiced by the town council of St Andrews. These accusations were well received, unsurprisingly since the chairman of the visitorial committee was also provost of the town. The citizens' complaints were mostly about disorderly and disloyal conduct by students. Here, as at the other Scottish universities, the commission proposed reforms to the organisation and curriculum of the university. Despite all its efforts, however, St Andrews remained Jacobite in sympathy, and in 1715–16 the students of St Leonard's College were responsible for a series of pro-Jacobite demonstrations which led to another visitorial commission in 1718. This commission was fairly easily satisfied about the loyalty of the university, suspending only one professor (Alexander Scrimgeour, Professor of Ecclesiastical History since 1713), who was allowed to continue to draw the emoluments of his chair for life. This was the last visitation the University of St Andrews was to see until the 1820s.[52] 'At any other time, there should be no special need to regret the absence of external interference. At this stage, however, what it meant was that the University went through a prolonged period of extreme difficulty, while the government, and indeed the country at large, remained aloof and almost totally indifferent to its fate.'[53]

The two universities of Aberdeen were much like St Andrews in their religious and political complexion.[54] Aberdeen, however, was treated much more leniently than St Andrews by the 1690 commissioners, perhaps because the Patron of Marischal College, the Earl Marischal, led the committee of visitation. Only one professor (James Garden, Professor of Divinity at King's College) declined to take the oath or sign the confession of faith, and even he was allowed to continue in office until 1696.[55] A much more serious situation arose in 1715. The Aberdeen area was one of the centres of Jacobite activity, and staff at both colleges were implicated. Two royal commissions working in 1716 and 1717 finally dismissed Principal George Middleton and three other staff at King's College, while at Marischal College they made a clean sweep of all the staff except Professor Thomas Blackwell, who became Principal. Teaching at Marischal College ceased for the two years 1715–16 and 1716–17.[56] The masters at King's College drew up a memorial in their defence which touched on the question of praying publicly for the King. The Principal had evaded the problem by stating that he had conducted no public prayers since August 1714. The professors of philosophy then:

> . . . being interrogat told that they were in constant use of saying dayly the publick and private prayers in the Schools dureing the sessions of the college, that they had still prayed as their predecessors had done To witt for the King and the Royal Family, that this was the method of praying the time of King William's visitation and was not so much as quarrelled then, and that it hath ever been the custome since to doe so.

Later in the same memorial the masters declared that:

> It may be thought both the first and last of these Commissions have been obtained without his Majesty's being fully appraised of the import thereof, For . . . nothing can be reasonablie thought more injurious and offensive in the publick Administration than those commissions, such commissions haveing been compted

Grievances in the reign of King James the Seventh whose proceedings as to the Universities of Oxford and Cambridge were considered as Incroachments of great moment.[57]

These arguments did not help the King's masters, and:

The Commission having after this manner purged the King's College of four members resolved to plant the same as unwarrantably . . . they sent the Lord Forglen to the North in order to treat with the members of the University yet remaining anent filling the vacancies and to know if they would agree to such persons as the Commissioners would name. But . . . the masters . . . still insisted on their privilege by the fundation to fill the vacancies.

Whereupon the masters were threatened with punishment for irregularities in the finances of the college before they would admit the commission's nominees.[58] When the Marischal College purge took effect, six chairs which had formerly been in the patronage of the Earl Marischal became regius chairs, the Earl Marischal having been attainted of high treason. Roger Emerson has shown how subject were all Aberdeen academic appointments to the workings of national and local politics throughout the rest of the century.[59] The severe measures taken by the 1716–17 royal commissions worked at least to the extent that Aberdeen's universities made no stirrings during '45.

J.M. Bulloch, in his history of Aberdeen University, saw the whole period from the Revolution to 1717 as bringing about a change from Church to State control of the Scottish universities. At Aberdeen this was marked by the election at King's College of the first lay chancellor, the Earl of Erroll, to replace the vanished bishop chancellors of the past. For the Scottish universities as a whole this same turn from Church to State control was seen in the work of the parliamentary commission of the 1690s, as well as the royal commissions which visited Aberdeen, St Andrews and Glasgow in the early Hanoverian period. State recognition came too, Bulloch suggests, when in 1709 the Scottish universities gained copyright privileges.[60] He might equally have quoted the clause in the Act of Union of 1707 which reads:

For the greater security of the foresaid protestant religion . . . the universities and colleges of St Andrews Glasgow Aberdeen and Edinburgh as now established by law shall continue within this kingdom for ever.

But Bulloch perhaps exaggerated the gap between Church and State in a period when religion was so much a continuing part of the texture of political life. The commission of the 1690s had been set up by act of parliament, but it was still a 'Presbyterian inquisition', and the Scottish universities remained very much under the control of Church and State during this period.

After the Revolution of 1688 the Scottish universities were slower than the English to gain a degree of autonomy from government. In part this may have been for cultural reasons – perhaps arguments about private and corporate property rights carried somewhat less weight in Scotland than in England? The union of the crowns in 1603 and the parliamentary union of 1707 had each had an effect in drawing wealthy and powerful men away from their Scottish roots. Though in the seventeenth century there was little sign of Scots seeking an English education, by the early eighteenth century some of the Scottish elite did send their sons to English schools and universities,[61] and this traffic was not wholly reversed or outweighed by the attractions of Edinburgh and Glasgow Universities at the height of the Scottish Enlightenment in the later eighteenth century. Whatever the precise balance between the education systems of the two kingdoms, it was clear that the national political game, in which all universities played some part, was centred in London. Even more obviously the difference between English and Scottish universities was one of relative power and importance: the Scottish universities were more numerous, but they were nothing like so large or so well-endowed as their English counterparts. In the post-Revolution period Oxford had three hundred or more resident Fellows, while the two universities of Aberdeen had less than a dozen masters each, and the other Scottish universities were not much bigger. Moreover Scottish universities lacked direct political representation: unlike Oxford and Cambridge, they had no right of sending MPs to Parliament until the nineteenth century. Thus the experiences of England and Scotland were no less different in the field of academic life than they were in so many other ways in the thirty years after 1688.

NOTES

1. E.N. Williams, *The Eighteenth-Century Constitution 1688–1815* (Cambridge, 1960), p.12; the draft form of the Declaration of Rights contained a clause stating: 'Cities, universities and towns corporate, and boroughs and plantations to be secured against *Quo Warrantos* and surrenders and mandates, and restored to their ancient rights': L.G. Schwoerer, *The Declaration of Rights, 1689* (Baltimore, 1981), p.299.
2. M.H. Curtis, *Oxford and Cambridge in Transition, 1558–1642* (Oxford, 1959), p.280.
3. V.H.H. Green, *The History of Oxford University* (London, 1974), pp.63–5.
4. *The Diary of Samuel Pepys,* ed. R. Latham and W. Matthews, 11 vols (London, 1970–83), vol.1, p.277 and n.1.
5. J.P.C. Roach, 'The University of Cambridge' in *Victoria County History, A History of the County of Cambridge and Isle of Ely,* vol.3, *The City and University of Cambridge* (London, 1959), pp.200, 203, 210, 211.
6. Gilbert Burnet, *History of His Own Time*, 6 vols (Oxford, 1833), vol.3, p.149.
7. Roach 'Cambridge', pp.212–13; M.B. Rex, *University Representation in England, 1604–1690* (London, 1954), pp.302–3.
8. G.V. Bennett, 'Loyalist Oxford and the Revolution', in L.S. Sutherland and L.G. Mitchell (eds), *The History of the University of Oxford*, vol.5, *The Eighteenth Century* (Oxford, 1986), pp.16–17; Green, *History of Oxford*, p.90. J. Miller, *Popery and Politics in England 1660–1688* (Cambridge 1973), pp.240, 243, says that at least eight Oxford fellows and one at Cambridge became converts, and that three chapels were opened at Oxford by newly converted fellows.
9. Bennett, 'Loyalist Oxford', p.17.
10. Bennett, 'Loyalist Oxford', p.18; Green, *History of Oxford*, pp.90–91.
11. Bennett, 'Loyalist Oxford', p.18.
12. On the six of clubs they are in confrontation with the Ecclesiastical Commission, whose president announces 'We will huff ye Dr Huff for all your huff',

while the eight of clubs depicts 'Magdalen College Scholars turned out':
R. Whiting, 'Among my souvenirs', *The Historian*, 18 (1988), p.12.

13. Burnet, *History*, vol.3, p.158.

14. Bennett, 'Loyalist Oxford', pp.19–20.

15. ibid., pp.21, 23; Roach, 'Cambridge', p.213, who gives the Oxford figure as fourteen, but admits the counts for both universities are uncertain.

16. A. de la Pryne, *Diary*, ed. C. Jackson (Surtees Society, 54), p.70, quoted by Roach, 'Cambridge', p.213.

17. Rex, *University Representation*, pp.14, 327–8, 345.

18. Bennett, 'Loyalist Oxford', p.16.

19. H.C. Foxcroft (ed.), *A Supplement to Burnet's History of My Own Time* (Oxford, 1902), p.214.

20. Roach, 'Cambridge', pp.213–4.

21. In 1726, 110 were awarded, and 286 when George II visited Cambridge in 1728. R. Sedgwick, *The History of Parliament, The House of Commons 1715–1754*, 2 vols (London, 1970), vol.1, p.202. I owe this reference, and much useful comment, to Dr Eveline Cruickshanks.

22. L.B. Namier and J. Brooke, *The History of Parliament, The House of Commons 1584–1790*, 3 vols (London, 1964), vol.1, p.220.

23. J. Saltmarsh, 'King's College', in *VCH, Cambridge*, pp.397–8.

24. Roach, 'Cambridge', p.213.

25. Bennett, 'Loyalist Oxford', p.26.

26. J.H. Monk, *The Life of Richard Bentley* (London, 1830), pp.294–5. Sedgwick, *The Commons 1715–1754*, vol.1, p.201, confirms that until 1727 'Cambridge University, like Oxford, returned Tories'; Green, *History of Oxford*, pp.93, 94; G.V. Bennett, 'The Era of party zeal 1702–1714' in *History of the University of Oxford*, vol.5, pp.62, 67.

27. Bennett, 'Loyalist Oxford', p.29, and 'Against the tide: Oxford under William III', in *History of the University of Oxford*, vol.5, p.31.

28. Bennett, 'Against the tide', pp.32–3, 34, 36, 50.

29. Bennett, 'The Era of party zeal', p.86.

30. Sedgwick, *The Commons 1715–1754*, vol.1, p.306.

31. P. Langford, 'Tories and Jacobites 1714–1751' in *History of the University of Oxford*, vol.5, p.99.

32. ibid., pp.103–6.

33. Anon., *Reasons for a Royal Visitation of the Universities* (London, 1717), quoted in R.O. Berdahl, *British Universities and the State* (Berkeley & Los Angeles, 1959), p.18.

34. Langford, 'Tories and Jacobites', p.107; Sedgwick, *The Commons 1715– 1754*, vol.1, p.306; Berdahl, *Universities and the State*, p.18.

35. Stratford to Harley, 20 Mar. [1717] and 24 Dec. 1719, quoted in Langford, 'Tories and Jacobites', p.107.

36. ibid., p.123; Sedgwick, *The Commons 1715–1754*, vol.1, p.307.

37. Rex, *University Representation*, p.350; Churton to Sidmouth, 31 Oct. 1806, quoted in R. Thorne, *The History of Parliament, The House of Commons 1790–1820*, 5 vols (London, 1986), vol.2, p.327; Namier and Brooke, *The Commons 1754–1790*, vol.1, p.360.

38. W. Ferguson, *Scotland 1689 to the Present* (Edinburgh, 1968), p.96; D.B. Horne, *A Short History of the University of Edinburgh, 1556–1889* (Edinburgh, 1967), p.34.

39. There are accounts of the work of the commission in all the Scottish university histories cited, and see also C. Shepherd, 'The Arts Curriculum at Aberdeen at

the Beginning of the Eighteenth Century' in J.J. Carter and J.H. Pittock (eds.), *Aberdeen and the Enlightenment* (Aberdeen, 1987), pp.146–54.

40. R.S. Rait, *The Universities of Aberdeen: A History* (Aberdeen, 1895), p.173; Horn, *Edinburgh*, p.36.

41. Horn, *Edinburgh*, p.38.

42. ibid., p.37, see also pp.71–2 and 73.

43. B.P. Lenman, 'A Client society: Scotland between the '15 and the '45', in J. Black (ed.), *Britain in the Age of Walpole* (London, 1984), pp.69–93, and see also D. Szechi and D. Hayton, 'John Bull's other kingdoms: the English government of Scotland and Ireland' in C. Jones (ed.), *Britain in the First Age of Party, 1680–1750* (London, 1987), pp.241–80, especially pp.241, 246, 253–9.

44. William Robertson to Gilbert Elliot, 15 & [20] Feb. 1762, quoted in R.B. Sher, *Church and University in the Scottish Enlightenment: the Moderate Literati of Edinburgh* (Edinburgh, 1985), p.113.

45. D.J. Withrington, 'Education and society in the eighteenth century' in N.T. Phillipson and R Mitchison (eds.), *Scotland in the Age of Improvement* (Edinburgh, 1970), pp.169–99, especially pp.184–5, 191–2; Ferguson, *Scotland*, pp.204–9; T.C. Smout, *A History of the Scottish People 1560–1830* (London, 1969), pp.476–9; T.M. Devine and R Mitchison (eds.), *People and Society in Scotland*, vol.1, *1760–1830* (Edinburgh, 1988), pp.130–1, 147.

46. J.D. Mackie, *The University of Glasgow 1451–1951: A Short History* (Glasgow, 1954), pp.133–5.

47. ibid., pp.153–4, 156, 177, 178, 190.

48. R.G. Cant, *The University of St Andrews: A Short History*, Revised ed. (Edinburgh, 1970), p.77–8, 78 n.1.

49. ibid., pp.78–9.

50. R.K. Hannay, 'The Visitation of St Andrews University in 1690', *Scottish Historical Review*, 13, (1915), p.3.

51. ibid., p.4.

52. ibid., pp.3, 7–15; Cant, *St Andrews*, pp.79–80, 86, 86 n.2.

53. Cant, *St Andrews*, p.87.

54. R.L. Emerson will shortly publish a detailed analysis of the eighteenth-century teachers at Aberdeen's two universities in the Aberdeen Quincentennial Studies series.

55. Rait, *Universities of Aberdeen*, pp.173, 177.

56. ibid., pp.190–2, 293–4; J.M. Bulloch, *A History of the University of Aberdeen, 1495–1895*, (London 1895), pp.139–42.

57. P.J. Anderson (ed.), *Records of the Aberdeen Universities Commission 1716–17* (Aberdeen, 1900), pp.36–7, 45.

58. ibid., 51, 52, 53–55.

59. R.L. Emerson, 'Aberdeen professors 1690–1800: two structures, two professoriates, two careers', in Carter and Pittock, *Aberdeen and the Enlightenment*, pp.155–67; 'Lord Bute and the Scottish Universities 1760–1792', in K.W. Schweizer (ed.), *Lord Bute: Essays in Re-interpretation* (Leicester, 1988), pp.147–79.

60. Bulloch, *University of Aberdeen*, pp.131–8.

61. B.R. Levack, *The Formation of the British State: England, Scotland, and the Union, 1603–1707* (Oxford, 1987), pp.185–6, 211–12; Lenman 'A Client Society', pp.84–5.

2

THE FIRST AMERICAN REVOLUTION, 1689

David S. Lovejoy

What role did the American colonies play in the history of England during the century of revolution? If one reads exclusively British historians, one's answer would be: 'Hardly any role at all.' But, of course, we are not discussing the whole century at this point—only its last few years. What is surprising to me is not only English lack of interest *then* in reverberations of the Glorious Revolution in America, but British lack of interest *today* in these same colonial events. This is not a scolding of anyone or any group. It is simply pointing out just after the tercentenary of that Revolution that British historians have tended to ignore the upheaval in the colonies despite its being a crisis in the early empire second only to the American Revolution.

The English empire in North America took on some kind of definition after the Restoration of Charles II in 1660. Already six colonies struggled to keep a foothold in the new continent, and five more were founded in the next twenty-one years. Along with additional settlements went an increasing attempt to direct and control them both economically and politically, even, in some cases, religiously. A mercantile frame of mind among the planners dictated a colonial policy which—if fitfully—took shape as colonies multiplied and trade expanded. Fundamental was the assumption—presumption, colonists said—that colonies existed for the benefit of the mother country. When a series of Navigation Acts, passed by Parliament, failed to convince colonists that the bulk of their trade should centre upon London and other English ports, the Crown brought pressure to bear upon colonial governments by political means to force them to mend their ways. Pressure ranged from royal commissions sent to warn, guide, and reform stubborn colonies, particularly Massachusetts, to an attempt to impose Poynings's Law in a couple of instances, one of them successful, to generous patronage to the King's friends who eagerly displaced hungry locals. The appointment of the Lords of Trade, a committee of the Privy Council, in 1675 brought a number of colonial loose ends under one body of policy-makers in London. The aggressive Bishop of London, Henry Compton, took colonial religious affairs under his wing, uninvited, and laid down law for the Anglican Church in Virginia and other royal colonies and vigorously pushed it in dissenting colonies. This effort was not at all appreciated in Massachusetts and Connecticut where governments discriminated against Anglicans and other sects outside the Congregational Church such as Quakers. Colonial policy after 1660 emphasised subordination, dependency, and consolidation along with a centralising of control in London.[1]

Before this tightening of the reins quite reached its peak in the final years of Charles II's reign, colonists reacted to it. In doing so they articulated a conception of empire different from the one they were increasingly subjected to. On neither side of the Atlantic was there precedent about how colonies and colonists should be regarded and governed, and planners in the realm as well as doers in America worked out their own ideas as needs of the kingdom and New World conditions dictated. Despite differences in America, say, between Virginia in the south and Massachusetts in the north, colonists came to surprisingly similar conclusions about their roles in the New World and their relationship to the Crown.

Provoked by Charles II's short-sighted gift of a large body of Virginia's land to loyal friends, the Virginia government in 1675 sought a charter from the Crown which would settle a number of political issues and also protect the colony from royal whim. At the heart of the new charter were a confirmation of the local assembly's authority, a guarantee against taxation without consent, and an assurance generally of the rights of Englishmen in Virginia. Colonies, Virginia's agents argued in London, were 'but in nature of an extension . . . of the realm', and Virginians should possess the 'same liberties and privileges as Englishmen in England'. Such a bold assertion clashed head-on with plans initiated in London to tighten and centralise authority, and Charles II and the Lords of Trade scrapped the charter before it received the Great Seal.[2] Maryland followed the next year. The Chesapeake colonies shared grievances in the 1670s, among them the drastically low price of tobacco and the demand that their crop be marketed only in England, which further depressed the price. Added to this were high customs duties in English ports and the act of 1673 which charged duties on tobacco when it was transported from one colony to another.[3] Settlers in both colonies suffered high local taxes to support their governments, and the Indian menace frustrated expansion and raised taxes still further for defence.

While Virginians sought protection from impositions of the Crown, colonists in Maryland found their proprietor, Lord Baltimore, and his Catholic government the cause of their difficulties. Maryland's charter of 1632 gave the proprietor absolute power, despite holding out at the same time promises of Englishmen's rights. To enhance control, he restricted suffrage and representation, held courts in his own name, not the king's, and taxed heavily, claimed Marylanders, to support the self-interested government and its Catholic favourites. After a small unsuccessful rebellion, the government hanged two of its leaders and fined others. The reaction of the colonists was a petition to Charles II and the people of England in a unique document called 'Complaint from Heaven and a Huy and Crye out of Virginia and Maryland'. This was a major statement which protested openly against the proprietor's government whose arbitrariness denied Marylanders 'liberty of the freeborne subjects of England'. They sought the king's protection under a royal government which, they assumed, wrongly as it turned out, would honour their rights as Englishmen. Once it reached London, 'Complaint from Heaven' died a quick death with Virginia's charter.[4]

Puritan Massachusetts was different. But, then, Massachusetts was always different, for in its seventeenth-century struggle a major role was played by God himself. A liberal charter of 1629, directing the colonists to elect all their officers, was part and parcel of a covenant with God, which defined the holy purpose of the Bible Commonwealth from its inception. In combination these special attributes made the Bay Colony, to say the least, difficult to deal with.[5] As English policy intensified in the 1670s and 80s, Massachusetts' charter came under siege. A Royal Commission, an imperious collector of customs—really a spy, colonists claimed, the Royal Navy enlisted to seize offending traders, besides serious threats to the charter itself, all these humiliations made the colony bristle in defence of the 'Lord's vineyard' in America. In 1678 the General Court answered charges against the colony in a state paper worthy of an independent republic. It plainly hinted at immunity from the Acts of Trade because the colony sent no representatives to Parliament, and registered a strong complaint against all trade restrictions, some of which it defined as taxation without consent. The 1678 statement publicised a deeply held conception of empire which admitted the colony's allegiance to the Crown, but questioned any interference with its trade and politics. Graciously, out of respect for the King, the General Court agreed to review its laws and repeal any it found repugnant to the laws of England except—and here Massachusetts exposed its very soul – 'except such as the repealling whereof will make us to renounce the professed cause of our first coming hither'. Dearer to them than any material advantage to the realm or to themselves, was the 'interest of the Lord Jesus, & of his churches.'[6]

If Massachusetts was unique in its divine purpose and sacrosanct charter, New York was unique in other ways. It was the only colony based on conquest (other than from the Indians) and therefore contained a majority of Dutchmen; it was a proprietary colony owned and governed by a member of the royal family, James, Duke of York; and from its outset, owing to the Duke's suspicions about government, New Yorkers were denied a representative assembly. Protests against arbitrary government were frequent from the beginning, based on political principle and self-interested needs.[7] When New Yorkers repeatedly dragged their feet over taxes and paying customs to the Duke, James reluctantly relented and permitted a legislature for the first time. This was in 1683, almost twenty years after the Dutch surrender. The first task the new representatives tackled was the drafting of the Charter of Libertyes which fashioned a frame of government and put control squarely into the hands of the governor, the council, and the 'people mett in General Assembly', subject only to the review of the Duke. While the Virginia charter of 1675 generally defined rights and liberties which all subjects ought to enjoy, the New York charter listed them at great length. It would guarantee individual liberties, the right of both freeholders and freemen to vote; it included Magna Carta's paragraph on liberty of persons, judgment by peers, and law of the land; and adapted the Petition of Right of 1628 to protect New Yorkers from taxation without representation. Excessive bail, quartering of troops in private homes and so on, were prohibited, suggesting the people's apprehension of such rights under the Duke's rule. The legislature emerged as a little parliament with measures to ensure triennial gatherings, times and places of meetings, judgement of the fitness of its members, and immunity from arrest along with three servants in travelling to and from their sessions. Drafters of the charter had a very definite idea of what colonists' rights ought to be, and they put together an instrument which, they believed, would protect them forever.[8]

The middle 1680s was the worst time possible for a radical colonial charter to come under scrutiny in London. As a result of the Popish Plot, the Exclusion Crisis, Shaftesbury's other carryings-on against the Crown, Charles II and his government were in no mood to be generous respecting domestic or colonial policy. The King's 'revenge' was felt all around, and a good deal of it spilled over to America. The Navigation Acts were tightened all along the line. The Crown went to court against Massachusetts' charter and managed to revoke it in 1684, as well as commencing actions against the charters of a half dozen other colonies. The Lords of Trade discussed a plan for Parliament to tax all the colonies directly.[9] From Charles's and James's deliberations with the Privy Council emerged a decision to consolidate colonial governments in the north into one large Dominion without trace of the usual representative assemblies. Then in February 1685 Charles II died, and James, who harboured even stronger convictions about the prerogative, succeeded him. It was at this point that the New York Charter was laid upon the table, and it was not long before James as king vetoed it and took the colony under the wing of the Crown. The next year he dispatched Sir Edmund Andros to Boston as Governor-General over all New England, now robbed of its local assemblies in favour of direct rule. Andros and his council restructured New Englanders' lives and livelihoods. The Dominion government taxed them and legislated without their consent; it revamped their system of justice, challenged their ownership of land, forced the Acts of Trade upon them, and pushed into their midst the King's Church and all its vanities. God, it seemed, had washed his hands of the Bible Commonwealth. In 1688 James added New York and New Jersey to the Dominion, and arbitrary government obtained from the St Croix in Maine to Delaware Bay. Among the bureaucrats in London there was serious talk of a southern Dominion to follow.[10]

Two conceptions of empire met face-to-face and the colonists' version collapsed by the wayside. Colonists had worried less about sovereignty in the realm, which was a chief issue at home, than about sovereignty in the empire. From experience, principle, and need, a good many of them, particularly in Virginia, Maryland, New York and New England, worked out schemes to protect themselves in which sovereignty was divided between the Crown and their own governments. Although they were outside the realm, colonists insisted they were entitled to the rights and liberties of Englishmen. It was the old issue of liberty versus order, rights versus control, the periphery versus the centre of things. In James's reign there was little doubt which was the winner.

But he was not the winner for long as we know. News of the dramatic events in England was blown across the Atlantic in the winter and spring of 1688–89, some of it directly, much of it by way of the West Indies. It was often garbled, and out of sequence, and some of it was even accurate. Colonists suffered several months of uncertainty, and it was not until the spring of 1689 that they pieced together the course of events, but only in few places with the help of the established governments.[11] Whether they acted before they were assured of William's success is a debatable point. But act they did, beginning in Massachussetts in the middle of April. Bay Colonists overthrew Governor-General Andros and his Dominion officers, threw the lot in prison, and set up for themselves on the bases of their former government, assuming, they said, that King William would reinstate the charter of 1629 and return Massachusetts to its holy state.[12]

A month and a half later merchant and militia captain Jacob Leisler and his followers toppled the Dominon government in New York. He represented a cross-section of New Yorkers and a large measure of Dutchmen. Leisler called an assembly which incorporated parts of the Charter of Libertyes of 1683 to justify colony taxes. He ruled as governor for almost two years before the previously dominant elite caught up with him.[13] In July Maryland's John Coode, at the head of a Protestant Association, forced out Lord Baltimore's people at gun-point and waited for William to recognise their commendable reduction of a Catholic regime which had illegally separated good Englishmen from the Crown.[14] In each of these colonies the rebels claimed that their former governments had deliberately suppressed the joyful news of William's and Mary's accession and no doubt were preparing to hold their colonies for James in a Catholic conspiracy – with help from Louis XIV and the French in Canada. This was particularly true in Massachusetts whose leaders were apprehensive, too, lest William confirm Governor Andros and the Dominion in place and leave them no better off than before. To prevent either possibility, they had pounced.[15]

Colonists in America spent two turbulent years or more between their rebellions and King William's eventual resettlement of their governments. Much of this time they spent justifying what they had done. In doing so they fell back upon their conceptions of empire generally agreed to in the previous decade or two. William had invaded the realm to rescue it from slavery and popery, they said, and the colonies were as much in need of rescuing as England, given their governments which sharply reflected James's absolute and Catholic rule. William had descended upon England to restore the charters revoked by James, and colonists, chiefly in New England, included their own in the new king's promise. Englishmen at home had rebelled to restore their ancient rights violated by Charles and James, adding a few new ones, according to the Declaration of Rights of February 1689. Colonists rebelled for the same reasons, to restore rights they either had enjoyed or ought to have enjoyed these many years as English subjects abroad. The Glorious Revolution was a shared revolution, they claimed, for colonies were part of the English nation in which colonists participated as equals. The Dominion of New England had grossly violated rights which the whole English nation laid claim to, according to a Boston writer. Jacob Leisler's soldiers in New York gloried in the part they played in a deliverance by 'so happy an instrument as Prince William', for they had groaned for so long under the 'same oppression as Englishmen at home'. In Maryland John Coode's Protestant Associators boasted of a 'proportionable Share of so great a Blessing' with their 'fellow subjects' in their 'native Country of England'.[16]

Under covenant and charter Massachusetts had established for some time its own reason for being, in accord with a holy purpose, as we have seen. But in *justifying* rebellion Bay Colonists told a different story. Gone was the charter by court action; the special arrangement with God had never won much respect among the powers-that-be in London. Coming late, then, to an appreciation of an empire of equals, Massachusetts' colonists quickly adjusted their argument to the revolutionary fashion. Sensitive to these changes, Increase Mather, in vindicating New England, put things very clearly: 'No Englishmen in their Wits', he wrote, 'will ever Venture their Lives and Estates to Enlarge the Kings Dominions abroad, and Enrich the whole English Nation, if their Reward after all must be to be deprived of their *English Liberties*.'[17]

Better to understand the underlying causes of the upheaval in 1689, we ought to remember that a prominent characteristic of colonial culture was its political and social instability. It was difficult, colonists discovered, to transfer to the New World the subtle but effective relationships which had existed for generations in England between wealth and social standing, on the one hand, and the exercise of political power and privilege, on the other. Given the unsophisticated, even crude circumstances colonists found themselves in, the consequences of colonisation were often unstable political and social conditions which frustrated and confused not only ambitious settlers who did the work, but even governors and governments chosen or appointed to rule over them.[18]

Therefore, if we swallow whole the purely political and constitutional view of the colonists' attempts to share the Revolution of 1688 with those who stayed at home, we would be telling only half the story. In each colony, accompanying rebellion, was a strike for supremacy by one group of colonists or another who half recognised the cultural imbalance of their lives and felt left out of a proper share of the rewards colonial governments and economies had to offer them. Lord Baltimore's Catholic oligarchy since the Restoration had discriminated against Maryland colonists, chiefly Protestants, who were a majority, in a government bent on extracting advantages for the proprietor and his favourites.[19] All New Yorkers resented a lack of an assembly in which both political and economic needs might better be accommodated, but a particular group of merchants and landowners had done very well under these conditions through close association with the proprietary government and then with the Dominion of New England. It was this group which was behind the Charter of Libertyes of 1683 with the hope that a guarantee of Englishmen's rights could only enhance its grip on the colony and its economics rewards. It was against these people, now entrenched in the Dominion, that Jacob Leisler rebelled, only to be undone by a set of circumstances he could not control in either New York or London.[20] In Massachusetts rebellion seemed almost unanimous. Bay Colonists 'did this day rise as one man', one report boasted. The Dominion under Andros had incensed a great many people, chiefly the Puritan Old Guard which pursued God's purpose through the old charter, but also more moderate colonists whose economic interests the Dominion had seriously upset. Both groups found relief in the Dominion's demise, or so it appeared at the time.[21]

The Revolution of 1688 in England, then, was a godsend to a large number of colonists who willingly exploited it for their own peculiar purposes. Self-interest and political principle combined to trigger rebellion against colonial regimes which, colonists insisted, violated a fair share in New World advantages besides an equal treatment from government. English rights and liberties, after all, protected property and economic opportunity as well as civil and individual rights.

Now, what do we make of all this? The English at home, including William's new government, awoke one morning to learn that several colonies three thousand miles away in America had shared the Glorious Revolution with them on grounds wholly inconsistent with any idea of empire familiar to them. Revolution, it seems, did not touch colonial policy. As true after 1688 as before was the hard fact that 'All plantations were of the King's making and . . . he might at any time alter or dispose of them at his pleasure', a statement attributed to the First Earl of Shaftesbury no less.[22]

Still, Maryland won its royal government. The Crown was as suspicious of Lord Baltimore's proprietary as were Marylanders, although for different reasons. A proprietary regime was a long step removed from control by the Crown, a Stuart objective William happily accepted. When John Coode and his Protestant rebels dispossessed the Catholic proprietor of his government, William approved; he commissioned a royal governor, selected a royal council, and agreed to an elected assembly. So far so good. It looked as if revolution in Maryland was a huge success.[23] But when the deputies shortly afterwards tried to nail down their conception of empire in a declaratory law, to ensure the very guarantees and rights they had struggled for against the proprietor, William vetoed the lot. Royal government, to be sure, but colonists 'were of the King's making'.[24]

Luckily for Massachusetts, William III made no effort to reimpose the Dominion. But war with France stirred up hostile Indians besides the French in the north, and the colony's defences, since Andros's hurried departure, were in shambles. The government languished; colony debt rose astoundingly; a former homogeneity among colonists appeared to fade. Indian attacks forced the evacuation of frontier towns; and then in 1692 the notorious witchcraft epidemic broke out at Salem. These together brought Massachusetts close to demoralisation. There was no doubt this time that God had turned his back on his people.[25] Still, things might have been worse, had it not been for the brilliant negotiating of Increase Mather, colony agent in London, who argued for Massachusetts' exceptionalism. Although unable to persuade William to return the charter, he brought home a new one which secured half a loaf at the very least. Granted God's people were from that time subject to the king's governor, they chose their own council and elected a lower house. Although they lost their capacity to evade the Navigation Acts – well, almost – to persecute Anglicans and Quakers and other dissenters, and to confine colony voting to Puritan saints, they survived the compromise, if chastened and humiliated. The addition of Plymouth Colony to Massachusetts brightened prospects in Boston if not in Plymouth.[26]

The consequences of revolution in New York could not have been more different. Jacob Leisler ruled as governor for almost two years on behalf of King William, but not without provoking a great deal of bitterness. The elite group of merchants and landowners, who had pretty much called the tune since proprietary days, angrily opposed Leisler's policies, such as taxing their land and trade and destroying the commercial monopolies which had benefited them at the expense of ordinary people. War with France and shortly an ambitious but disastrous joint expedition with Massachusetts and Connecticut against Canada called for new taxes, more troops, and in some cases forced seizure of supplies.[27] Virulently anti-Catholic, Leisler purged New York of remnants of James's rule and damned as 'papishly affected' all who opposed him, his policies, and his increasing arbitrariness. He had no luck with agents in London and won no friendly support there. Support in New York dwindled as his government hardened, all the while alienating many of its earlier friends.[28] When William, his hands full at home and on the continent, got around to resettling New York and commissioning a royal governor, Leisler hesitated long enough to give his enemies opportunity to cry treason against the King. In short order he was tried and hanged along with his deputy. Thus ended Leisler's Rebellion, but not the sharp division between factions which persisted and poisoned politics in New York for the next generation.[29]

At the very time the new government hanged Leisler, its legislature translated the charter of Libertyes into statute law. It enacted the whole list of guarantees against arbitrary government which New Yorkers had struggled to revive during Leisler's short time in power. Once the new legislation surfaced in England, King William promptly dismissed it for the same reasons James earlier had scuttled the charter.[30] There was no room in the English empire for a colony whose legislature had presumed to guarantee its people the same rights and liberties Englishmen enjoyed at home.

In the short run the Glorious Revolution in America, contrary to the tenor of political and constitutional changes in the realm, taught colonies that they were dominions of the Crown, dependent and subordinate and subject to the royal grace and favour of the king. But what colonists did not win in 1689, by attempting make the Revolution theirs, too, they tended to assume over the long pull of the eighteenth century. Then when colonial policy from London took a new twist in the 1760s and 70s, imposing direct taxation, admiralty court justice, and all the rest of it, colonists revived their seventeenth-century idea of empire—if they had ever buried it. It was strongly evident in the Declaration of the First Continental Congress which met in Philadelphia in 1774.[31] Allegiance to the Crown, yes, but other interference violated colonists' rights and made them second-class citizens in what they assumed was an empire of equals. King and Parliament ruled in Britain, and king and local assemblies ruled in America. This was divided sovereignty, an answer to the conflict between liberty and control. But the Revolution of 1688 had made Parliament supreme at home, and in the eighteenth century supremacy had spread across the ocean. When colonists denied it, when king and Parliament sent troops to enforce it, colonists gave up the struggle and by independence established themselves equal to the English as members of the human race.

Notes

1. For English colonial policy, see Charles M. Andrews, *The Colonial Period of American History* 4 vols. (New Haven, 1933–38). For a brief discussion of colonial policy as it affected the colonies in the latter half of the seventeenth century, see David S. Lovejoy, *The Glorious Revolution in America* (New York, 1972, reprinted Middletown, Conn, 1987) chs. 1–2. Bishop Compton's connection with the American colonies is described in Edward F. Carpenter, *The Protestant Bishop, Being the Life of Henry Compton, 1632–1713, Bishop of London* (London, 1956), ch. XIV.

2. John D. Burk, *History of Virginia* 4 vols. (Petersburg, Va., 1804–16), II, Appendix, pp. XI–LX. See, too, *Virginia Magazine of History and Biography*, 56 (1948), 264–6; W. Noel Sainsbury (ed.), *Calendar of State Papers, Colonial Series, 1675–1676* (London, 1893), nos. 602, 603, 696, 697, I–II, 834, 835, hereafter cited as *CSPC*.

3. 25 *Car*. II, c. 7, *Statutes of the Realm*, V, 792; Leo F. Stock (ed.), *Proceedings and Debates of the British Parliaments Respecting North America, 1452–1727* 5 vols. (Washington, 1921–41), I, pp. 398–400, 399n.

4. For Maryland's charter, see Samuel Lucas (ed.), *Charters of the Old English Colonies in America* (London, 1850), pp. 88–97. See, too, W. H. Browne, et al. (eds.), *Archives of Maryland* 72 vols. (Baltimore, 1883–1972), I, pp. 262–6; ibid., II, pp. 159–60, 168–9, 174–84; ibid., V, pp. 134–152; *CSPC, 1675–1676*, no. 937.

5. Perry Miller, 'From the Covenant to the Revival', J. W. Smith and A. L. Jamison (ed.), *Religion in American Life* 3 vols. (Princeton, 1961), I, pp. 322–68; Edmund S. Morgan, *The Puritan Dilemma: The Story of John Winthrop* (Boston, 1958), ch. VII.

6. 'Diary of John Hull', American Antiquarian Society *Transactions and Collections*, III (1857), 202–3, 212, 216–17; E. B. O'Callaghan and B. Fernow (eds.), *Documents Relative to the Colonial History of the State of New-York* 15 vols. (Albany, 1853–1887), III, pp. 51–5, 57–61, hereafter cited as *N. Y. Col. Docs.*; N. B. Shurtleff (ed.), *Records of the Governor and Company of the Massachusetts Bay in New England, 1628–1686* 5 vols. (Boston, 1853–54), V, *1674–1686*, pp. 198–201, 202.

7. *The Colonial Laws of New York from the Year 1664 to the Revolution*, 5 vols. (Albany, 1894–96), I, pp. 1–71; *N. Y. Col. Docs.*, XIV, pp. 632, 580; *Ibid.*; III, pp. 230, 235, 221–3, 246.

8. For the Charter of Libertyes, see *Col. Laws of N. Y.*, I, pp. 111–16.

9. David Ogg, *England in the Reign of Charles II* 2 vols. (Oxford, 1934, reprinted, 1963), II, ch. 17; J. P. Kenyon, *Robert Spencer, Earl of Sunderland, 1641–1702* (London, 1958), ch. 3; Blathwayt Papers, Colonial Williamsburg, vol. XIV; Philip S. Haffenden, 'The Crown and the Colonial Charters, 1675–1688,' *William and Mary Quarterly*, 3rd ser., XV (1958), 297–311, 452–66; *CSPC, 1681–1685*, no. 1902; Viola F. Barnes, *The Dominion of New England* (New Haven, 1923, reprinted New York, 1960), pp. 23–4 and n.

10. For demise of New York's charter, see *CSPC, 1685–1688*, no. 37; *N. Y. Col. Docs.*, III, 354, 357–9, 360–61. For the Dominion of New England, see Barnes, *Dominion*; Lovejoy, *Glorious Revolution in America*, chs. 9–10.

11. For colonists' uncertainty about events in England, see Colonial Office Papers, Public Record Office, 1/65/90, 5/905, pp. 41–2, hereafter cited as C. O.; Livingston Family Papers, General Correspondence, 1661–1695, Frankling Delano Roosevelt Library, Hyde Park, New York; Blathwayt Papers, vols. XVI, XVII.

12. Events in Massachusetts are reported in John Riggs's Narrative, C. O. 5/905, pp. 85–7, and *CSPC, 1689–1692*, no. 261; C. O. 5/855, nos. 2, 15; C. M. Andrews, ed., *Narratives of the Insurrections, 1675–1690* (New York, 1915), pp. 215–19; 'Diary of Lawrence Hammond', April 18, 1689, Massachusetts Historical Society *Proceedings* (1891–1892), 2nd ser., VII, 149–50; *Hinckley Papers*, Mass. Hist. Soc. *Collections*, 4th ser., V, 192–6; *An Account of the Late Revolutions in New-England*, by A. B., in W. H. Whitmore (ed.), *Andros Tracts*: Being a Collection of Pamphlets and Official Papers . . . *of the Andros Government* 3 vols. (New York, 1868–1874), II, 189–201; *New-England's Factions Discovered*, by C. D., in Andrews (ed.), *Narratives*, pp. 253–67.

13. Documents describing the rebellions in New York are in E. B. O'Callaghan (ed.), *Documentary History of the State of New-York* 4 vols. (Albany, 1849–51), II, 3–4, 7–8, 10, 11–13, 55–6, and Introductory, hereafter cited as *Doc. Hist. N. Y.*; *N. Y. Col. Docs.*, III, pp. 636–48; Andrews (ed.), *Narratives*, pp. 323–329; C. O. 5/855,no. 16; *CSPC, 1689–1692*, no. 242.

14. For events in Maryland, see 'Narrative of Coll. Henry Darnall' in J. Thomas Scharf, *History of Maryland* 3 vols., (Baltimore, 1879), I, pp. 338–9; *Arch of Md.*, VIII, 101–10, 156; Beverly McAnear (ed.), 'Mariland's Grevances Wiy The Have Taken Op Arms', *Journal of Southern History*, VIII (1942), 405–7; Andrews (ed.), *Narratives*, pp. 305–14, *CSPC, 1689–1692*, nos. 290 315.

15. 'Diary of Lawrence Hammond', pp. 149–50; R. N. Toppan and A. T. S. Goodrick (eds.), *Edward Randolph: Including His Letters and Official papers . . . 1676–1703* 7 vols. (Boston, 1898–1909), VI, pp. 312–13.

16. *Andros Tracts*, I, pp. 71, 72, II, 77, 191–2; *Doc. Hist. of N. Y.*, II, pp. 10, 58; Andrews (ed.), *Narratives*, pp. 181, 310–11, 313; *Arch. of Md.*, VIII, pp. 143–4; M. G. Hall, L. H. Leder, and M. G. Kammen (eds.), *The Glorious Revolution in America: Documents of the Colonial Crisis of 1689* (Chapel Hill, 1964), pp. 48, 103, 109.

17. *Andros Tracts*, II, pp. 76.

18. Bernard Bailyn, 'Politics and Social Structure in Virginia', in James Morton Smith (ed.), *Seventeenth-Century America*: Essays in Colonial History (Chapel Hill, 1959), pp. 90–115.

19. See again 'Complaint from Heaven', *Arch. of Md.*, V, pp. 134–52.

20. *Loyalty Vindicated from the Reflections of a Virulent Pamphlet* (1698), Andrews (ed.), *Narratives*, p. 382.

21. 'Diary of Lawrence Hammond,' pp. 149–50; Lovejoy, *Glorious Revolution*, pp. 244–5.

22. *CSPC, 1681–1685*, no. 1087.

23. *Arch of Md.*, VIII, pp. 312, 425–561 *passim*; Michael G. Kammen, 'Causes of the Maryland Revolution of 1689', *Maryland Historical Magazine* (Dec. 1960), p. 330.

24. *Arch. of Md.*, XIII, pp. 425–30; Eugene R. Sheridan, 'Maryland as a Royal Colony, 1689–1715' (Unpubl. A. M. thesis, Univ. of Wisconsin (1968). ch. II; Richard A. Gleissner, 'Religious Causes of the Glorious Revolution in Maryland,' *Maryland Historical Magazine* (Winter, 1969), 332–41.

25. John Palmer, *An Impartial Account of the State of New England*, in *Andros Tracts*, I, p27; Andrews (ed.), *Narrative*, p. 208; *New England's Faction*

Discovered, ibid., p. 257; 'Diary of Lawrence Hammond', p. 160; C. O. 5/905, pp. 176–7; C. O. 5/855, no. 56; *CSPC, 1689–1692*, no. 741.

26. Increase Mather, 'Autobiography,' ed. M. G. Hall, Am. Antiq. Soc. *Proceedings,* 71 (1961), pt. 2, pp. 333–7; Increase Mather, *A Brief Account concerning Several of the Agents,* in Andrews (ed.), *Narrative,* pp. 276–97. The Massachusetts charter of 1691 is in Hall, Leder, and Kammen (eds.), *Glorious Revolution,* pp. 76–9. *Hinckley Papers,* pp. 299–301; *CSPC, 1689–1692,* no. 1731.

27. For Leisler's troubles, see *CSPC, 1689–1692,* no. 840; *Col. Laws of N. Y.,* I. p. 218; *Doc. Hist N. Y.,* II, pp. 50, 243; *N. Y. Col. Docs.,* III, pp. 717, 762; Andrews (ed.), *Narratives,* pp. 350, 388. For Leisler's role as wartime leader, see *Hinckley Papers,* pp. 232–3, 239, 247, 249–52; *Doc. Hist. N. Y.,* II, pp. 1–65, 242, 390. L. H. Leder, '". . . Like Madmen Through the Street," the New York City Riot of June 1690,' *The New York Historical Society Quarterly,* 39, no. 4 (Oct. 1955), 405–15.

28. *CSPC, 1689–1962,* nos. 458, 365; *Doc. Hist. N. Y.,* II, pp. 23, 268; C. O. 5/1081/50; C. O. 5/1081/64; Andrews (ed.), *Narratives,* pp. 324 and n., 398n.; *N. Y. Col. Docs,* III pp. 629–32; Jerome R. Reich, *Leisler's Rebellion, a Study of Democracy in New York* (Chicago, 1953), pp. 85–6.

29. Blathwayt Papers, vols. IV, VIII, IX, XV; *Hinckley Papers,* pp. 282–4; Andrews (ed.), *Narratives,* pp. 248n., 391 and n.; *N. Y. Col. Docs,* III, pp. 757–9; *Doc. Hist. N. Y.,* II, pp. 376–80, 382.

30. *Col. Laws of N. Y.,* I, pp.244–8; *CSPC, 1969–1697,* nos. 846, 952, 1010, 1012; *N. Y. Col. Docs.,* IV, pp. 263–5.

31. Merrill Jensen (ed.), *English Historical Documents,* IX, *American Colonial Documents to 1776* (London, 1955), pp. 805–8.

3

JACOBITE LITERATURE: LOVE, DEATH AND VIOLENCE

Murray Pittock

Statues of King James II and VII are hard to find. Those of us who have not seen, or who have forgotten, the Augustan ones of the King outside the National Gallery in London or in the niche high up in University College, Oxford, may perhaps still associate that age with the time after the Revolution. The old uneasy straitjacket definitions of eighteenth-century studies are loosening; but it still seems that the intellectual history of that time in England or Scotland is directed away from sources of conflict to myths of consensus. The Enlightenment is there to enlighten; trade to humanise or aggrandise, depending on one's perspective. Fielding's aim is justice in life and art; Johnson canonises the canon; the bitterness of satire only reflects that transitory world of Walpole, and does not disrupt the Whig consensus. Wolfe recalls Gray's 'Elegy' before Quebec, won with British Highlanders; and the ghosts of judgment, wit, and taste haunt us with the suggestion of the inevitability of progress.

Above the entrance to Pope's grotto was carved the motto 'JR 1696', with stigmata and a crown of thorns.[1] This poignant image of suffering and sacrifice, combined with the name 'Jacobus Rex', and the political implications of the Resurrection, was one of the dominant motifs in the continuing cause of Jacobitism. We are beginning to realise that the struggle to restore the Stuarts was not a narrow quarrel of absolutists and 'barbarians' (Trevelyan's word for Highlanders) against history.[2] In this paper I shall be arguing for the importance of one aspect in what was a much broader ideological battle. The literature of the Stuart cause, if its symbols and ambiguities are identified, poses a marked challenge to our concepts of the tendencies inherent in eighteenth-century literary history. In the long run its identity may heighten the fading charms of Augustanism, by portraying it as a keener struggle than those who popularised the concept would have dared to confess.

During the 1650s, the Horatian ode had been a popular form because of its very ambivalence towards the role of Augustus, an ambivalence intensified by Marvell's poem, where 'Augustus' is the republican who has slain 'Caesar': a double reversal of history.[3] Times of political trouble breed such literary ambiguity. Such 'Augustan' double irony can be found in Dryden's translation of Virgil, the ultimate expression of his quietist Jacobitism, and in

Pope's ascribing to Dulness, the surrogate of 'Dunce [George] the second', the sentiment:

> Oh, (cry'd the Goddess) for some pedant Reign!
> Some gentle JAMES, to bless the land again . . .[4]

Thus the Hanoverians invoke those whom they have deposed to 'bless the land': the verb is bitter in the light of the religious oppression 1688 had engendered. By 1723, five separate new penal laws had been passed against Catholics, and the apostolic Kirk in Scotland had been disestablished for the last time.[5] Subsequently, both were the target of further legislation, and the Episcopalians in Scotland earned a distinction unique in the Anglican communion when they were effectively proscribed by a parliament sitting in the very country in which Anglicanism was the established religion.[6] Such were the restraints and contradictions inherent in the post-Revolution settlement, after the Tory Augustus, Dryden's 'Heroick *James*', was overthrown, and the Virgilian prophecy in *Eclogues* (taken as referring both to Augustus and Christ) was thwarted.[7] The land was not blessed: Scotland had to endure severe famine, and 'laughing Ceres' would 're-assume the land' no more.[8] Prices rose, at first rapidly. Between the accession of Charles I and 1688, they had risen by 12½ per cent; between 1692 and 1702, by 17 per cent. More significantly, land prices (the Tory measure of stability) rocketed.[9] The *Res Gestae* of brick and marble had become a commercial burlesque, oppressive in its implications:

> See Britain sunk in lucre's sordid charms . . .
> . . .Blest paper credit! last and best supply!
>   That lends Corruption lighter wings to fly!
>   A single leaf shall waft an Army o'er,
>   Or ship off Senates to a distant Shore . . .
> . . .Pregnant with thousands flits the scrap unseen,
>   And silent sells a King or buys a Queen.[10]

The instability of money and of government were related. The real international conspirator is not Jacobitism, but capital. Yet the accusations of corruption levied at the Whig ascendancy were symbolic, as well as actual. The concern with 'lucre' is simoniac, wrought from the death of the spiritual: the Church has sacrificed itself to the interests of the State, to those of the Emperor, 'George our Nero' as one song has it.[11] This of course Christians in the early Church would not do, and were martyred for it. The failure of the Stuart cause is not just the loss of the Augustus, but the loss of fertility associated with God's approval (compare 'Windsor Forest', *The Rape of the Lock*, and *The Dunciad*), and the loss of faith itself. The 'Moody, Murmuring' Jews of Dryden have killed their Christ, not the son but the nephew of David.[12] No resurrection was forthcoming in 1692, 1696, 1708, 1714, 1715, or 1719:

> Then rose the Seed of Chaos, and of Night,
> To blot out Order, and extinguish Light . . .
>
> (Pope, 766)

The religious interpretation of the Jacobite cause also suggested that attempts such as those of Harley and Bolingbroke to return James III to power in 1713-15, were blasphemous because they demanded the King's apostasy.[13]

Bolingbroke's *Patriot King*, written shortly after he had re-opened vain negotiations with the Stuarts,[14] is a call for a restored organicism, which, naturally enough given his track record, ignores the religious question of Stuart support. It shares a significant heritage with other 'Augustan' Jacobite literature in its doubleness (it could be addressed either to Frederick or James), and its nostalgia. 'Nostalgia', Brean Hammond tells us, 'was built into Bolingbroke's ideology'.[15] It was part of all Jacobite ideology; increasingly so as the King did not return. The defiant subtexts of the Tory satirists, which struggle in irony against the ostensible tone, are attempts to reclaim the vanishing ideal of the sacred Augustus. Like the early Christians, they had their codes and signs. Their king was the heavenly one, *de jure* as the Jews broke their own Law to crucify Christ. Their faithfulness was of the spirit; their ambitions (perforce perhaps), not of this world: hence the glorification of the country retreat, perhaps with echoes of Marvell's 'Appleton House', which could simultaneously contain the ideals of Roman and Christian retreat with the comfort of a fantasy polity in which poetic Toryism could operate. Events like the arrest of Bishop Atterbury on 24 August 1722 strengthened the correspondence between Whig hegemony and pagan oppression.[16] Offers like that of John Pointer, of St John's College, Oxford, to die at the block in place of Lord Lovat expressed the sacred nature of Jacobite martyrdom and its selflessness;[17] while public executions after the Risings, and actions like Cumberland's firing of Episcopal chapels only further emphasised the parallels with the early Church. The prominent involvement of women in the Stuart cause may also have been significant in this respect: in the histories and typologies of a society where women are regarded as having little place, the early martyrs and the Jacobite heroines were two of the only groups in which they figured notably.[18] Even Whig songs took account of this phenomenon, as does this one on 'Colonel' Anne Mackintosh, aligning her with both Biblical and classical precedent:

> Of all the Rebel Beauties here,
>   There's one I will not name, Man,
> Who there did head five hundred Men,
>   For which she's much to blame, Man . . .

> No *Bathsheba*, nor *Venus* fair,
>   Could e'er so well appear, Man,
> As she did in her Feelabeg
>   Before the *Chevalier*, Man . . .[19]

The Oaths of Abjuration were to the Jacobites simple invitations to act the part of Judas for the same kind of reward, and only served to complete the symbolic picture of sacrifice and martyrdom. Their king's kingdom had been shown (emphatically) to be not of this world; he was 'over the water', a metaphor in itself for death and spiritual change.

Such conclusions are beginning to emerge from study of the 'hidden agenda' of Augustanism. But what is so surprising is that this literature, the literature of the Augustan struggle, is echoed in its concerns by popular Jacobite songs and poems. The approach of Pope and Swift is shared, only with a more intense bitterness. Take 'For Mr S.M. on his turning Evidence,' a poem first published in 1747, which echoes the sentiments of Pope's 'Memory of an Unfortunate Lady,' and the tone of the end of his 'Epistle to Dr Arbuthnot':[20]

> Go wretch enjoy the purchase you've gained
> Scorn & reproach you every step attend
> By all Mankind neglect & forgot
> Retire to solitude, retire & rot . . .
> . . . Whenever thou goest wild anguish & dispair
> And black remorse attend with hideous stare
> May fear your Hellish Sould [sic] with torments fill
> Your Passions Devils, & your bosom Hell
> Thus you may drag your Heavy Chains along
> Some Minutes more your glorious Life prolong
> And when the fates shall cut a Coward's breast
> Wearying yet of being afraid of Death
> If Crimes like these hereafter be forgiven
> Judas & M, both may go to Heaven[21]

Who would not weep, if such a man there be? The man of course is Murray of Broughton, Charles's secretary, whose King's Evidence helped to send Lord Lovat to his death. Secretary Murray's characterisation as a Judas is made doubly appropriate by the story that it was his attempt to embezzle French funds which led him to linger too long after Culloden, and be apprehended.

Elsewhere we find the same concerns in popular literature as shown by the Augustans over the growth of a money-based society, and the suppressed violence of Pope or Swift is brought out into the open. The 'Scafold' is 'sick with Blood;' 'Oppression, Murder Tyranny/All keen in Triumph ride;' 'Villains' have 'for pelf forsook/Their Country', which faces 'Corruption Bribery breach of Law'. Reference is made to anti-Walpole declarations like that made by James in 1741 (James also offered indemnity for all Tories and Opposition Whigs).[22] In 'Whigg teachers desist from your banters', probably written in Scotland about 1746, the Presbyterians are mocked for their commercialism:

> But if our young Hero was crowned
>   As yet I trust I owe I will see
> You'll then change your cant and be crying
>   Give stipends and loyal we'll be. . .

The Presbyterian clergy inhabit an anti-world; their 'Religion' is 'the contrivance of Pluto', both the underworld of darkness/dullness and the god of riches; they are themselves 'Burlesq'. Elsewhere, George is 'Jupiter's King of ye frog', a cynical and cunning simile which suggests that his log-like intransigence will turn to a stork-like attack on his subjects. Pope makes exactly the same point in *The Dunciad* (Pope, 735 ff.). George is seen as restoring the 'brave happy Days/ Like those of fourtie nine': a common theme found also in Swift, to whom the Whigs are the modern representatives of the Covenant.[23] 'Our Parliament's turned rump,' the song says.[24]

The point I wish to make does not depend on specific (and common) kinds of reference to Whig society, but on the general ironic characterisation of the nature of that society and its development, which Pope, Swift, Gay, and the meanest Jacobite scribbler can share. *The Beggar's Opera* is not a Jacobite play, but it attacks the basis of Whig society not just, as Brecht thought, from a revolutionary perspective, but from a reactionary one too. The highwayman was an archetypal underground Cavalier/Jacobite figure: many had been displaced Royalists (and remain so in fiction as late as *Lorna Doone*), and his way of life was of the heroic mould, that of the horseman. *Mac*heath is a native hero; and we must not forget the large number of contemporary Jacobite criminals such as the Windsor Blacks.[25]

The Jacobite song or poem was by no means always dependent on the models provided by its betters, however. A poem of 1747, 'Eternal mind by whose most just Commands', is one of the earliest known examples of the dramatic monologue, dating from the same time as Warton's 'Dying Indian', which Philip Hobsbaum has argued is the first true example.[26] It is spoken by James II and VII in approximately 1690. Making use of Drydenesque typology (the Absalom story remained a popular Jacobite one), the poem mourns Britain's loss of loyalty and the death of Dundee:

> And thee thereon who dutiful & brave
> Could generous attempts renew
> And nigh my foes Subdue
> Yet all the victory lyes buried in the grave. . .

James ends his monologue on a note which characterises the active world of Jacobite struggle as it does the passive one of Pope's grotto: sacrifice, blood, and passion. Here, however, we are not intended to recall Christ:

> That I may thee release from thy Distress
> All Danger, care and Labour Ill embrace
> Ill fight my way thro' Seas of blood & goar
> That I may thee to freedom once restore

James is here the 'tender hearted parent', *pater patriae*, the true Augustus living up to his title.[27] Other songs and poems would be written showing

him, his son, and his grandson, not as parents but as lovers, the lovers of
Scotland:

> Oh hey! oh hey! sang the bonny lass,
>   Oh hey! and wae is me!
> There's siccan sorrow in Scotland
>   As een did never see.
>
> Oh hey! Oh hey! for my father auld!
>   Oh hey! for my mither dear!
> And my heart will burst for the bonny lad
>   Wha left me lanesome here.[28]

Jacobite poetry mostly lacks the protective irony of the Tory satirists: it
is much closer to the frontiers of anger and loss. Its keynotes are love,
death, and violence, the naked, frontiersman side of the Augustan struggle. In that sense, it has remained one of Scotland's most popular literary
forms. Unfortunately, just as the Whig approach to history and literature
has affected notions of Augustanism,[29] so the sentimentalism of what we
may perhaps call 'Ossianisation' has undermined the integrity of Jacobite
literature. Writers like W.G. Blaikie Murdoch and Bernard Kelly created
a mush of 'the white rose of the Stuarts . . . enshrined for ever in . . . all
generous hearts in the realms of song'.[30] Today there is a reaction against this
kind of thinking (or dreaming), which points out that much of the 'literature'
of Jacobitism was 'written as an act of self-conscious nationalism' by Burns,
Hogg, Lady Nairne, and others.[31]

Now this is true, but its implicit corollary, that there is no genuine Jacobite
literature to be had in Scots or English, is not. Some of the most famous
and popular songs, such as 'Cam ye by Athol' and, notoriously, the Skye
Boat Song, are not contemporary, but many are. Contemporary songs can
be hard to identify, partly because of the criminal overtones of possessing
Jacobite literature at the time (who can be surprised at the ambivalence of
the Tory satirists?); but I have been quoting from them, and not from later
compositions.

As I have suggested, the mark of this literature is its closeness to the
analytic dimensions of the Tory world-view. I have discussed the implications this may have for aspects of the study of Pope and Swift; and I shall
now try to establish a simple framework in which contemporary Jacobite
literature might be studied.

The study of popular Jacobitism generally is still in its infancy. But it
appears that certain symbols and rituals (dress, language, flowers, sermons,
effigies) were embodied in song and popular celebration. Nicholas Rogers
mentions some of these in action in his pioneering essay, 'Riot and Popular
Jacobitism in Early Hanoverian England'.[32] These symbols and rituals,
embodied in English literature through irony and the mock-polities of
Dulness, Liliput, or *The Beggar's Opera*, were more directly reflected in
the songs and poems of the open Jacobites. These forms concentrated the

experience diffused in symbol and ritual into the distillation of theme; and
the loyal theme was expressed on three major levels, matching the concerns
of popular (indeed all) culture. There are poems of political action and satire; poems of sacred love (King as Divine Person, Christian Augustus); and
poems of erotic or familial love: king as fellow-citizen, not remote Whig
oligarch. For political reasons perhaps, erotic songs were popular in early
printed collections. It is easier to disguise a poem such as 'The Blackbird' as
a love-song than it would be to do the same for some of the rabid Jacobite
material to be found in private collections:

> Britain may rejoyce and sing
>   It's once a happy Nation,
> Governed by a German thing,
>   Our Sovereign by Creation,
> And whensoever this King fails,
>   And drops into the Dark Sir
> O then we have a Prince of Wales
>   Begot by Cunning Smark Sir.
>   (MS. 2222)

The adaptation of Jacobite words to popular airs, a custom long practised in
Scotland,[33] was a further means of rendering a popular, perhaps patriotic,
tune successfully subversive (Gay also adapted popular airs for his own
purposes). Such a practice helped to keep popular Jacobitism popular, and
rendered the tunes concerned happily ambivalent. Although verses like those
quoted above could seldom see the light of day, the erotic tradition could
spread its influence more unhindered. Perhaps that is why later Jacobite
songs had a bias towards this tradition, vulnerable as it became to easy
sentimentality.[34]

Nationalist, other political, and sacred Jacobite verse dating from the
period, can be found often in manuscript collections. It is verse in these
traditions which tends to be richer in intellectual and ideological Jacobitism.
The erotic tradition, continued in songs adapted like 'By the bonnie bonnie
banks of Loch Lomond', and even perhaps ostensibly non-Jacobite songs like
'Wild Mountain Thyme', merged closely into Scottish popular tradition. The
sacred and political traditions establish a picture of fortitude and sacrifice.
They show an older, nobler society losing life to save it, casting away all, in
the style of Montrose, in the battle against a mercantilist society in the grip of
foreign interests and meaningless wars. The ethic of Lovelace is preserved to
combat that of Defoe.[35] Nobleness, honour, and heroism (these are Lowland
compositions we must remember, devoted to the Highland ideal before it
became popularised), are exalted in their last struggle with forces about to
overwhelm them. Recent work such as Bruce Lenman's may have cast doubt
on the reality of a heroic culture in the Highlands, but the image at least of a
self-sacrificing timocracy was valuable to the Jacobite cause.[36]

The compositions on these themes display a passionate sense of feeling and
commitment less distant from actual passion than the erotic lyrics seem to

be. The attachment is not to the beloved, but to the Divine Person of the sacred king:

> O James, O James, O Sacred James,
> Our King whom we adore,
> We'll undertake this for thy sake,
> And suffer yet much more. . .

Sometimes the great is linked to the intimate, to emphasise the strength of allegiance to the man and his right (in this case Charles is referred to):

> His Princely endowments & virtues that shine
> Proclaim him descended of antientest Line
> Let Samuel make haste with Oil to anoint
> Whom Subjects wish for, & God seems to appoint
> 3. He is our Bone & our flesh whom should we desire
> But our own whom all ever we did admire . . .

In this way the king could be a type both of the sacred majesty and the earthly husband. The social implications of this sacred status are usually clear: to protect the true Church, the suffering remnant which in Scotland was now Episcopacy.[37] As a variant on the use of popular airs in Jacobite song, actual psalms were adapted:

> The Lord's my targe I will be stout
> My Durk and trusty blade –
> Tho Cambles come in flocks about
> I will not be afraid.

William Donaldson has shown that both Whig and Jacobite used biblical typologies as part of their argument;[38] but those emanating from the oppressed Church are especially poignant in their sincerity:

> For since they got the ruling power
> Our Loyal patriarchs they devour
> No honest man can live secure
> No prey but they pursue at . . .
>
> God's home they rob'd & set on fire
> Our own they pillag'd & took our gear
> And left us neither Horse or Mare
> Both Cow and Ewe they slew it. . .
>
> O King of Kings to thee we fly
> Compassionate our misery
> Exalt the Low pull down the high. . .
>
> (MS. 2222)

The great Jacobite families were seen as the Israelites in Egypt, the land of bondage. What Bruce Lenman has called the 'sacramental view of life' held by the Episcopal (and indeed High Anglican) clergy was symbolised again and again in the language of suffering and sacrifice.[39] 'With blood deal Right to Stuart' was simultaneously a call to battle and to martyrdom. It was perhaps this ambivalence which showed itself in the willingness of Stuart leaders to take arms, even when they thought defeat far more likely than victory, as did Pitsligo and Lord George Murray. Indeed, the worldly defeat which the ideology of martyrdom assumed may in the end have been a self-fulfilling prophecy. Charles was unjust to Lord George after the '45, but his belief that the Lieutenant-General did not really want to win is not inconsistent with the facts of the campaign.[40] Lord Balmerino's instructions to his friends to drink him 'ain degrae ta haiven' on the scaffold, are more consistent with the implicit pathos of sacred Jacobitism, itself not always far removed from the erotic tradition of longing, loss, or consummation.[41]

The obverse of the call to martyrdom was the call to war, which is reflected in the third major theme of Jacobite literature: politics. The nationalist element in Jacobitism has been played down by those who have sought to marginalise it, but it would be fair to say that (*pace* the odd Cameronian), it was the only serious nationalist force in Scotland from 1715 onwards. Charles's landing in the far west, almost alone, was an echo of Bruce's, made in similar circumstances in 1307.[42] Speeches like Lord Belhaven's against the Union contrasted the decay of the present with the heroes of the past, and this was yet another recollection of the loss of a golden age, the age of the apostles, the age of heroes:

> Oh fy for *Bruce* and *Wallace* now
> For *Randolph, Montrose, Airly;*
> This wicked generation's curst
> And hes done nothing fairly;
> Come, let us have our king again
> And set us as we were, jo,
> Then every man will have his ain
> And ill we need not fear, jo.[43]

This nostalgia had its long-term dangers. The romanticisation which overtook Scotland, Jacobitism, and in particular the Highlands almost immediately after the last attempt of 1759, led to a vast upsurge in a nationalism of sentiment. As soon as Scotland ceased to be a military threat, its political aspirations devolved into history. In Aberdeen, there is a Victorian statue of Wallace, covered in anti-English sentiments: but such monuments were depoliticised by the fear sentimentalists often suffer, when the objects of their affection become responsibilities. The nostalgic basis of Jacobite ideology may have done the nationalism it so long voiced much permanent damage. As clearly as Scott, it was dwelling only on the dying fall, and Prince George's appearance in Highland dress at a masquerade ball in 1789 showed how thoroughly emasculated the past had become.[44] Modern Jacobite sentiment was born. It is imperative to recover the ideology of what we now tend to think of as a lament; but we must always be aware that this ideology may have carried the seeds of its own obsolescence in a self-conscious identification with other-wordly and nostalgic concepts of political value.

From our perspective, perhaps the most successful political poems are those akin to the topograpical nationalism of 'Windsor Forest'.[45] The return of Charles is a rebirth: 'laughing Ceres' once more will have the opportunity to 're-assume the land' in a poem such as 'Come, all brave Scotsmen':

> Come, all brave *Scotsmen*, and rejoice
>   With a loud Acclamation;
> Since Charles is come over the Main
>   Into our Scottish Nation.
>
> Let Hills, and Dales, and Mountains great,
>   And every Wood and Spring,
> Extend your Voices to the Clouds
>   For Joy of Stuart our King.
>
> Ye Nightingales and Lav'rocks too,
>   And every Bird that sing,
> Make haste and leave your doleful Notes,
>   And Royal Stuart sing.
>
> All Beasts that go upon all Four,
>   Go leap and dance around;
> Because that the curst Union's broke,
>   And fallen to the Ground.[46]

The return of 'Peace, and Plenty' to Scotland requires not only the restoration of the sacred king in his Christian and nationalist role, but also as a fertility representative, an organic healer. The theme is repeated in poems like 'To daunton me':

> But to wanton me, to wanton me,
> O ken ye what it is that wad wanton me?–
> To see guid corn upon the rigs,
> And banishment amang the Whigs,
> And right restored whare right sud be,
> I think would do meikle to wanton me.[47]

As in the work of Pope and Swift, the land was a potent symbol of Tory values overtaken by commercialism,[48] so in more explicit Jacobite literature the earth itself waits for political rebirth which will render it fruitful once more. Only when the forces of disorder, the Whig Lords of Misrule, are banished will the land once more regain its organic, generative power. Only when Dulness is overthrown will the Horatian ethic be born again. Virgilian and Christian visions of kingship merge in the image of the lost Augustus, the Stuart icon that looms over eighteenth-century literature, and whose influences linger on to the present day.[49] I do not propose to discuss the literary legacy of the Stuart myth here. But an example of how closely Stuart and other myths may be intertwined in literary constructs is found in this poem of Andrew Lang's, 'The Tenth of June 1715':

> Day of the flower and the King!
>   When shall the sails of white
> Shine on the seas and bring
>   In the day, in the dawn, in the night
>   The King to his land and his right?[50]

Here the return of James is linked to the return of Iseult, and the sign of the white sail which was not unfurled, itself a potent story of the neo-Jacobite elements of the Celtic Twilight.[51] The flower reference is to the white rose, sign of the organic king who never returned as monarch to his native Scotland. All his cause brought was the black sail of death, and perhaps the most potent myth of loss in native literatures, English and Scottish, metropolitan and provincial.

In this essay I have tried to integrate, as far as possible in so brief a space, the various kinds of Jacobite literature. The provision of a thematic framework in which to study popular songs and poems, does, I think, make it easier to see how they conjoin with the greater literature of the period, with which they have not normally been associated. The passionate struggles identifiable in Stuart literature may lend a far gloomier tone to certain aspects of eighteenth-century studies, but that tone belongs to those from whom it is frequently withdrawn. The paradoxes of the couplet and the bitterness of *saeva indignatio* have their ideological as well as their literary audience.

The Celtic heroic myth, whether derived from the Stuarts or elsewhere, is an enduring one. Howard Erskine-Hill ends his 'Literature and the Jacobite Cause' with a quotation from Yeats's 'Black Tower', about the loss of an exiled king.[52] The intellectual Jacobitism of Ruskin, Whistler, or MacGregor Mathers may echo the peculiar legacy of a lost golden age and a continuing nostalgia, whose executors were the Jacobites themselves. 'Traditional sanctity and loveliness' have fallen, whether to 'Paudeen's pence' or Walpole's bribes:[53] but the myth of the patriot hero, Cuchulain or Tearlach, continues to generate itself:

> Why should we celebrate
> These dead men more than the dying?
> It is not to ring the bell backward
> Nor is it an incantation
> To summon the spectre of a Rose . . .
> . . . Whatever we inherit from the fortunate
> We have taken from the defeated
> What they had to leave us – a symbol:
> A symbol perfected in death.[54]

Despite his own disclaimer, it has been regarded as odd that Eliot should choose to celebrate so old a cause in the middle of the Second World War.[55] But the importance of that pervading myth to the two greatest poets of our century is a tribute to the level of consciousness of the Stuart cause bequeathed.

Notes

1. Brean Hammond, *Pope* (Brighton, 1986), p. 28.
2. G.M. Trevelyan, *England Under the Stuarts,* 14th edn. (London, 1928), p. 455.
3. Andrew Marvell, *The Poems and Letters*, ed. H.M. Margoliouth, 2 vols, 3rd edn. (Oxford, 1971), I, pp. 92–4.
4. Alexander Pope, *The Poems,* ed. John Butt (Bungay, 1963), pp. 350,775.
5. Cf. Alexander Pope, *Imitations of Horace,* ed. John Butt (London, 1939), p. 168n.
6. Andrew L. Drummond and James Bulloch, *The Scottish Church 1688–1843,* (Edinburgh, 1973), pp. 28–29.
7. John Dryden, *The Poems and Fables,* ed. James Kinsley, (Oxford, 1962), p. 330.
8. Pope, *The Poems,* p. 594.
9. John Burnett, *A History of the Cost of Living* (Harmondsworth, 1969), pp. 61, 104, 140.
10. Pope, *The Poems,* pp. 574, 579.
11. Ms. 2222, Aberdeen University Library. This is a commonplace-book in which a number of songs and poems from the 1740s and earlier are contained. A fully annotated edition of these songs will shortly be forthcoming from the Voltaire Foundation.
12. Dryden, *The Poems,* p. 191.
13. Cf. H.N. Fieldhouse, 'Bolingbroke's share in the Jacobite Intrigue of 1710–14', *English Historical Review,* vol. 52 (1937), pp. 443–59.
14. Hammond *Pope,* p. 46. Cf. Simon Varey in *Journal of the British Society of Eighteenth-Century Studies* 6:2 (Autumn, 1983), pp. 163–72.
15. Ibid., p. 47.
16. Cf. Bertrand A. Goldgar, *Walpole and the Wits* (Lincoln, Neb., 1976), pp. 28ff.
17. W.R. Ward, *Georgian Oxford: University Politics in the Eighteenth Century* (Oxford, 1958), p. 169.
18. Flora MacDonald is only the most famous example in a hagiography which includes Anne Mackintosh, the Countess of Winchelsea, and Jane Barker.
19. National Library of Scotland, Ms. 488.f.64–67.
20. Pope, *The Poems,* pp. 262, 612.
21. Ms. 2222, Aberdeen University Library; cf. *To Mr. S— M— on his 'Turning Evidence'* (London, 1747).
22. Eveline Cruickshanks, *Political Untouchables* (London, 1979), pp. 28, 47.
23. Jonathan Swift, *Poetical Works,* ed. Herbert Davis (London, 1967), p. 509; F.P. Lock, *Swift's Tory Politics* (London, 1983), pp. 66, 71, 79, 119.
24. Ms. 2222, Aberdeen University Library.
25. Hammond, *Pope,* p. 36.
26. Ms. 2222, Aberdeen University Library; cf. Philip Hobsbaum, 'The Rise of the Dramatic Monologue', *Hudson Review* 28 (1975), 227–45.
27. Ms. 2222.
28. *Jacobite Songs and Ballads,* ed. G.S. Macquoid (London, n.d.), p. 75.
29. Cf. W.A. Speck, *Society and Literature in England 1700–60* (Dublin, 1983), pp. 11, 167, 209, and *passim.*

30. Bernard Kelly, *The Conqueror of Culloden*, (London, 1903), p. 75. Cf. W.G. Blaikie Murdoch, *The Spirit of Jacobite Loyalty*, (Edinburgh, 1907), *passim*.
31. David Johnson, *Music and Society in Lowland Scotland in the Eighteenth Century*, (London, 1972), p. 4. Cf. p. 146 also.
32. Nicholas Rogers, 'Riot and Popular Jacobitism in Early Hanoverian England', in *Ideology and Conspiracy*, ed. Eveline Cruickshanks (Edinburgh, 1982), pp. 70–88.
33. Cf. William Donaldson, *The Jacobite Song*, (Aberdeen, 1988), pp. 31ff.
34. Cf. ibid. pp. 49 ff.
35. Cf. Daniel Defoe, *The Complete English Tradesman* (Gloucester, 1987), *passim*.
36. Bruce Lenman, *The Jacobite Risings in Britain 1689–1746*, (London, 1980), pp. 246ff.
37. Cf. Bruce Lenman, 'The Scottish Episcopal Clergy and the Ideology of Jacobitism', in *Ideology and Conspiracy*, ed. Eveline Cruickshanks (Edinburgh, 1982) pp. 36–48.
38. Donaldson, *The Jacobite Song*, pp. 20–22, 30, 45, 47.
39. Lenman, 'The Scottish Episcopal Clergy', p. 47.
40. Winifred Duke, *Lord George Murray and the '45*, (Aberdeen, 1927), pp. 71–73, 204, 210–11.
41. Cf. *Seasonable Reflections on Arthur, late Lord Balmerino* (London, 1746), p. 12; *An Account of the Behaviour of . . . Arthur, late Lord Balmerino*, (London, 1746), p. 6.
42. Cf. Geoffrey Barrow, *Robert Bruce*, 2nd edn., (Edinburgh, 1976), pp. 234ff.
43. Donaldson, *The Jacobite Song*, p. 12.
44. ibid., p. 92.
45. Cf. Douglas Brooks-Davies, '"Thoughts of Gods": Messianic Alchemy in *Windsor-Forest*', *Yearbook of English Studies* 18 (1988), pp. 125–42.
46. Donaldson, *The Jacobite Song*, p. 65.
47. Cf. Macquoid, *The Jacobite Songs*, p. 153.
48. Isabel Rivers, *The Poetry of Conservatism 1600–1745*, (Cambridge, 1973), pp. 188, 192–3, 196, 200.
49. Cf. Lucy McDiarmid, *Saving Civilization* (Cambridge, 1984), pp. 34ff; Murray Pittock, 'Decadence and the English Tradition', unpublished D. Phil. thesis, (Oxford, 1986), pp. 133–48.
50. Andrew Lang, 'The Tenth of June 1715', *Everybody's Magazine*, June 1901.
51. A.C. Swinburne, *Tristram of Lyonesse*, (London, 1920), p. 147.
52. Howard Erskine-Hill, 'Literature and the Jacobite Cause', in *Ideology and Conspiracy*, ed. Eveline Cruickshanks (Edinburgh, 1982), pp. 49–69.
53. W.B. Yeats, *Collected Poems*, 2nd edn. (London, 1950), pp. 119, 276.
54. T.S. Eliot, *Complete Poems and Plays* (London, 1969), p. 196.
55. McDiarmid, *Saving Civilization*, p. 59.

WILLIAM SMITH IN ABERDEEN (1745) AND PHILADELPHIA (1778): FRATRICIDE AND FAMILIALISM

Robert Lawson-Peebles

On 17 June 1778 William Smith wrote from Philadelphia to Lady Juliana Penn in London:

> Figure to yourself, Madam, the dreadful situation of this City, which in 24 Hours is again to change Masters; for by that Time we are told it will be wholly evacuated; and with what Spirit or Temper our former Citizens, who have been near Nine months expelled from it may return, God only knows. I must take my Chance with my dear Wife & seven Children, full of Apprehensions around me. But I was left a Prisoner by my Countrymen when they went out, & here they shall find me, without any Thing they can charge on me as Criminal. The Rest I leave to the good Will of Providence.

The letter, which must have been dispatched with the departing British soldiers, vividly reveals the problems confronting a moderate in revolutionary times. Smith had become the first Provost of the College of Philadelphia (which later became the University of Pennsylvania) in 1754, and he had been extremely active in the affairs of the city and the colony. When discord grew between Britain and America, Smith tried to mediate. It did not please the revolutionaries. He was briefly imprisoned in 1776 and then released on parole. He remained in Philadelphia when British troops entered it on 26 September 1777. When they left he could have joined the 3,000 or more Loyalists who left with them. Once again he decided to take his chance, and he was present in Philadelphia when, as he had anticipated, the Continental forces reoccupied the city on 18 June 1778. He was accused of Sedition, and in 1779 lost his job as Provost of the College.[1]

The case of William Smith is interesting for three reasons. First, he provides an unusual view of revolution, not as a heroic tournament but rather as fratricidal strife—hence the references in the letter to 'our former Citizens' and 'my Countrymen'. Secondly, Smith's life provides a link, probably unique, between three periods of social unrest and military conflict which, because of their varying outcomes, are often treated differently by historians, as is indicated by their differing titles: the Second Jacobite *Rebellion*, the French and Indian *War*, and the American *Revolution*. Thirdly, and most importantly, Smith's experiences in these three periods prompted him to develop a robust but malleable social and educational philosophy which could be accommodated to changing conditions and which therefore was both serviceable and tenacious.

Smith was born in 1727 at Slains, a small village north of Aberdeen, on Scotland's north-eastern coast. In 1743 he was admitted to King's College, Aberdeen, and was granted a bursary, for his father had limited means. It was not a propitious time for study and reflection. For much of the preceding century north-eastern Scotland had been marked by political and religious unrest. It was a conservative area dominated by the Episcopalian Church, which believed in order, deference and the divine right of kings, symbolised by the Stuart succession. The Restoration of 1660 had therefore been greeted with the greatest fervour in Aberdeen. James Garden, Professor of Divinity at King's College, looked back on it as a blessed release from God's just punishment for 'an unhappy, (dismal) Revolution'. In common with the Scottish bishops, Garden regarded the so-called 'Glorious Revolution' as somewhat less than glorious. William III quickly took his revenge. In 1690 he ratified a new constitution for the Church of Scotland which vested power in the Presbytery and excluded the bishops. A separate Episcopalian Church was formed, but it suffered from suspicion and repression. In 1696 Garden was deprived of his chair at King's, and the College went through a period of decline that was still evident when Smith arrived there.[2]

Aberdeen and the North East were a fertile ground for Jacobitism. There is no need here to walk again over the well-worn paths of Jacobite history; in any event, the map has lately been redrawn. Bruce Lenman has suggested that the Rebellions may be seen less as a culture-clash between Gael and Anglo-Saxon, broadsword and musket, Catholic and Protestant – although those elements are still there – than as a response to political changes in the island as a whole. Those political changes had their origin in London, and the fulcrum of response was in Aberdeen. For if, as Dr Lenman contends, it was the Scottish Episcopal clergy who 'were the most significant single group of men creating and transmitting articulate Jacobite ideology', then Aberdeen and the surrounding countryside were its home territory. It is entirely appropriate, therefore, that during the abortive Jacobite invasion of 1708 a French emissary should meet the Earl Marischal and the Earl of Erroll at Erroll's castle in Slains – Smith's village. It is appropriate, too, that James Garden should be one of the delegation who in 1716 presented a loyal address from the Episcopal clergy of Aberdeen to the Old Pretender at the Earl Marischal's house at Fetteresso, a few miles south of the city. He was accompanied by several of the senior members of King's, who lost their posts once the Rebellion was over.[3]

During the Second Jacobite Rebellion Aberdeen changed masters several times. Initially it was garrisoned by detachments of Sir John Cope's army. They left the city to take part in his fruitless pursuit of the Jacobite forces into the Highlands. Cope's entire army of some 2,000 men returned to Aberdeen on 11 September 1745 and camped there until 15 September, when they left by boat, bound for the Firth of Forth and the Battle of Prestonpans. Cope had impounded all of Aberdeen's weapons to prevent them from falling into Jacobite hands, and then lost them himself at that ignominious rout. On 25 September Aberdeen was claimed for James VIII. The city and its environs provided a force of some 1,100 men who marched to Inverurie and on 23 December defeated units sent by Lord Loudoun, the Hanoverian commander in the Highlands, to retake Aberdeen. Thereafter Jacobite fortunes waned. On 22 February 1746 a French transport slipped by the British Navy and brought reinforcements, and the next day the Jacobite forces left the city. Aberdeen was reoccupied, this time by the army of the Duke of Cumberland, on 27 February. They camped there until 8 April, when they marched north to decimate the Pretender's army at the Battle of Culloden.[4]

The Brutality of the British Army during and after the '45 is too well known and too unpleasant to need repeating. Cumberland quickly became known as 'The Butcher', even by his supporters. Loyalist and rebel alike were slaughtered. The military commanders considered mass deportation. Aberdeen houses were plundered, even by senior officers. On 1 August 1746 the troops, urged on by their officers, celebrated the King's birthday by going on a window-smashing spree. Fear and suspicion lasted for several years afterwards. In 1749, for instance, the Principal of King's joined with his counterpart at Marischal College in presenting a memorial to the government. It claimed that those members of the professiorate who had been purged, particularly after the '15, had opened schools in the north-east and had 'poisoned the greatest part of the Young Gentry of those Parts with Principles that have since thoroughly appeared'. The rhetoric of conspiracy – the fear of a hostile environment, of the enemy at the gates – will be familiar to those who have read the literature of the Illuminati Scare and the McCarthy Trials. It was in these adverse and unpleasant circumstances that Smith completed his studies at King's in 1747.[5]

There were two further, personal, circumstances which would have contributed to the discomforts of Smith's early life. His father was a small landholder in an area where the large land-owners were a limited and exclusive group and where those of lesser means occupied precarious, marginal positions.[6] Secondly, although he was an Episcopalian, Smith was not a Jacobite. This latter conflict must have been particularly painful to him, in view of his Episcopalian beliefs in hierarchy and deference. In all, he was doubly excluded, at odds both with the Presbyterians in power and with many Episcopalians. He must have felt, in the words of his 1778 letter, a prisoner of his countrymen.

Smith escaped to London in 1750; yet even London was not far enough away from Aberdeen. After the '45 the English revealed a dislike and fear of the Scots unparalleled even in the unhappy history of Anglo-Scottish relations. It was not confined to the Jacobites; Scots generally were regarded as 'scum', 'barbarous and lawless ruffians' and (in a reference to Swift's *Gullivers' Travels*) 'a ragged hungry rabble of Yahoos'. Not even the loyal Scots in London were exempted from such vilification. As one complained, 'the guilty and the innocent are confounded together, and the crimes of a few are imputed to the whole nation'.[7] Smith's course was clear: he left London for the American Colonies on 3 March 1751.

2

Smith's attitudes in the years before his departure can be deduced from two documents. The first is a letter which was published as a Preface to a sermon by his Episcopalian colleague Thomas Barton, who had taught at the College of Philadelphia before becoming a missionary on Pennsylvania's western frontier. The sermon, *Unanimity and Public Spirit*, clearly conveys the sense of present danger felt by Barton during the French and Indian War. It was preached shortly after the defeat on 9 July 1755 of General Edward Braddock's British army by a force of French Coonskinners and Indians less than half their number. In the ensuing months the settlers in western Pennsylvania lived in constant fear of imminent attack. Barton met the fear head on. He issued a ringing call for 'united Resolution and true *British* Spirit'. Smith's prefatory letter praised Barton for his militancy, his refusal 'to appear cold in the Interests of his God, the Interests of his King, or the Interests of his Protestant Country'. If ministers:

> Had not . . . from Time to Time boldly raised their Voice, and warned and exhorted their Fellow-Citizens, mixing temporal and eternal Concerns, most certainly Popish Error and Popish Slavery (perhaps Heathen Error and Heathen Slavery) had long ere now overwhelmed us! Where then would have been the Blessings purchased by our Reformation and glorious Revolution?

He then made an explicit comparison with the fears expressed in England less than ten years earlier after Cope's defeat at Prestonpans. He cited the example of the Archbishop of Canterbury who, when Archbishop of York, made a 'noble stand . . . for his King and Country during the late Rebellion.'[8]

Thomas Herring was translated to the See of York in 1743. Two years later, according to his life long friend the writer William Duncombe, he 'was the first who gave the Alarm, and awakened the Nation from its Lethargy' after Prestonpans. Herring revealed attitudes just as forthright and aggressive as Barton's: he called a meeting at York Castle of the nobility, gentry and clergy, and treated them to a rousing harangue. They must prepare themselves, he said, 'to guard against the mischievous Attempts of these wild and desperate Ruffians', who were being manipulated by England's old enemies, France and Spain, in a plot to install 'Popery and arbitrary Power'. The speech had its effect. £40,000 was immediately subscribed for the defence of the country, and Herring became a national hero. The speech was published in *The Gentleman's Magazine* and subsequently, at the insistence of the King, in the *Gazette*. Horace Walpole remarked that Herring's speech 'had as much true spirit, honesty and bravery in it: as ever was penned by an historian for an ancient hero'.[9]

Smith met Herring when he arrived in London. The Archbishop, now holding the See of Canterbury, made a strong impact. In the letter to Thomas Barton, Smith asserted that he had 'Reason to count his Favour and Protection the happiest Circumstance of my Lot'. Certainly, Smith adopted Herring's attitudes. While he recommended Herring's York speech as a prescription for preserving the 'public Liberty' of Britain, he advocated a later sermon preached in London as a prescription 'for the preservation of its public Virtue'. Herring gave the sermon on 7 January 1747, the Fast Day proclaimed after the conclusion of the Jacobite Rebellion. He warned that stable government could exist only if it was based on 'Principles of Order, and Peace, and Justice, and a Sobriety and Temperance in the Morals of all its Members'. If any of the 'Orders' of society became corrupt, the corruption would spread like a virus and bring about the downfall of that society. He pointed to the decline of earlier empires, and concluded that 'Union at Home, and Loyalty and Affection to the King and his Royal Family, are our great and sure Defence'.[10]

In this, as in other sermons, Herring advocated a familial ideology which had, by the 1740s, become commonplace. The ideology was rooted in a correspondence between the human body, the family and the body politic. It has been discussed recently by Jonathan Clark, and its American transformations have been examined by Jay Fliegelman and Melvin Yazawa. There is no need to discuss it at length here, except to indicate that terms like 'liberty' and 'tolerance' were important components of the ideology and were ardently subscribed to, sometimes in the face of some starkly contrasting and unpleasant facts. When Cumberland returned from Culloden, Herring presented him with an address which thanked him for restoring 'the public Tranquillity', and having achieved it 'in every amiable Light'. Many Scots had reason to think differently about Cumberland's amiability.[11]

Familialism was constructed on a constellation of concepts revolving around the word 'Union'. The word occurs frequently in Herring's sermons, and was eloquently defined by Thomas Barton in 1776 when he remarked that 'Union, and good Agreement, give a double Relish to Prosperity; sooth [sic] Adversity, and call forth all the humane and generous Affections, all the soft and endearing Actions, which can alone render Man useful and *sociable* to Man!'. Barton emphasised sociability because it allowed him to make the leap from the nuclear to the national family, to show that 'Affections' and 'endearing Actions' were efficacious in the public as well as the private sphere. One of the consequences was that civil strife was looked on with particular horror, as fratricide. Barton anticipated Smith's 1778 letter when, in 1776, he lamented the insults offered to ministers when they offered 'Prayers for the King & Royal Family'. 'Some of them,' he said, 'have been dragged from their horses, assaulted with stones & dirt, ducked in water; obliged to flie for their lives, driven from their habitations & families, laid under arrests & imprisoned!'. In 1755, though, sociability prompted Barton to make the sharpest distinction between the British empire and the Catholic states. In carefully paired and balanced phrases, he asked: 'Must the free-born Subjects of a generous King, the dutiful Children of an indulgent Parent, become the base Servants of a haughty Master, the suspected Slaves of a revengeful Tyrant?'[12]

The second document which gives an insight into Smith's early beliefs is a commonplace book. It is not dated, but its appearance and contents indicate that Smith started it when he was quite young. At first glance the book reveals that Smith's tastes in poetry were unexceptional, and that he was assiduous in indulging them. The book contains Young's *Night Thoughts* in its entirety and lengthy extracts from Milton's *Paradise Lost* and Thomson's *Seasons*. It is on closer inspection that Smith's attitudes begin to emerge. For instance, the stanzas he chooses from Addison's 'A Letter from Italy' both support the political contrast drawn by Thomas Barton and provide a cultural consolation for an Aberdonian:

> On foreign mountains may the Sun refine
> The Grape's soft juice, and Mellow it to wine,
> With Citron groves adorn a distant soil,
> And the fat Olive swell with floods of oil:
> We envy not the warmer clime, that lies
> In ten degrees of more indulgent skies,
> Nor at the coarseness of our heaven repine,
> Tho' o'er our heads the frozen *Pleiads* shine:
> 'Tis Liberty that crowns Britannia's Isle,
> And makes her barren rocks and her bleak mountains smile.

The most comprehensive statement of Smith's beliefs is provided by the extract which proved to be the hardest to identify. He copied two brief pieces from the text he identified simply as 'W. Ral. a little alterd'. It turns out to be George Sewell's *The Tragedy of Sir Walter Raleigh*.[13]

George Sewell is described in the *Dictionary of National Biography* as a 'controversialist and hack-writer'. *The Tragedy of Sir Walter Raleigh* was his greatest success. Its first production took place in 1719 and its popularity was doubtless in part due to the revival of anti-Spanish feeling following the abortive Spanish-supported Jacobite invasion of that year. By 1722 the play had gone through five editions, and it may well have prompted the antiquarian William Oldys to write his life of Ralegh. The sixth edition was published in 1745, no doubt in response to the Rebellion. The play was revived for one night in 1789 but has since, as far as I know, disappeared. To an extent it trades in stereotypes. It deals with the imprisonment and death of Ralegh, and suggests that the hero's decline and demise were engineered by a circle of conniving Catholic courtiers led by Gundamor, a double-dealing Spanish ambassador. One of Ralegh's supporters is his former lieutenant, Howard, who is portrayed as a bluff sea-dog and who bellows some of the more garish lines in the play:

> Blue Pestlience and Poison blast their Lips!
> O! how I hate his Tribe of kissing Courtiers.

The characterisation of Howard is in strong contrast to that of Ralegh. Indeed, Sewell's portrait of the English hero is markedly different from the image we have of him today. It provides a strong insight into familialism.

Today we probably tend to think of Sir Walter Ralegh as Queen Elizabeth's randy dandy, the man who took time out from spreading cloaks over puddles to invent the tobacco trade. In part, no doubt, we owe this stereotype to Erroll Flynn and countless swashbuckling films. In part, however, we owe it to John Aubrey, whose 'Brief Life' of Sir Walter endowed him with such potency that he could deprive girls of their language as well as their virtue:

He loved a wench well: and one time getting up one of the mayds of honor against a tree in a wood ('twas his first lady) who seemed at first boarding to be somewhat fearful of her Honor, and modest, she cryed Sweet Sir Walter, what do you me ask? Will you undoe me? Nay, sweet Sir Walter! Sir Walter! At last, as the danger and

the pleasure at the same time grew higher, she cried in the ecstacey Swisser Swatter!
Swisser Swatter! She proved with child and I doubt not but this heroe tooke care of
them both, as also that the product was more then ordinary mortall.

Sewell's Ralegh seems to be an entirely different man. He is so irreproachable
that, according to Gundamor, he fills the British nation with 'the love of Virtue'. Otherwise, he is an ordinary mortal, a family man who would prefer 'the
Charities of Social Love' to a martyr's death. Indeed, he specifically eschews the
fate of the most famous tragic hero in English Literature:

> Think not I hold what vain Philosophy
> Of proud Indifference, that pretends to look
> On Pain and Pleasure with an equal Eye.
> To *be* is better far than *Not to be*
> Else Nature cheated us in our Formation.

The theme is etched into the structure of the play: we are introduced to his wife
and son before we meet Ralegh, and we see him in the limited circumstances of
his home and the Tower of London. The final Act presents Ralegh alone with
his son. He tells Young Ralegh that he is now 'Heir and Father of our Race'.
Ralegh is then removed and beheaded.

Ralegh's opponents are noted for their hatred of the family. Salisbury damns
'the base mixture of Connubial Love' and praises the rule of celibacy for the
priesthood, so that 'no tender look of Love/Disarms [Rome's] holy Butchers
in their Wrath'. Yet, all the power of Rome's holy butchers and their acolytes
is powerless against familialism because it is too deeply rooted in the British
Constitution. It is to be found, firstly, in the exemplary text. In the long years
that Ralegh awaits the execution of his sentence he completes his *History of
the World*. He has written it, he says, so that men may 'grow wiser in their
Father's Follies'. Secondly, familialism is defended by the exemplary monarch.
This becomes clear when Ralegh addresses a eulogy to the memory of Queen
Elizabeth:

> grateful Piety enbalm thy Dust,
> With kind, religious Tenderness and Love!
> With dear Remembrance, and with dread Regard,
> Visit her Ashes, ye succeeding Monarchs;
> From her transcribe the Model of your Power,
> And leave the Blessings of a righteous Sway.

In view of Elizabeth's marital status, it seems at first sight rather odd to make her
a defender of the family. But it did not seem odd to William Smith, for this is one
of the passages that he copied into his commonplace book.[14]

3

Recent analyses of eighteenth-century Scottish thought have shown that it
was sufficiently flexible to be modified under the press of events. The belief in
the divine but inflexible right of kings which had for so long upheld Jacobite

claims was gradually abandoned in favour of familialism. Even such a staunch Jacobite as Lord Forbes of Pitsligo, who at the age of sixty-seven mustered a troop of cavalry to support the Young Pretender, justified his actions in terms of 'the good of England'. When he denounced 'arbitrary government' he was adopting precisely the same language as his arch-enemy Thomas Herring.[15] The dispute, in other words, had become one of fact and interpretation rather than one of philosophy.

In the view of Sewell and Smith the Virgin Queen was legitimated as a monarch not by the strong yet rigid claims of divine right, but by the weak yet pliable claims of familialism, 'religious Tenderness and Love'. She was the metaphorical father of a metaphorical family. The notable, and useful, thing about a metaphorical family is that its membership can change. Smith's earliest American publications show him extending the family. In *Indian Songs of Peace* (1752), his first American work, he proposes enlarging the family, by means of education, to include the Indians. *A General Idea of the College of Mirania*, published the following year, links the New World with the Old in a transatlantic family. It attracted the attention of Benjamin Franklin and led to the post in Philadelphia.[16]

The French and Indian War, and then Pontiac's Rebellion, caused Smith to revise his model of the family. We have already seen some evidence of his new militancy in the 'Letter' which prefaced Thomas Barton's *Unanimity and Public Spirit*. That militancy made a more extensive appearance in two sermons and two pamphlets that Smith published in the years 1755–57. The first sermon, preached in Philadelphia on 24 June 1755, and therefore before Braddock's defeat, proposed a version of familialism with some backbone. The King was still the father of his people, but unless they heeded his authority they shall be, he said, 'as a Body without a Head, our Strength uncollected, and ourselves an easy Prey to every Invader'. Twenty-one months later it had so much backbone that it was ramrod-stiff. In a sermon on 5 April 1757 to the First Battalion of the Royal American Regiment, which had been formed as a result of Braddock's defeat, Smith presented the soldiers with a stark choice. Either they could enjoy the benefits of a civilisation such as that envisaged in his *Mirania* pamphlet, or they could suffer 'popish Perfidy, French Tyranny and savage Barbarity'. He called the soldiers 'the Avengers of Liberty' and, after a graphic description of Indian torture, concluded with the rallying-cry, 'Let our enemies know that Britons will be Britons still, in every clime and age!' The Indian Songs of Peace had disappeared. Smith's words now echoed those of the martial Archbishop Herring, and also the genocidal attitudes of the English against his own people ten years earlier. It is a wonder that the soldiers refrained from smashing windows.[17]

The detail of Smith's revised familial ideology was set out in the two pamphlets published in 1755–56. *A Brief State of the Province of Pennsylvania* and *A Brief View of the Conduct of Pennsylvania* caused a furore because they attacked the Colony's Assembly for failing to protect it. *A Brief State* quickly went through three London editions and was also published in Dublin. *A Brief View* was promptly translated in French, no doubt for the benefit of Smith's Popish enemies. The pamphlets contain some of the features apparent in the sermons, and in material published during the Second Jacobite Rebellion: a fearful sense of growing threat, garnished with detailed accounts of atrocities. They also contain a series of proposals which anticipate the totalitarian state of the twentieth century. Smith's mildest proposal was that the Protestant ministry should be extended. Perhaps he imagined the ministry as a form of police, for his other proposals included a compulsory oath of allegiance; the suppression of foreign-language newspapers; and compulsory English lessons for the Pennsylvania German community together with the withdrawal of the franchise from them. Above all, he asserted that 'we must look to our Mother-Country for succour'. The alternative was 'civil and religious persecution'. One wonders what the German community felt about the double standards apparent in Smith's pamphlets. Certainly, the words 'tolerance' and 'mildness' had, for the time being, disappeared from his familial lexicon.[18]

Smith's proposals were developed further in his *Historical Account* of Bouquet's expedition against the Ohio Indians. The Swiss officer Henry Bouquet had adopted techniques of fighting in the woods which were quite different from the set-piece confrontations deployed on the fields of Europe. He anticipated some of the flexible methods of more modern warfare, and in consequence he inflicted a crushing defeat on the Indians. Smith wrote up the account of the expedition, and took the opportunity to introduce further ideas about the nature of his family. The Indians were now excluded. They had been kicked down the Great Chain of Being. Smith asserted that 'like beasts of prey, they are patient, deceitful, and rendered by habit almost insensible to the common feelings of humanity'. They are kept at the periphery, therefore, of his family; and in this resemble the Scottish Highlanders, held at the periphery of the British insular family.

The remaining members of the family were now distinctly martial in nature. The younger males were soldiers first; farming was still important, but took second place in time of war. Even in times of peace military exercises should be undertaken regularly, because they helped 'to inculcate and preserve purity of manners, obedience, order and decency'. He then proposed a plan for frontier settlements which would be self-sustaining and which, as they advanced, would push the Indians further and further away from the centre of civilisation, and the head of the family. Townships would be laid out in grids of 34,500 acres, placed alongside each other in a defensive chain not unlike the plans proposed by the British Army for the defence of the Highlands. The new element devised by Smith, however, was the grid pattern. It would later be developed by his student at the College of Philadelphia, Hugh Williamson, and by Thomas Jefferson, and it would make a deep impact on the North American continent.[19]

The Historical Account of Bouquet's Expedition was one of Smith's most popular publications. First published in Philadelphia in 1765, it was reprinted the next year in London by the Geographer Royal, came out in three different editions in Dublin between 1766 and 1770, and appeared in French translations in 1769 and 1778. It is Smith's most comprehensive attempt to revise his model of the family. He had already tried to strengthen its cultural bonds. In 1757 he began *The American Magazine*. He was seeking, he said, to establish something which, like newspapers, would keep alive 'the spirit of liberty' but which, unlike them, would be 'durable in its nature'. He was therefore trying to create an exemplary text which moved towards the status of Ralegh's *History of the*

World. He also tried to instill in the people of Philadelphia an admiration for the exemplary monarch. In January 1757 his students mounted several performances of James Thomson's *Alfred: A Masque*. The play presents King Alfred not only as the saviour of his country from the Danish yoke, but also as 'the father of the state', the hero who never despaired of fulfilling his task. The play is now forgotten, which is perhaps a pity, since the music is by Thomas Arne. One of its songs lives on, a monument to British chauvinism:

> When Britain first, at Heaven's command,
> Arose out of the azure main,
> This was the charter of the land,
> And guardian angels sung this strain:
> 'Rule, Britannia, rule the waves;
> Britons never will be slaves.'[20]

4

Understandably, songs such as 'Rule Britannia' were injurious to Smith's familial vision during the American Revolution. Smith had great difficulty in sustaining the spirit of King Alfred and Sir Walter Ralegh. He therefore reformulated his vision in three pamphlets which were widely read. In the first, *A Sermon on the Present Situation of American Affairs* (1775), Smith tried to pay respect to the rights both of the Mother Country and the colonists. He denounced British attempts at taxation and hoped for a restoration of American liberty within the empire. Americans, he said, had never sold their birthright, and were in consequence entitled to the privileges of their father's house, 'peace, liberty and safety.' As the French and Indian war had demonstrated, they would not submit to violence. Instead, they sought '*Order* and just *subordination*'. Once this had been achieved, unity would be restored and the utopian conditions anticipated in *A General Idea of the College of Mirania* would once more be possible: 'behold British Colonies spreading over this immense Continent, rejoicing in the common rights of Freeman, and imitating the Parent State in every Excellence'.[21]

Such sentiments were repeated in *Plain Truth* (1776), the response to Paine's *Common Sense* written by Smith (possibly in collaboration with others). In the third pamphlet, *An Oration in Memory General Montgomery* (1776), Smith adopted a different approach. Richard Montgomery had died on 31 December 1775 leading an abortive American attack on Quebec. Smith portrayed him first as Cincinnatus, and then as an exemplary British hero in the tradition of Alfred and Ralegh. Montgomery's loyalty to his King, he said, remained 'firm and unshaken'. Unshaken too was his 'love to our brethren whom we must oppose'. The general was therefore forced to pursue a course which would have been abhorrent to him but for his greater love of liberty. Once liberty had been reestablished he would have wished to return the colonies to the British Empire. This portrait of the general allowed Smith to place a particular interpretation upon recent events:

The resistance made at Lexington was not the traitorous act of men conspiring against the supreme powers; nor directed by the councils of any public body in America; but rose immediately out of the case, and was directed by *self-preservation*, the first great law of Nature as well as Society.[22]

Smith's view of Montgomery was shared by Burke and Fox when they spoke of the battle in the House of Commons. A quite different view was put forward by Thomas Paine, who depicted Montgomery as a martyr in the cause of Independence. Hugh Henry Brackenridge took Paine's side. Brackenridge, who was later to become well-known as a frontier jurist and the author of *Modern Chivalry*, was at the time a chaplain in the Continental Army. His tragedy, *the Death of General Montgomery*, was written quickly, shortly after the event. It presents a much less moderate view than Smith's. Brackenridge's Montgomery wishes to rid Quebec of

> This scorpion progeny, this mixed brood
> Of wild-wood savages, and Englishmen,
> Who 'gainst their brethren, in unrighteous cause,
> With cruel perfidy, have waged war.

Britain is portrayed as 'a mad mother' who 'doth her children stab'. Like Pitsligo and Herring before them, Brackenridge and Smith are employing the same ideological terminology, but to opposing ends. Their depiction of James Wolfe is likewise at odds. The earlier hero of Quebec still exercised a potent charm, as the recent portrait by Benjamin West demonstrated; and there were obvious parallels to be drawn with the death of Montgomery. Smith regards Wolfe as a friend to liberty and the loyal subject of the King. Brackenridge asserts that had Wolfe survived, he would have been disgusted at the decline in the British polity and would himself had led an army to Quebec 'to drive the tyrants out'. As if in confirmation, the ghost of Wolfe appears towards the end of the tragedy to celebrate 'the grand idea of an empire new', an independent America.[23]

Brackenridge's interpretation of the death of Montgomery became the authorised version. After the Declaration of Independence Smith could no longer claim that the clashes between the Americans and the British Army were spontaneous events. Smith, as we have seen from his letter to Lady Juliana Penn, found himself isolated. The events at Philadelphia must have seemed like a dreadful reprise of those in Aberdeen some thirty-two years earlier. Yet this time Smith did not quit. The familial ideology which had provided an answer to the fratricide of 1745 now helped to heal the wounds of 1778. Just over six months after the Continental troops marched in Philadelphia, Smith preached in the city's Christ Church. The theme of his sermon was a familiar one: if harmony were learnt in the home and then applied outside it 'Nation would no more rise against Nation in dreadful Havoc and Oppression'. It was now clear to Smith that the actions of the British government had disqualified it from its place in the family circle. He praised those who had fought for 'Liberty and Peace', and he set their actions within a historical framework. The comparison now was not with 1745 and Herring but rather with 1755 and Smith himself. Throughout his 1778 sermon Smith referred back to an earlier occasion in the same church: the occasion just before Braddock's defeat when he had issued the call to defend the colony. Doubtless, in drawing attention to his role in the French and Indian War, Smith was trying to ingratiate himself with the new 'Masters' of Philadelphia. But the comparison was also justified. The group that had listened to Smith on 24 June 1755 had been the Free and Accepted Masons of Pennsylvania. Benjamin Franklin had been one of their number. Now, on 28 December 1778, that same body were meeting, for the first time since 1755, in Christ Church. The most renowned member of the congregation, to whom Smith transferred the laurels of Cincinnatus, was George Washington, who would soon be better known as the Father of his Country.[24]

Notes

1. Smith, MS letter to Lady Juliana Penn 17 June 1778, Historical Society of Pennsylvania, by whose kind permission the letter is quoted. Albert F. Gegenheimer, *William Smith, Educator and Churchman, 1727–1803* (Philadelphia, 1943), pp. 179–80. John W. Jackson, *With the British Army in Philadelphia 1777–1778* (San Rafael, CA, 1979), pp. 16, 257–65. Edgar F. Smith, 'William Smith', *General Magazine and Historical Chronicle* vol. 29, no. 2 (Jan. 1972) pp. 160–1.

2. Gegenheimer, *William Smith*, 1–3. University of Aberdeen, matriculation and bursary records 1743–1747. Bruce Lenman, *The Jacobite Risings in Britain 1689–1746* (London, 1980), pp. 25, 69, 71. Roger L. Emerson, 'Aberdeen Professors 1690–1800', *Aberdeen and the Enlightenment*, ed. Jennifer J. Carter and Joan H. Pittock (Aberdeen, 1978), p. 156.

3. Lenman, 'The Scottish Episcopal Clergy and the Ideology of Jacobitism', *Ideology and Conspiracy: Aspects of Jacobitism*, ed. Evelyn Cruickshanks (Edinburgh, 1982), pp. 36, 45; and *The Jacobite Risings, passim.* Alexander Keith, *A Thousand Years of Aberdeen* (Aberdeen, 1972), pp. 178, 275.

4. Keith, *A Thousand Years*, pp. 276–8. James Fergusson, *John Fergusson, 1727–1750* (London, 1948), p. 159. W. A. Speck, *The Butcher: The Duke of Cumberland and the Suppression of the 45* (Oxford, 1981), pp. 29–35, 49, 107, 121–30.

5. Speck, *The Butcher*, pp. 141–62. Lenman, *The Jacobite Risings*, pp. 175, 268–9. Keith, *A Thousand Years*, pp. 278–9.

6. Ned Landsman, *Scotland and Its First American Colony, 1683–1765 (Princeton, 1985), pp. 24–36.*

7. Speck, *The Butcher*, pp. 95–7, 185–8.

8. Smith, 'A Letter' in Thomas Barton, *Unanimity and Public Spirit, A Sermon, Preached at Carlisle . . . soon after General Braddock's Defeat* (Philadelphia: B. Franklin and D. Hall, 1755), pp. vi,ix-x, xv.

9. Thomas Herring, *Seven Sermons on Public Occasions*, ed. William Duncombe (Dublin: G. Faulkner, 1763), pp. xviii-xix, xxi-xxv. Horace Walpole, *Horace Walpole's Correspondence with Sir Horace Mann*, ed. W. S. Lewis et al (New Haven, 1954) III, 126. See also Speck, *The Butcher*, pp. 55–6; Norman Sykes, *Church and State in England in the XVIIIth Century* (Cambridge, 1934), pp. 75–7; and Cedric Collyer, 'Yorkshire and the "Forty-Five"', *Yorkshire Archaeological Journal* 38 (1952–5), pp. 71–95.

10. Smith, 'A Letter' in Barton, *Unanimity*, p.xv. Herring, *Seven Sermons*, pp. 203, 206–12, 225.

11. Jonathan Clark, *English Society, 1688–1832: Ideology, Social Structure and Political Practice During the Ancien Régime* (Cambridge, 1985). Jay Fliegelman, *Prodigals and Pilgrims: The American Revolution Against Patriarchal Authority* (Cambridge, 1982). Melvin Yazawa, *From Colonies to Commonwealth: Familial Ideology and the Beginnings of the American Republic* (Baltimore, 1985). Herring, *Seven Sermons*, p. xxix.

12. Barton, *Unanimity*, pp. 6, 12 (Barton's emphases); letter 25 November 1776, *Historical Collections Relating to the American Colonial Church*, ed. William Stevens Perry 5 vols., (Hartford, Conn., 1870–78; reprint New York, 1969) II, p. 490.

13. Smith, notebook headed 'Excerpts', William Smith Collection, item No. 11, Van Pelt Library, University of Pennsylvania. The notebook is in a worse condition than most of Smith's MSS. It is worn and its outer pages are crumbling. The handwriting of the opening extracts is large and looks juvenile. Only after several pages does the writing resemble Smith's mature hand. None of the extracted items were first published later than 1735. The notebook is not paginated, but the Addison quotation appears on [p. 29]. Joseph Addison, 'A Letter from Italy' (1701), *Works*, ed. A. C. Guthkelch (2 vols, London, 1914) I, pp. 51–61, II, pp. 131–40.

14. George Sewell, *The Tragedy of Sir Walter Raleigh* (London: John Pemberton, 1719), pp. 7, 10, 36, 39, 50–51, 58. John Aubrey, *Brief Lives and Other Selected Writings*, ed. Anthony Powell (London, 1949), pp. 331–2. Smith, 'Excerpts,' [p. 60].

15. Peter J. Diamond, 'The Scottish Philosophy in Revolutionary America,' *Scotland and America in the Age of Enlightenment* ed. Richard B. Sher and Jeffrey Smitten (Princeton, and Edinburgh, forthcoming). I am grateful to Professor Diamond for letting me see an advance copy of his essay. Murray G. H. Pittock, 'Jacobitism in the North East: The Pitsligo Papers in Aberdeen University Library', *Aberdeen and the Enlightenment*, ed. Carter and Pittock, pp. 74–5.

16. [Smith], *Indian Songs of Peace: With a Proposal, in a Prefatory Letter, for Erecting Indian Schools* (New York: Printed by J. Parker and W. Weyman, 1752); *A General Idea of the College of Mirania*, (New York: Printed by J. Parker and W. Weyman, 1753). For discussions of *Mirania*, see Diamond, 'The Scottish Philosophy', and Lawson-Peebles, 'The Problem of William Smith: An Aberdonian in Revolutionary America', *Aberdeen and the Enlightenment*, ed. Carter and Pittock, pp. 56–7.

17. Smith, *A Sermon, Preached in Christ-Church, Philadelphia, Before the . . . Masons* (Philadelphia: B. Franklin and D. Hall, 1755), p. 19; *The Christian Soldier's Duty . . . A Sermon, Preached* April 5, 1757 (Philadelphia: James Chattin, 1756), pp. 27, 29, 31.

18. [Smith], *A Brief State of the Province of Pennsylvania* (London: R. Griffiths, 1755) pp. 23, 38–42; *A Brief View of the Conduct of Pennsylvania* (London: R. Griffiths, 1756), pp. 22, 45–6.

19. [Smith], *Historical Account of Bouquet's Expedition Against the Ohio Indians* (1765; reprint Cincinnati: Robert Clarke & Co., 1868), pp. 96, 118–21. For a discussion of the grid, see Lawson-Peebles, *Landscape and Written Expression in Revolutionary America* (Cambridge, 1988), pp. 183–188.

20. [Smith], *The American Magazine and Monthly Chronicle for the British Colonies* (Philadelphia: William Bradford, 1758) I, pp. 3–4. James Thomson, 'Songs in the Masque of "Alfred",' *Poetical Works* 2 vols. (Boston, 1854) I, pp. 66, 69. See Gegenheimer, *Smith*, pp. 56–60 for an account of Smith's production of *Alfred*.

21. Smith, *A Sermon On the Present Situation of American Affairs* (Philadelphia, 1775), pp. 13–14, 29, 19.

22. Smith, *An Oration in Memory of General Montgomery* 2nd ed., London: J. Almon, 1776), pp. 23, 33. Smith's emphasis.
23. Burke and Fox, Debate in the Commons 11 March 1776, reported in William Cobbett, *Parliamentary History* (London, 1813), XVIII, Cols. 1239–40. [Paine], *Dialogue Between the Ghost of General Montgomery, Just arrived from the Elysian Fields; and An American Delegate* (1776; reprint New York: Privately reprinted, 1865). [Brackenridge], *The Death of General Montgomery, at the Siege of Quebec* (Philadelphia: Robert Bell, 1777) 'Preface', pp. 10, 26–7, 40.
24. Smith, *A Sermon Preached In Christ-Church, Philadelphia ... before the ... Masons* (Philadelphia: Printed by John Dunlap, 1779), pp. 7, 14–16, 20–2, 26. On Washington as the father of his country, see Yazawa, *From Colonies to Commonwealth*, pp. 195–8, and Marcus Cunliffe, *George Washington; Man and Monument* (New York, 1958), pp. 20–23.

5

EVOLUTION AND REVOLUTIONS IN THE PURSUIT OF HAPPINESS IN FRANCE FROM 1688 TO 1750

Micheline Cuénin

In order to respect the chronological limits of this book while at the same time treating a question dealing with the history of *mores* and sensibility, I have chosen a vast subject, but I propose to limit myself to a few diverse but convergent evolutionary factors, without however *betraying* the complexity of lived experience.

The chronological commencement of this book, chosen with the history of Great Britain in mind, happens also to be appropriate, in a certain way, for France. 1688 marks both the exile of James II to Saint-Germain, the beginning of the so-called war of the League of Augsburg, and the first edition of a book which created a sensation, the *Caractères* of La Bruyère, a critical observer of the Parisian society of his day. As a terminal point, I have chosen the death of a transitional figure, our first sociologist, the président de Montesquieu, who is also the first to have preoccupied himself with defining happiness in relation to the internal upheavals which affect the period in which he lived. With him ends a generation which witnessed one of the greatest changes in modern history.

If, for the sake of clarity, we define the kind of happiness which we are examining as *joie de vivre* (the joy of living), a preliminary remark is necessary. At the end of the seventeenth century, according to Vauban's figures,[1] there were seventeen million true peasants, that is, eighty per cent of the population of the country, and only one-and-a-half to two million are qualified as 'well-off'; that is to say, they have enough to eat. The wider France of the period is another universe, indeed several other universes, if one bears in mind that the provinces retained their individual identities. By contrast, the Parisian world, where the social revolution which began around 1690 was practically completed within thirty years, represent a minuscule, but prodigiously active intellectual centre.

Although it is voiceless, the France of the provinces is of great importance and the word 'happiness' in French, which in 1688 was universally taken to mean social success, luck and favour, cannot be applied to it, unless we consider that people were indeed lucky to have reached the age of forty or forty-five after having overcome the hurdles of infant mortality, epidemics, incurable illnesses, or mutilating accidents. It is true that in the second half of the seventeenth century we see the final retreat of the plague, which had been endemic in the first half. The famous plague of Marseille in 1720 was exceptional and can be attributed to a tragic fraud during a sanitary check. The pillaging, raping soldiers are quartered, around 1685, under the direction of Louvois and Vauban, and are mustered at frontier fortifications which are models of their kind. Fiscal pressures are still high, but revolts have ceased to occur, for the national territory will henceforth remain constantly protected. The peasant will be able to work in peace and, in the richest regions, enjoy the fruits of his labours. He does not ask for more, especially since on holidays he can give himself over to ribald feasting. *His* job of living is simply the absence of calamities. He does not go out of his way to better his condition by working more than necessary, whence the surprise of the *intendants* (provincial royal representatives) in their reports, which unanimously call him lazy, while recognising his capacity for energy in cases of necessity.[2] These great state representatives understood little of peasant sensibilities. Indeed, on the tenant farms, when there is enough to eat, people prefer to 'taste the coolness of the shade', as La Fontaine says, who knew it so well. There remain such diseases as dysentery which still wreak havoc, not to mention smallpox which makes all men equals. The physician Helvetius, the father of the philosopher, discovered an effective formula against that dysentery and, from 1706 onwards, during great epidemics, Louis XIV, through his *intendants*, was to have the 'king's remedy' distributed everywhere. It is the beginning of a long educational policy directed at the peasantry through the supplying of free medicine whose effects were not to be felt till around 1750,[3] thus showing just how resistant the country dweller was to hygiene and novelty.

Similarly, according to one interpretation, his faith was profound and almost instinctive, and the theme of the prayer of the peasant, from the Le Nain brothers to Chardin's *Bénédicité* ('Grace Before the Meal') shows that the burden of inclement weather trained these humble folk to turn first to the Creator, and especially to thank him for their being still alive and able to nourish their families. On to this sort of spontaneous religion was grafted that great missionary effort of the Catholic Reformation around 1630. The clerics were to have no difficulty in persuading their country audiences that stable happiness did not exist on earth, that hell would punish present injustices, and that they were assured of felicity later, once they had left this vale of tears. This was a lesson they had learned at first hand and at their own expense. In any case, many modern historians agree that it was only around 1720 that the Catholic Reformation finally set up the ecclesiastical guidelines for the nation. From 1690 onwards, except in the case of the highest nobles, the bishop is generally resident. It was not to be long before there would be a seminary in each diocese, and a *curé* (parish priest) in each village. Vocations were very numerous, and priests were educated, therefore respected. Perfect unanimity was seen to exist between His Most Christian Majesty, who had become very pious since the death of the queen in 1682, and the humblest of his subjects, beginning with the landed nobility. Such happiness as the common people enjoyed was therefore simple, stable, and, in a certain sense, continuous, since to place oneself in the hands of providence allows one to accept misfortunes with resignation.

But for the remaining twenty per cent, inhabitants of large cities and especially of Paris, happiness resided in social success, and the idea that progress to it could be very rapid. Very significant in this respect is the translation in 1684 of the manual of Balthazar Gracian, the Spanish Jesuit.[4] It does not deal at all with *joie de vivre* but with how to succeed:

> There are rules for happiness, and happiness is not always fortuitous [. . .] Industriousness (that is wiliness) can be helpful. Some people content themselves with standing at Fortune's door waiting for her to open it. Others do better: they press forward, and sooner or later they win over fortune by dint of cajoling her.

Of course the author hastens to add that 'boldness' must be sustained by merit and perseverence, but it is instructive to note the appearance of a new idea here: man has a hold on his destiny, and, through actively planning and preparing the future, he even finds a pleasure which mobilises his intelligence. The translator, Amelot de la Houssaye, belongs to the world of Parisian lawyers, and this has wide implications. The magistrature had in fact constituted the rising class for almost a century, but its ascendancy was to gather momentum with the beginning of the fierce battles which marked the end of the reign, and which resulted in the decline of the dominance of the upper ranks of the nobility (the nobility of the sword), except at Versailles. This ancient order upheld and transmitted hereditary values were to be progressively eroded with it.

These values are encapsulated in the last words of Léonor de Rabutin, count of Bussy, to his son Roger, the memorialist who, in 1636, welcomes his father's regiment: 'the fear of God, honour dearer than life, service to the king.' It will be noted that the third of these imperatives comes last because this service is not obligatory in principle. But war was a passion, a violent pleasure at the beginning of the century. At the end of that same century glory, that 'extension of one's being', as Montesquieu was to say,[5] no longer resided exclusively in battle. It could also be encountered without endangering one's life, in the company of 'one of the greatest kings who ever existed' (Leibniz). In any event, it was so costly to equip oneself, to maintain six horses and three valets, and to purchase uniforms (with one's own money) that the survivors inevitably remained at home in penury.

The happiness of this formerly dominant class consisted in respect for its traditions (which, incidentally, were international) in the intimate satisfaction of duty accomplished, with the ambition of increasing the patrimony of heroism of one's house. This conception of life still held good among country gentlemen, at least among a certain number of them. When war was resumed under Louis XV, some authentic noblemen were unable to pay their expenses[6] or buy their equipment, and hence volunteered as ordinary soldiers, under an assumed name, of course, for fear of dishonouring the real one.[7]

As this class, the sword nobility, sank little by little, it appeared to be replaced by two types of war profiteers: the financiers and the nobility of the robe. The latter began, back in the sixteenth century, to grow rich with the spoils of the 'sword' class, by buying land and domains at low rates. When the King ordered a declaration of income under the first general capitation tax of 1695, Molé the first President of the Parlement, was revealed to be the richest man in the realm, on a par with the dukes and peers, as well as the official in charge of the sale of offices. Immediately above them were the princes of the blood, the ministers and the general tax collectors. Taken as a group, the marquises, counts, viscounts and barons, the 'small fry', proved to be less well-placed than the chief clerk of the criminal department of the Parlement.[8] The remodelling of society seemed to be nearing completion by 1695.

The robe nobility (the magistrature), whose richly endowed daughters were able to use prestigious titles, increased its power and imposed its values. It was always the intellectual elite of the realm, speaking and writing Latin. It cherished classical antiquity and the wisdom of pagan philosophies, encouraged by Jesuit masters. For fifteen years from 1663 to 1677 the first Président de Lamoignon, Guillaume, assembled a private academy at his home.[9] When scientific discoveries, mathematical analysis, the tools of optics (miscroscopes and astronomical telescopes) appeared, the magistrates and their clientele were the first to come together to scrutinise nature and debate the consequences of these discoveries. They were the ones to spread the pleasures of the intellect, to mix social classes, and to discern personal merit independently of birth. That is what the Lamoignons were to do from father to son right down to the minister of state and protector of the Encylopedists, Malesherbes, Guillaume II de Lamoignon.

But the joy of study presupposes leisure and seclusion, which are imcompatible with high office. Nicholas de Lamoignon, the youngest son of Guillaume I, was *intendant* of Languedoc,[10] and he lamented having to administer that province during the war against the Protestants. He wrote to the bishop of Nîmes, his childhood friend Fléchier: 'I have entirely forgotten the sweetness of possessing one's soul in peace, which should be the only happiness in life.' This is a very significant indirect confidence. Already it describes happiness as terrestrial, yet formed from a continuous thread, and based on a great, very stoic, moral precaution: the mastery of one's impulses. This sensation of being master of oneself is a refined pleasure, but subject to one condition: withdrawal. Indeed, as soon as one enters into the world, it evaporates! We can understand why Montesquieu, the first President of the Parlement of Bordeaux and founder of its Academy did not even reside in town and chose his domain of La Brède as the best place to reflect at his leisure and write his works. Already La Fontaine, considered an outcast, felt this necessity intensely. Around 1678, we find him praising that 'solitude', where he finds 'a secret sweetness, far from the world and noise, far from courts and cities'.

In 1711 the duke of Beauvilliers, a minister of state, resigned in order to spend his final years both in piety and in a restful life.[11] The Chevalier de

Forbin, after having been the terror of the seas with Duguay-Trouin and Tourville, was only too happy to ask for his 'absolute leave' in order to enjoy the sweetness of his country house near Marseille:

> I breathe a very healthy air, I spend a sweet life in honest abundance, solely occupied in serving God, in cultivating friends whose company I prefer to the most brilliant fate Fortune might have offered me . . . Far from complaining of the injustices I experienced at Court, I admit in all Candour that they were more profitable than harmful for me, since I owe them a happiness which I did not know before, and which I might perhaps never have tasted in my life.[12]

In short, he adopts the slow rhythm of country life, its refreshing virtues, relieved at no longer having to 'pay his court'. He died in 1733, no doubt quite happy. Indeed, more and more the city bourgeois and those in Paris in particular were to return as soon as possible to their country homes in order to enjoy a balanced existence.

This retreat becomes all the more understandable when we consider that the Church, at least in Paris, was in decline. Narrow Gallicanism divided the clergy. Jansenism became a political credo. Quietism was condemned, but not before permeating even the King's entourage and offering the sorry spectacle of the opposition between the two great men of the French clergy, Bossuet and Fénelon. Could it be that this phenomenon of division, for which Protestants were criticised, was also prevalent among Catholics? The spectacle brought smiles from the 'free thinkers' who until then had remained underground, but now spoke quite loudly. La Bruyère, a convinced Catholic, attempted in a long chapter to answer them. Through this long-neglected text we can discern the extent of their audience at the time. True believers were deeply grieved. If atheism showed itself openly, a rhetorical and theatrical preaching style scarcely helped correct the situation. A revealing anecdote is recounted by Louis Racine (the son of the great playwright). Around 1685, a certain abbé Le Tourneux, shortly to be dispatched into accelerated retirement, was attracting all of Paris. The King learnt of it and questioned Boileau, his historiographer: 'Who is this preacher named Le Tourneux? They say everyone is running to him: is he that learned? – Sire, replied Boileau, Your Majesty knows that people always seek out novelty: he is a preacher who preaches the Gospel.'[13]

Religious belief in Paris was being undermined at the very moment when a social group, which was not in the least worried about possessing its soul, as Lamoignon had said, saved France from disaster. By lending millions of pounds to the King, the Legendre Bank (named after the renowned Protestant financier who created it) opened the way for the final levy of troops commanded by the old Marshal of Villars who at Denain (1712) was to save the national territory from an invasion. Without the necessary funds, this desperate exploit would not have been possible, nor the honourable peace which followed, signed immediately at Utrecht. In reality, His Majesty had been 'cajoling' the corporation for a long time. When the War of the Spanish Succession broke out, the King treated the extremely rich Samuel Bernard as an equal and a friend and issued a special invitation to him to visit Marly. Thereupon, the favourite posed for Rigaud, the royal family painter, his chest bedecked with the great sash of Saint-Louis, the highest *military* award!

During the last three decades of the reign, the private services of the great tax farms became positively tentacular. That is why, immediately after the economic recovery following the peace, their liquid assets were invested in shipbuilding, an enterprise which had itself been stimulated by the naval war. The naval construction sites for a mixed fleet, now reconverted, launched ships of larger and larger tonnage. What for Great Britain was usual, for France was almost miraculous. Expensive, rare or prohibited merchandise, such as coffee, sugar and chocolate, relished by the powerful and at the court, became available in all the Parisian shops. And in as much as this massive influx of goods coincided with the death of the King and the unheard-of decision of the Regent to close Versailles, Paris 'became king'. At one stroke, all the daily habits were transformed in a new-found joy. Let us take a simple example. Louis XIV 'dined' at one o'clock. The courtiers and the capital did so at ten, in order to go afterwards to Versailles. But henceforth the city was in command. It was Paris that ate at one o'clock, and since that meant a long wait on an empty stomach, people borrowed from the innumerable convents the habit of taking breakfast, which included, besides the 'croissants' introduced in 1683,[14] the famous and unchanging *café au lait* (coffee with milk) distributed on all street corners, in preference to the traditional rustic wine of the old-style taverns.

In addition to this amusing upheaval, which involves the whole of Parisian society, the better-off legal and financial circles and a few great lords began to derive profit from the relaunching under new auspices of the silk industry in Lyon. A new technique had just revolutionised production. Based on the decomposition of the light spectrum by Newton and mixtures obtained by the German Mayer in Göttingen, the artists and artisans of Lyon succeeded in weaving threads dyed with ninety-one principal shades. The ancient, heavy brocades gave way to shimmering, watered *failles* which no modern word can adequately describe. It was a veritable Aladdin's cave. One could gaze upon baskets containing twelve to fifteen metres of coloured cloth with such names as 'pigeon breast', 'crushed flea', tones of pink and mauve, like those which could be seen in the dress with which Watteau enfolds the rich client of Madame Gersaint. Despite all that, the workshops of Lyon did not abandon their speciality: plain brocaded silks and large floral designs, such as De Troy shows us in the *Declaration of Love*.[15] How could such splendours not invite one to embark for Cythera?

And that was not all. There was no longer a court, nor any etiquette, nor were there any constraints. No more tall wigs like that of the king, no ridiculous metal-bound corsets. These went out of fashion instantaneously. Montesquieu notes, in 1717, in the hundredth *Persian Letter*: 'Sometimes the hair styles rise imperceptibly and a revolution makes them drop suddenly.' Now, the fashion went for plain natural hair, simply adorned with shining ribbons, allowing one to glimpse irresistible necks, like those created by the brush of Watteau. Similarly, even if their parents remained faithful to the old styles, the trendsetting young men adopted the small 'rat's-tail' wig which appeared around the time of the death of the great King, and which finally permitted men to wear a hat, destined for a long career, and whose shape was at that point still undecided: was it to be 'purse-shaped', 'poodle-dog's ears' or was it to correspond to some other picturesque name?[16]

From now on, anything goes, and the first thing people did was to go off to applaud the Italian actors. Louis XIV was hardly dead in his grave when the Regent, who desired nothing better, called them back in triumph in 1716. The troupe maintained its impertinent repertoire but also created Marivaux's plays, while the Comédie Française stood by and watched its receipts decline. The Italians sang, laughed, and embodied the gaiety and unconcern of the moment. People danced at the Opera, and anyone could go there.

This new Paris was reckoned worth the visit. An illustrious provincial was already there: Montesquieu, who was twenty-six years old at the time of Louis XIV's death and witnessed as a tourist the birth of a new world. He saw the general prosperity blossom forth. Order-books were full. The most astute cabinet-makers set about following the tastes of a society eager to buy, and manufacture new furniture adapted to the current frivolity: low 'commodes', 'chiffoniers', 'bonheurs-du-jour' (little davenports) whose very names require no commentary. They created hitherto unheard-of forms based on the curved line which appeared at the end of the preceding century, and produced marvellously delicate pieces, small ceremonial or utilitarian furniture, harmonising the fanciful novelty of the content with the originality of the container. The standard of living rose everywhere in Paris and the large cities, which, except for Lyon, were also seaports, and Lyon itself had for long been the capital of the book trade.

And certainly Lyon was not idle. It spread the ideas of Locke and of Spinoza; it diffused applied mathematics. The use of the four operations became widespread along with the extension of commerce. In the face of these facts, who would have dared maintain that happiness was possible only in a silent retirement? There was a feeling that one should go out and see what was going on, and then revise the outdated definitions. Pleasures seemed so numerous that happiness could be constituted simply by accumulating them. It was felt that even profit should no longer arouse misplaced scruples. Encouraged by the English example, Montesquieu bought shares in naval armaments at Bordeaux and, as opposed to La Bruyère, took care not to scorn money: 'Business is so necessary for pleasures that each individual must procure for himself as many happy moments as possible.'[17] And now the impoverished upper nobility (the nobility of the sword) found a providential way out of the dilemma of derogation or decline, something which allowed it to avoid total eclipse. There are immemorial texts which state clearly that the glass industry is not beneath the dignity of nobles. So rare was this astonishing Italian invention that it was deemed worthy of landed gentry. In the Vivarais area, the Voguë family developed it as far as possible and it came to be used everywhere.

What had become of the ancient interdicts now, then? The universe had changed. It had become open to human knowledge; but the consequence of this very understandable exhilaration was that each individual had to construct of his own happiness for himself, 'according to the dispositions of his "machine" [body and mind].' First of all, he had to achieve the proper balance of his physiological functions, and then go on to find the formula adapted to his own case. This rapid 'personalisation' of happiness certainly caught the best minds unawares, and this explains the surprising quantity of treatises on happiness which appeared during the eighteenth century,[18] whereas not one exists from the seventeenth century. Disappointing treatises, it must be said, since that generation, brought up by the Jesuits, took its inspiration from antiquity, and failed to ascribed its conduct to principles which were in fact less novel than its mentors supposed. People thereupon gave themselves over to the pleasure of trying out ideas, of bouncing them around like a ball, without putting too much of themselves into them, so that – paradoxically – they lived in a state of improvisation. This seems to me to be the character of the *salons* of the beginning of the century, where anything was allowed as long as a person had wit.

But meanwhile, what was going on in the streets? One would have been able to see large building sites in the direction of the Faubourg Saint-Germain, where architects like Boffrand and Robert de Cotte were incorporating larger windows to take the bigger sheets of glass currently being produced. One might see also very well-dressed lackeys, and servant girls who could well be taken for their mistress. Daniel Roche's investigation of the people of Paris[19] shows that domestics lived well, their quarters were tastefully decorated, and Madame, who changed her dress several times a day, habitually gave to her maid the clothing she no longer wanted. Of all the salaried employees in the town, the *soubrette* (maid) was the classiest and the sharpest, as Marivaux quite accurately informs us. Lesage, in his *Turcaret*, had not exaggerated the rapacity of this upwardly mobile class in the least. All the inventories of the property of those women fortunate enough to live through this period note the possession of at least a hand-mirror. Whereas the great mirrors intensifed the light of candles and reflected the heat from fire-places in the houses of well-off families, the small mirror was something anyone could afford.

Of course the mirror was known in the seventeenth century: Colbert had created the royal factory of Saint-Gobain which produced the *Galerie des Glaces* (Hall of Mirrors) at Versailles, but these expensive products did not penetrate the ordinary market. A young woman contemplated herself in the eyes of her lover. Novels and poetry of the first half of the seventeenth century showed lovers such as we find in *l'Astrée*[20] vying with each other in fidelity. The faces of women might be marred by smallpox, but this misfortune did not prevent the princess of Conti, the daughter of Louis XIV, from being the most 'beautiful' woman at Court. But when the mirror became faithful, love became more realistic. In the opinion of women, the beauty of the body counted for more than the beauty of the soul. In order, so they thought, to camouflage the ravages of time, they now started to use and abuse make-up. Literary scholars have always considered La Bruyère to be a misogynist or, at least, as less than totally gentlemanly; but this is an error. He saw certain of his contemporaries transform themselves into masked dolls. In order to make people think they had a white complexion, they plastered their faces with a thick layer of ceruse, the white lead used by painters which has strong coating properties. On top of that, they painted their cheeks with bright red rouge (see, for example, the paintings of Lancret and Boucher). But what the artists

do *not* show are 'the false teeth in the mouth; the balls of wax in the jaws':
'what trickery', says our moralist, 'just to make oneself ugly!'.

That is why, as the century advanced, and still following the English example, they preferred to delay the onset of old age by taking care of their health.
After the enormous eating and drinking bouts of the Regency came the fashion for sobriety, for dietetics, and around 1750 a large number of hygienist
treatises were published. The first to launch this genre was the indefatigable
abbé de Saint-Pierre, nephew of the Marshal of Villars, in his observations
on sobriety, written in 1735.[21] He enumerated seven advantages: a very long
life, fewer and less critical illnesses, fewer pains and sufferings, a life more
open to gaiety and to the enjoyment of innocent pleasures, and hence a
life which allowed one to work better for the benefit of one's family, one's
friends, one's country, and consequently a more benevolent life and one more
worthy of paradise. Finally, bodily vigour also meant moral courage. And as
for women, they were thus able to preserve for longer 'what they consider to
be their greatest merit: their external charms'. Quality of life, and also quantity. A Maupertuis seeks the secret of prolonging life and even of achieving
immortality: chemistry and alchemy would, it was thought, combine to fulfil
this wondrous purpose. It should be no surprise, then, that Cagliostro, in this
context, succeeded in persuading Mme de Pompadour and others that he was
two thousand years-old. On a more serious note, I should obviously not omit
the work of John Gregory, born here in Aberdeen, who appears to have been
the ancestor of modern eugenics.

In this new perspective, Christian values were secularised in order to make
them fit into the universe of pleasure. Fine wits, readers of La Bruyère, retained the idea that the most delicate [refined] pleasure is that of giving it to
others.' 'Let us then no longer be charitable but benevolent,' as the abbé de
Saint-Pierre had already put it. Let us no longer talk of the love of one's neighbour, which sounds too religious, but of the love of humanity: the expression
is already found in the famous scene of the poor man in Molière's *Dom Juan*.
And we have already seen how good health led to the notion of service, to
activities which put one in harmony with oneself, a view with stands in contrast to that of the Augustinian moralists of the seventeenth century, who, had
analysed that attitude as an effect of self-esteem.[22]

Now people were being told they must love themselves, flatter their
inclinations, seek diversion. The young Montesquieu followed the others,
but at the end of his life he recoiled instinctively before the audacity of the new
generation, both for moral and physiological reasons. Against Maupertuis,[23]
he argued that the scramble for pleasures necessitates a constant increase in the
dose, because muscles slacken, and stimulants, we would say today, lead to an
overdose.[24] And 'since want engenders pain, not only have we gained nothing, but we have lost everything.' Maupertuis 'included in his calculations
only pleasures and pain', utilising a mechanical application of a misplaced
mathematical method. Perhaps feeling somewhat responsible, for he followed
this path in his *Essay on Taste*,[25] Montesquieu writes: 'Despite what I may
have said concerning happiness founded in my machine, I do not maintain
for all that that our soul cannot contribute to our happiness by the direction it
takes.'[26]

Clearly, we can reintroduce the values of the will which are the basis of the whole Greco–Roman heritage and the Cartesian outlook of the *Treatise of the Passions of the Soul*. It is a return to the self-possession recommended by Nicholas de Lamoignon . . . .

Thus the old traditions of the nobility of the robe resurface at the end of their existence among those who have been witness to a great mental revolution at the turn of the century. Closing his now sightless eyes, Montesquieu clung to continuity, the faultless pleasure which only the soul (he does not even say 'spirit') is able to give.

But the solution did not only apply to those whose childhood was formed by the teachers of the preceding century. The deep, personal, unadmitted anxiety was no less real for the others. Since the history of mores is irreversible, they were later to seek elsewhere, notably in nature, recognised at last, a fixed reference and a transcendent beauty capable of bringing an uninterrupted happiness.

NOTES

1. In *La Dîme royale*, 1690. See the commentaries of Jean Meyer, *La vie quotidienne sous la Régence* (Paris, Hachette, 1979), pp.324–326.
2. ibid., pp.307–17; following the findings of Louis Trénard, *Les Mémoires des intendants pour l'instruction du duc de Bourgogne* (1695–1710) edited in 1968, 1975.
3. François Le Brun, *Les hommes et la mort en Anjou*, (Paris, Flammarion (collection 'Sciences') 1975), pp.209 ff.
4. 1601–1657. The original title, *Oraculo manual. . .* was variously translated throughout Europe. It is maxim XXI that is cited here. In French: *L'Homme de Cour*, 1684.
5. *Lettres persanes*, letter 89.
6. It will be recalled that military posts were as venal as the civil ones, with the exception that they were not hereditary in a corps in which one was called upon to die. If the dead officer left a male heir, the king might give this gift to the child, but this only happened when his finances were in good shape.
7. See François Bluche, *La vie quotidienne de la noblesse française au XVIIIe siècle*, (Paris, Hachette, 1973), pp.137–42.
8. See François Bluche and J.P. Solnon, *La Véritable Hiérarchie sociale de l'ancienne France, le tarif de la première capitation*, (Geneva, 1983).
9. See R. Zuber and M. Cuénin, *Littérature française, le Classicisme*, (Paris, Arthaud–Flammarion, 1984), p.266 ff.
10. Nicholas de Lamoignon, lord of Basville, marquis of La Motte, count of Launay-Courson, born in Paris in 1684, died in Basville in 1724.
11. Paul, son of the duke of Saint-Aignan, born in 1648, died in his domain of Vaucresson in 1714.
12. Claude de Forbin-Gardanne, born and died at Saint Marcel, near Marseille, 1656–1726. These lines close his *Mémoires*. 1729.
13. Louis Racine, *Mémoires . . .*, in Jean Racine *Oeuvres*, ed. R. Picard, (Paris, Gallimard (collection de la Pléiade)), I, p.109.
14. They were made in honour of Jean Sobieski's victory over the Turks at the gates of Vienna. The future King of Poland had spent many years in France, and married a Frenchwoman, Marie de la Grange d'Arquien, whence the rejoicing.

15. Jean-François De Troy, (1679–1752), Director of the French Academy of Rome in 1738. This canvas, painted in 1731, is still in Berlin. It forms the book-jacket of Jean Meyer's work. See also n.16 (below).

16. François Boucher, *Histoire de costume*, (Paris, Flammarion, 1965), pp.312, 297.

17. *Mes pensées*, VI, 'Plaisirs et bonheur', in *Oeuvres*, (Paris, Seuil (Collection 'L'Intégrale')), p.985.

18. Robert Mauzi, *L'idée du bonheur au XVIIIe siècle*, (Paris, Armand Colin, 1969), pp.9–10.

19. See the investigation of ordinary objects according to the records of notaries in Daniel Roche, *Le Peuple de Paris*, (Paris, Aubier-Montaigne, 1981); 'Savoir Consommer', pp.148–154.

20. See M. Cuénin, *L'Idéologie amoureuse*, (Paris, Aux Amateurs de Livres, 1981, 1987).

21. Abbé de Saint-Pierre, *Observations sur la sobriété*, quoted and commented on by Robert Mauzi, op.cit., p.304.

22. La Bruyère, *Des Jugements*, Maxime 98 (7th ed.). A long tradition beginning in France and in Savoie with François de Sales is taken up again by Port-Royal, in the perspective of the 'interior Christian'.

23. Maupertuis 1698–1759. His *Essaie de philosophie morale*, here under attack, appeared in 1751.

24. *Mes pensées*.

25. *Encylopédie* article 'Goût'; but Montesquieu's text is modified.

26. *Mes Pensées*. These 'notes' are a collection of 'thoughts' dictated at various dates and gathered together haphazardly after the death of the author.

6

THE REVOLT OF THE *PHILOSOPHES* AGAINST ARISTOCRATIC TASTES

John Pappas

French classical aesthetic values are basically aristocratic values. In the seventeenth century, and particularly during the reign of Louis XIV, artists, musicians and men of letters sought above all the favour of the King, and it was thanks to his generous support that they achieved fame and honour in their time. Although Louis XV was less interested in the theatre, the nobility continued to set the tastes of the nation in aesthetic matters.

Anyone who has visited the château of Versailles or other aristocratic houses in the Loire valley, for example, will recall the paintings and frescoes decorating their walls and ceilings; allegorical representations of gods and goddesses from antiquity, idealised portraits where all warts and wrinkles have been eliminated, beautifully clothed shepherds and shepherdesses surrounded by cupids and floral garlands; certainly not the realistic bourgeois paintings that Diderot would propose in the second half of the eighteenth century.

The theatre too reflected the same refined tastes. Classical tragedy required a subject worthy of its distinguished audience. The themes were generally taken from antiquity and dealt with kings and queens, or at least princes and princesses. In his *La Nouvelle Héloise*, Rousseau complains of the Paris theatre, 'there are in that large city five or six hundred thousand souls you never see on the stage . . . Today authors would consider themselves dishonoured if they knew what went on at a merchant's counter or a workman's shop; they must have only illustrious interlocutors.' The nobility, he continues, 'are like the only inhabitants of the earth.' Those who do not have the aristocratic trappings of a coach and a *maître d'hôtel* 'are not of this world; they are bourgeois, men of the populace, people from another world . . . Thus there is a handful of insolent individuals who count only themselves in the whole universe . . . It is exclusively for them that plays are written'.[1] Seven years later, Beaumarchais was to echo him while pleading for a bourgeois drama: 'What have the revolutions of Athens and Rome to do with me? What real interest can I have in the death of a Peloponnesian tyrant, in the sacrifice of a young princess in Aulis? There is in all that nothing for me to see, no morality suited to my condition' (*Essai sur le genre dramatique sérieux*, 1767).[2]

Rousseau's criticism is well taken. Not only were plays written for the aristocracy; their success depended on aristocratic approval. We know from Lancaster that audiences refrained from applauding when the king was present until, like the Caesars of old who turned thumbs up or down on a gladiator, he had shown his approval or disapproval. D'Alembert complains of the need to bow to high-ranking nobles in literary matters and he refuses to go through the process of currying favour by dedicating prefaces to aristocratic 'protectors'. Molière had already mocked that necessary procedure by having the valet, Mascarille, disguised as a nobleman in the *Précieuses ridicules*, declare:

> It is the custom here that authors come to read their new plays to us men of condition in order to engage us to find them beautiful and to make their reputation; and you can well imagine that when we read something, the pit doesn't dare contradict us. As for me, I'm very conscientious; and when I've made a promise to some poet, I always cry out 'How beautiful!' even before the candles are lit. (scene 10)

It is no wonder that D'Alembert could complain bitterly about 'those proud and vile men, who look upon men of letters as a species of animal destined to combat in the arena for the pleasure of the multitude'.[3]

The same can be said of the novel. In 1731 Marivaux finds it necessary to defend the quarrel between a coachman and a merchant in his *La vie de Marianne* by decrying, in a subsequent chapter, the exclusion of the bourgeoisie from artistic creation:

> There are some people whose vanity enters into all they do, even in their reading. Give them the story of the human heart in high ranks, and that makes it for them very important; but don't talk to them about middle ranks, they only want to see lords, princes, kings or at least people of renown. That's all that exists for the nobility of their taste. Don't bother with the rest of men; let them live, but let's not talk about them. They will gladly tell you that nature could have done without them and that the bourgeoisie dishonours it.[4]

And Diderot was later to attack the conventional novel in his *Jacques le fataliste* and claim the right for the author to insert coarse language and scabrous incidents in his writings.

As with other forms of artistic expression, classical theatre was circumscribed by numerous conventions – which we call 'the rules' – which prevented the introduction of the realism Diderot, Rousseau and others demanded. Finally, music too had to be elevated and dignified. Louis XIV required appropriate music for all state functions. His superintendent of music, Lully, composed pieces for the King's suppers, for court ceremonies, for jousts, for religious observances and as a distraction for the court. Lully's operas were in reality classical tragedies set to music and, as with the theatre, reworked the traditional subjects of classical antiquity found in the plays of Corneille and Racine.

The eighteenth century continued this aristocratic preference and, although Voltaire was avant-garde in his philosophical views, he presented himself as the staunchest defender of seventeenth century courtly taste in aesthetic matters. For example, when Diderot and others proposed bougeois characters as subjects of tragedies, Voltaire rejected the idea saying: 'What would be a tragic plot among commoners? It would simply vilify the tragic genre; it would miss the objective of both tragedy and comedy; it would be a sort of bastard, a monster born of the inability of producing a true comedy or tragedy'.[5]

In the classical vision, art was not to imitate brute nature but *la belle nature*, that is, an embellished nature. Realism was not the goal, but art, that is, artifice, which would create a beauty worthy of the delicate tastes of a refined audience. Thus, in the preface to his play *Zaïre*, Voltaire attacks a speech in Dryden's *Antony and Cleopatra* as being too vulgar:

> It is very likely that Cleopatra often spoke in that taste, but it is not such indecency that ought to be represented before a respectable audience. Some of your (English) compatriots will reply in vain: 'But that's the way pure nature is'; we must reply that it is precisely that nature which must be carefully veiled. It is that veil which makes the charm of proper people (*honnêtes gens*): there is no pleasure for them without propriety (*les bienséances*).

And he insists that the rule of *bienséances* is not an arbitrary one; it is a 'natural law'. 'You should subject yourselves to the rules of our theatre', he tells his English friend, Faulkner, 'as we should embrace your philosophy'.[6]

One of the targets of both Diderot and Rousseau is precisely the affected dignity required by the *bienséances* upheld by Voltaire as a natural law. Rousseau attacks the 'false delicacy' which leads Frenchmen to neglect 'naturalness and illusion'. The Frenchman values embellishment and not imitation; he states:

> The actors in turn neglect entirely the creation of an illusion, since they see that nobody cares about it. They place heroes of antiquity between six rows of young Parisians; they superimpose French styles on Roman clothes; the tearful Cornelia is seen wearing two inches of rouge, Cato a white powdered wig, and Brutus a hoop skirt.[7]

And he calls out to Voltaire: 'Tell us, celebrated Arouet, how many male and powerful beauties you have had to sacrifice because of our false delicacy, and how much the spirit of gallantry, so fertile in petty things, has cost you great ones'.[8]

Diderot reflects the same attitude. Decrying the 'fairy-land' atmosphere and the 'insipid mythology' in the art of his day, he turns to the theatre: 'But wonder at the peculiar ways of civilized peoples. Their delicacy is at times pushed to the point where they forbid their poets from utilizing the very circumstances which are in their custom, and which have simplicity, beauty and truth'.[9]

One criticism which had been levelled against Diderot's play *Le Fils naturel* (*The Natural Son*) was that he had the actors drink tea on stage, and he had replied that he did not want to be judged by arbitrary conventions but by what went on in his own living room. We recall that in attacking

Shakespeare as a barbarian, Voltaire had pointed out as evidence in his *Dissertation on Tragedy*: 'Hamlet, his mother and his step-father drink together on the stage. They sing at the table, they quarrel, they fight, they kill each other; one would believe that this work is the fruit of the imagination of a drunken savage'.[10] On the French stage, all these events were taboo, and killing had to be done offstage and described to the audience afterwards by an eye-witness or a messenger. In the face of such limitations on playwrights, Diderot cries out:

> Oh ridiculous and superficial people! what limits you place on art! what constraints you impose on your artists! and of what pleasures you deprive yourselves by your delicacy! . . . Woe to the man born with genius who will try to present a spectacle which is in nature but which is not in prejudices![11]

And, echoing Rousseau, he decries the ostentatious costumes worn by actors and their lack of concern for more realism. When Mademoiselle Clairon appears on stage without the traditional hoop skirt, he is overjoyed:

> An actress has courageously got rid of the hoop skirt . . . Ah! if she would only dare one day to show herself on stage with all the nobility and simplicity of attire that her roles require! let us say more; in the disorder into which an event as terrible as the death of a husband, the loss of a son, and the other catastrophes of the tragic stage should throw her; what around a dishevelled woman, would all those powdered, curled, dressed-up dolls become? They would sooner or later have to conform. Nature, nature! she cannot be resisted. We must either ban her or obey her.[12]

Sixty-nine years later, Victor Hugo was to echo Rousseau and Diderot by attacking classical rules in the preface to his play *Cromwell* (1827) in very similar terms: 'Let us insist on this point; the poet must take advice only from nature, from truth and from his inspiration which is also a truth and a nature.' The rules, he goes on to say 'have curbed the flight of our greatest poets. It is with the shears of the unities that their wings were clipped.' And he attacks 'that painted, ornamented, powdered poetry of the eighteenth century; that literature wearing hoop skirts, tassels and flounces. They offer an admirable résumé of a period with which the greatest geniuses could not have contact without becoming petty.'[13]

The same requirement of following nature applies to the other arts. In *Rameau's Nephew* Diderot sets forth his general principle. When asked what is the model for song, he explains:

> Song is an imitation, through sounds of a scale invented by art or inspired by nature, as you wish, either through the voice or an instrument, of physical noises or the accents of passion; and you see that by changing therein what needs to be changed, the definition applies exactly to painting, to eloquence, to sculpture or to poetry.[14]

Let us test this all-embracing definition by applying it to painting. As with the theatre, the aristocratic taste in painting tended towards a fairy-land atmosphere, allegory based on antiquity, and excessive decorative effects rather than a natural simplicity. Watteau's *Pilgrimage to Cythera*, painted in 1717, is a good example. First it deals with a mythological subject from antiquity. The people depicted are nobles dressed in fine clothing. The painting is embellished with Cupids hovering over the ship. Even the woods are made more civilised by the statue draped with garlands of flowers. Boucher's *The Triumph of Venus*, has the same features of escape from reality into a fairy-tale world. Such paintings adorned the walls and ceilings of aristocratic houses.

Writing of Boucher's rococo style, Diderot exclaims: 'That man is the ruin of all young students of painting. They scarcely learn to handle a brush and hold a pallet when they busy themselves trying to weave children's garlands, . . . and launch into all sorts of extravagances'.[15] Boucher's well-dressed, prettified shepherds in his allegory entitled *Springtime* is a good illustration of the genre. Calling Boucher a 'hypocrite' in art, Diderot calls for greater simplicity, insisting: 'we need naiveté. Without naiveté there is no true beauty'. What is naiveté? he asks: 'It is water taken from a stream and thrown on the canvas.'[16] This is almost photographic realism is what he admires in Chardin's still lifes. In describing his *The Olive Jar* (1760) Diderot marvels:

> It is nature itself; the objects come out of the canvas and with a truth which deceives the eyes . . . the fact is that that porcelain vase is porcelain; those olives are really separated visibly by the water in which they are swimming; we have only to take those biscuits and eat them, that orange and open it and press it, that glass of wine and drink it, those fruits and peel them, that pâté and sink one's knife into it.[17]

But it is not only a matter of realism: Diderot also reacts against the rules of the *bienséances* (standards of decorum) which only allowed a refined and embellished subject. Chardin's *Disembowelled Ray* says Diderot, 'is disgusting, but it is the very flesh, skin and blood of the fish', and he adds, in anticipation of Baudelaire, that Chardin's talent teaches us 'how to avoid the disgust that certain still lifes can evoke'.[18] Finally, Chardin's lower class subjects satisfy Diderot's desire for bourgeois art. *Back from the Market* is an example, as is *Grace before Meals*, which adds the moral edification so dear to Diderot.

If Chardin's still lifes represent the first half of Diderot's aesthetic principle, the exact imitation of nature, Greuze's sentimentality and emotivity illustrate the second, the imitation of human passion. In addition to such touching scenes as the *Girl with Dead Canary* or the *Young Girl Caring for her Paralytic Father*, Greuze also painted dramatic scenes pointing up a moral lesson. Two of these evoke ecstatic exclamations of admiration from Diderot. They are *The Father's Curse* (*La Malédiction paternelle*) and its sequel, *The Punished Son* (*Le Mauvais fils puni*, 1765). In the second, the mother, pointing to the dying father, is, according to Diderot, saying to her son who has just returned: 'See what you've done!' Despite what I would call 'grand opera' poses of suffering – hands extended, eyes raised heavenward, etc., in other words Romanticism *avant la lettre,* Diderot can say of this painting which today we might view as highly exaggerated and histrionic: 'there are no tormented or artificial attitudes, the actions are true, as befits a painting'.[19]

As opposed to the often erotic and suggestive paintings enjoyed by the aristocracy and exemplified by Boucher's buxom nudes disguised as goddesses, Diderot sees in Grueze the one who brings back virtue to art:

> What! has not the brush been devoted long enough to debauchery and vice? Should we not be pleased to see it cooperating at last with dramatic poetry in touching us, instructing us and inviting us to virtue? Courage my friend Greuze, give us morality in painting, and do it always this way.[20]

In music too, the dual obligation of art to imitate the physical world and human emotions applies. Indeed, D'Alembert, in the Preliminary Discourse to the *Encyclopedia* declares: 'All music which does not paint anything is only noise', and he places music last among the arts because it is capable of fewer and less accurate imitations of nature. We might dismiss such a view as too narrow, but the fact that it is presented as the official position of the Encyclopedists makes it worthy of note. And the popularity of such harpsichord pieces as Rameau's imitation of the flight of a butterfly or the hooves of a horse indicates that it was not a point of view limited to a few *philosophes* but represented the changing tastes of the nation.

In his *On Dramatic Poetry*, Diderot imagines a ballet in which the orchestra imitates a storm – a theme which Beethoven and Rossini were later to exploit – while the strings express the fear and terror of two young peasant children caught in the woods during the tempest. But it is perhaps the opera which furnishes the best example of the contrast between an aristocratic and a bourgeois aesthetic, because the genre was closely linked to classical theatre and thus underwent the same restrictions decried by Diderot and Rousseau, as we have seen. French opera was developed by Lully, who called it 'lyric tragedy' – an apt name because the music was the handmaid of the libretto, which was judged by the same rules as a classical play. In fact, Voltaire states that the only justification for opera is that early Greek tragedies had choruses. The music had to be elevated to correspond to the tone of tragedy, and Lully attended the Comédie Française to study the declamation of Alexandrine verse the better to reflect its intonations in his music. Diderot was later to write in his *Rameau's Nephew*, 'Do not think that actors in the theatre and their declamation can serve us as models. Fie! we need something more energetic, less affected, more true'. That model for the musician will be an 'animal cry or the cry of a passionate man'.[21]

It will be recalled that Voltaire resisted the trend toward a more passionate declamation when he complained that actors were beginning to recite verse as if it were everyday conversation, thus ruining its dignity. And in the preface to *Zaïre,* he chides English actors for expressing themselves 'more as poets overcome by enthusiasm than as men inspired by passion'; they declaim verses 'with a fury and impetuosity which is to natural beauty what convulsions are to a noble and dignified walk'. It is of course precisely this aberration that Diderot will espouse, and the 'fury' and 'impetuosity' of poets 'overcome by enthusiasm' will be his formula for imitating the 'animal cry of passion'.

The arrival of a troupe of Italian musicians in Paris in 1752 to present Pergolese's *The Maid as Mistress* (*La Serva Padrona*), was the occasion for a violent controversy between the exponents of the traditional French opera versus the more passionate and bourgeois Italian opera. The one-act piece was played as an Interlude with Lully's *Acis and Galatée*. The contrast was all the more striking and the audience was carried away by the liveliness and emotivity of the Italian production. Rousseau wrote a pamphlet declaring the French language unfit for music, which resulted in his being chased from the opera house by the French musicians. In general the *philosophes* backed the Italianists while the aristocracy upheld traditional French opera.

The Italian tendency to subordinate the text to the music is strongly rejected by Voltaire in the famous episode of the Venetian senator in *Candide,* where Pococurante declares:

> I would perhaps like opera better if they had not found the secret of making of it a monster which revolts me. Let whoever wishes go and see miserable musicalized tragedies in which the scenes are only created to lead into two or three ridiculous songs which show off the vocal chords of an actress . . . I have long ago given up that poor stuff [*ces pauvretés*] which nowadays constitutes the glory of Italy.[22]

But for the *philosophes* in general, if French music was to achieve the passion and vivacity of the Italian opera, it would have to abandon the classical themes defended by the aristocracy and championed by Voltaire. It must abandon what Diderot calls its 'ingenious sentences, its light, tender and delicate madrigals . . . which are cold, languishing, monotonous. I would just as soon have to set to music La Rochefoucauld's *Maximes* or Pascal's *Pensées*', and he adds sarcastically, 'What do we need then? We need exclamations, interjections, suspensions, interruptions, affirmations, negations; we call out, we invoke, we cry, we sob, we weep, we laugh openly'.[23] This is not to say that French opera did not have such elements, but, as I have suggested, it was not the cries 'in the street', as Diderot put it, which served as a model for the musician in French opera but the measured, noble declamation of the French tragic theatre.

When Pergolese's opera was presented on the same occasion as Lully's, the contrast was all the more startling. The 'facility, flexibility, harmony, prosody, ellipses and the inversions' in the Italian language, notes Diderot, make the French opera appear 'stiff, dull, heavy, weighty, pedantic and monotonous'; and he grows more heated:

> Yes, yes, (French audiences) thought that after mixing their tears with those of a mother lamenting the death of her son, after having shuddered at the order of a tyrant commanding a murder, they would not be bored by their own fairy-tales, their insipid mythology, their sticky little madrigals which show no less the bad taste of the poet than the poverty of the art which adapts itself to it. The poor fools! It is not so and cannot be. The true, the good, the beautiful have their rights. We may contest them, but we end up admiring them. Anything out of keeping with

them may be admired for a time, but we end up yawning. Go ahead and yawn, gentlemen; yawn to your heart's content, be my guest![24]

The same is true of poetry. In his *Dialogue between Poetry and Philosophy*, D'Alembert rejects the 'outdated imagery', with its clichés like 'Flore' and 'Zephyre', exclaiming: 'It is the endless repetition of these trivialities, with which we have been so often been bored, that causes the disgust of our century for poetry in general – a disgust which is impossible to hide'.[25]

As we have seen in theatre, poetry, art and music, Diderot and his associates attacked the traditional genres and aesthetic values upheld by the aristocracy as being stilted, unrealistic and unrelated to everyday life, and they proposed a more realistic, more emotional mode of expression which would reflect bourgeois life and values. It was not simply a theoretical quarrel over aesthetics. It was a power struggle in which the *philosophes* sought to wrest from the nobility the right to dictate literary and artistic rules to the nation. In the quarrel over opera, the King had simply banished the Italian troupe from the kingdom and thus arbitrarily ended it. During that same quarrel, Diderot's friend Grimm had written in his *Correspondance littéraire*:

> In matters of taste, the court gives the nation fashions and the *philosophes* laws. All they need is the courage, which they do not always have, to confront the most generally accepted, and often the most absurd opinions, and to attack them with all the force of reason, to exterminate them everywhere they find them. The philosopher who wrote the *Preliminary Discourse* to the *Encyclopedia* has given them the signal.[26]

He is of course referring to D'Alermbert's *Essay on Men of Letters and the Great* in which he denigrates the nobility as incompetent in such matters and insists that men of letters should make the rules. They can achieve this goal by presenting a united front and winning over public opinion. I have treated this question in a recent article on 'D'Alembert and the New Aristocracy'.[27] Suffice is to say here that D'Alembert is simply echoing a general movement toward a greater dignity for the writer. In his *Lettres philosophiques* (*Letters on the English Nation*), for example, Voltaire had demanded greater respect for the man of letters. Rousseau is his *Discourse on the Sciences and the Arts* had called upon kings to 'renounce the old prejudice invented by the pride of the great, that the art of leading the people is more difficult than that of enlightening them',[28] and D'Alembert in the *Essay* already quoted declared that the aristocracy regards the term 'men of letters' as 'an inferior state; as if the art of instructing and enlightening men were not, after the so rare art of governing them well, the noblest apanage of the human condition'.[29]

As we have seen from Diderot's artistic theories, this instruction was not only to be aesthetic but moral. Already at the end of the seventeenth century, Molière had depicted in his *Dom Juan* a certain type of hedonistic young aristocrat who lives only for his own pleasure without any moral scruples. This character would proliferate in the comedies and novels of seduction of the eighteenth century. The unrestrained pursuit of pleasure, often to the detriment of the other classes of society, is evoked in the Encyclopedia article 'Luxury' ('*Luxe*') in which Saint Lambert points to the dissolute life of the aristocracy as compared to the industriousness and usefulness of the bourgeoisie, which he calls the 'Second Estate'. It is precisely this exemplary class which must bring about the moral regeneration of the nation. '[This class] will be proud because evil mores will not have vilified it; jealous of the great who will not have corrupted it, it will watch over their conduct, it will be pleased to enlighten them, and from it will emanate the light which will filter down to the people and will rise up to the great.' (p. 769). Marmontel's moral tales published towards the end of the century, are precisely the implementation of this desire of the Encyclopedists to preach bourgeois morality, and they are in a way precursors of the novels of social utility conceived by George Sand in the nineteenth century.

By way of conclusion, I will point out that this campaign eventually succeeded, as the Marquis de Ségur attests in his *Mémoires*. He describes the enthusiasm of young noblemen for the *philosophes'* cause, saying: 'We criticised the powers at Versailles, and we paid court to those of the *Encyclopedia*. We preferred a word of praise from D'Alembert, from Diderot, to the most brilliant favour of a prince'.[30]

The nineteenth-century view of the writer as prophet of the nation, as Vigny's *Moses* illustrates, stems directly from this campaign. We have quoted briefly from Hugo's *Preface to Cromwell* to show that he is heir to the movement. In the preface to his *Human Comedy* Balzac calls the writer 'an instructor of men' who is 'equal to and perhaps superior to the statesman'. And, echoing D'Alembert's *Essay on Men of Letters and the Great*, he publishes his own 'Letter to French Writers' in the *Revue de Paris* (*Paris Review*) in 1834; 'Civilisation is nothing without its expression. It is we, the scholars, the writers, the artists, the poets, who are in charge of expressing it. We are the new pontiffs of an unknown future, whose actions we are preparing. This proposition, the eighteenth century has proved it. United we are at the same height as the power which kills us individually.'[31]

And when the writer today, at least in France, is listened to with respect, whether he voices an opinion on aesthetics or politics, it is in no small measure thanks to the eighteenth century *philosophes*, who won that privilege for him.

Notes

1. Rousseau, *Oeuvres completes* (Paris, Pléiade, 1962), vol.II, p.252. All translations are my own.
2. Beaumarchais, *Théâtre complet* (Paris, Gallimard), (Bibliotheque de la Pléiade, 1949), p.18.
3. *Oeuvres de D'Alembert* (Paris, Delin, 1822), vol.IV, p.365.
4. Marivaux, *La vie de Marianne* (Paris, Garnier Frères, 1963), p.57.
5. *Théâtre de Voltaire* (Paris, Garnier Frères, 1870), p.529.
6. ibid., pp. 156–8.
7. op.cit., p. 254.
8. Rousseau, *Du Contrat social* (Paris, Garnier Frères, 1962), p.16.
9. Diderot, *Oeuvres esthétiques* (Paris, Garnier Frères, 1959), p.263.

10. Voltaire, op.cit., p.462.
11. Diderot, op.cit., p.263.
12. ibid., p.267.
13. Hugo, *Préface de Cromwell* (Paris, Larousse, 1972). pp.69, 78, 109.
14. Diderot, *Oeuvres romanesques* (Paris, Garnier Frères, 1962), p.464.
15. Diderot, *Oeuvres esthétiques* (Paris, Garnier Frères, 1959), p.453.
16. ibid., p.825.
17. ibid., pp.483–4.
18. ibid., p.484.
19. ibid., p.550.
20. ibid., p.524.
21. ibid., p.471.
22. Voltaire, *Romans et contes* (Paris, Garnier Frères, 1960), p.205.
23. Diderot, *Oeuvres esthétiques* pp.470–1.
24. ibid., pp.466–7.
25. D'Alembert, op.cit., IV, p.376.
26. Grimm, *Correspondance littéraire* (Paris, Garnier Frères, 1877–82), XVI, pp.301–2.
27. 'D'Alembert et la nouvelle aristocratie' *Dix-Huitième Siècle*, 15 (1983), pp.335–43.
28. Rousseau, *Du contrat social* (Paris, Garnier Frères, 1962), p.23.
29. D'Alembert, op.cit., p.360.
30. *Mémoires souvenirs et anecdotes*, par M. le comte de Ségur (Paris 1859), vol.XIX of Barrière's *Mémoires*, pp.97–9.
31. Quoted by Louis de Royaumont, *Balzac et la société des gens de lettres* (1833–1913), (Paris, Dorbon, 1913), p.25.

7

POLITICS AND THE THEATRE: THE FINANCIER AND THE MERCHANT ON AND OFF THE STAGE IN EIGHTEENTH-CENTURY FRANCE

John Dunkley

This chapter examines the French theatrical portrayals of the financier and the merchant in the light of dramatic 'philosophical' and political developments in the latter half of the eighteenth century.

Let us begin by glancing backwards. The only plays to deal with contemporaries in Louis XIV's France were comedies. Comedy and tragedy were rigidly separate genres. While the term 'comedy' did not necessarily imply a frivolous treatment of theatrical subjects, it excluded the passionate emotions and major existential problems which were seen as the province of tragedy. Tragedy for its part excluded contemporary subjects and characters of other than princely rank and their entourage. Comedy, which did use contemporary characters, did not, however, exclude seriousness in either the subject matter or in its ethical implications. If we take the case of the best known comic dramatist of all, Molière, we find that, while the greatest proportion of his output consists of one-act farces and three act plays in the Italian tradition, those for which he is best remembered – and not only by academics – are the five-act plays where a serious statement is being made behind any laughter the play may provoke. Plays such as *L'Ecole des femmes*, *Le Misanthrope* and *Tartuffe* are particular examples.

But in all Molière's plays, even the most serious, the bourgeois and his world are the butt of satire. As the critic Paul Bénichou once observed, any other tone in the theatre of the day, most especially in plays written for performance before an aristocratic audience, would have spelt disaster for the dramatist. He was not expected to preach, let alone preach bourgeois values in a society where the court aristocracy set the tone – to which the bourgeoisie in any case aspired. A writer's status was low; he was an artisan, patronised even by actors, whose own social position was marginal, and he was not expected to try to tell his betters how to behave. The status of the bourgeois was low too. Parsimony, thrift, incremental coping with life, work, family preoccupations, dependence were all the marks of a life-style far removed from aristocratic insouciance, honour, bravura and display. Not only did the bourgeois not set the social norm, he did not set the ethical norm either.

But Molière died in 1673 and, as the reign wore on, financial problems became ever more acute. Devalued by the king and emasculated by the Versailles court system, the nobles' prestige waned in relative terms. It would be a mistake to overstate the degree to which it waned. Titles were still sought after, and though royal promotions were rarer in the eighteenth century than before, those gained through marriage or the purchase of legal offices brought, as time passed, social prestige comparable to all but the highest hereditary ones. And privilege, most especially fiscal privilege, did not disappear until the Revolution. But an increasing preoccupation with money and an awareness of what money could do for people's social position and economic and political influence offered the perspective of alternative satisfactions to those which the accident of birth, the absence of a legal career or an advantageous marriage denied.

Some of these doors were traditionally closed to Protestants, and naturally economic goals appealed especially to those who, as international traders living in coastal centres and forming part of a supra-national network, carried on their work on French soil in the full knowledge of the government and despite the Revocation of the Edict of Nantes in 1685. If they were allowed to carry on their activities with a minimum of official interference, this was simply because the state saw where its own best interest lay. Admittedly, Protestantism could be seen by the king as a caucus within the state, and distrusted as such, especially given its international base. But for all the misery and hardship brought by the Revocation and the *dragonnades* which preceeded it from around 1680 onwards, it was in no small measure a propaganda exercise, and there is no point in turning a propaganda exercise into a self-inflicted wound. As the tide of religious bigotry receded with the end of the reign, so it became clear that the best way of limiting commercial damage to France and the corresponding advantage to its competitors (which was real enough, despite the fact that established communities of craftsmen sometimes resented an influx of similarly skilled refugees from France, whom they saw as competitors in the local market) lay in leaving the Protestants unmolested and in deriving profit from their activities through the taxation to which they were liable as members of the Third Estate.

As a stimulus to the prosperity of the French economy, Colbert oversaw the establishment and regulation of a number of manufacturing ventures, mostly in the luxury trades such as glass-blowing and lace-making. Though some of them were of limited long-term success, they served to underline the need for internal investment, provided employment and stimulated a broader demand than had existed previously. Though the reluctance of the nobility to become involved in trade was by no means total, the fear of derogation from noble status – and hence loss of privilege – which was consequent upon retail trading, was allowed to spill over into the areas of wholesale and maritime trading as well. Despite repeated royal encouragement to the nobles to involve themselves in these latter types of venture (which would have brought profit while still preserving tax exemptions) the take-up, though not negligible, was less wholehearted than had been hoped, and it was predominantly members of the Third Estate who seized the opportunities available.[1]

Another of Colbert's innovations was the reorganisation in 1681 of the four old tax farms into one General United Farm. The tax-farming principle was that a group of people would join together and bid for the lease on the right to collect indirect taxes (*perceptions*) for a specific period. Once the bid was accepted, the tax farmers paid the Treasury a rent on the farm, in regular instalments, and possessed the lease on it, that is, the right to collect the revenues and to add in their administrative costs and a profit margin. In addition, the bidders to whom the lease was granted had to pay the Treasury a surety bond (in effect, an interest-bearing loan) to prove their financial solidity. Naturally the opportunity for profiteering lay open, and the general feeling was that the tax farmers took it. The French population traditionally believed that all taxes were unjustified, and some believed that, at the very most, taxes should only be levied on what remained once one's living expenses had been met. Moreover, they also thought that any assessment of tax liability was an intrusion into a family's financial affairs and that these were, as of right, a domestic secret. Armed with attitudes as logically untenable as these, they not unnaturally resented the tax farmers and their agents to the highest degree. These people were loathed by the population at large as extortionists, and the visible opulence of some tax farmers in the face of general economic hardship fuelled this feeling. They were also despised by the old, but often impecunious, nobility as rich upstarts. Only the state appreciated them, and that only because Louis XIV's policies could not function without them.

The result of these economic and political developments on the literature of the closing years of the reign is interesting. Some prose works appear in which the manipulators of French finance are criticised: *Les Soupirs de la France esclave,* for example, which is a dense and bitter analysis of all the evils of the French state machine. It was published in Amsterdam in 1689 and is generally attributed to Pierre Jurieu. A very amusing prose satire, *Pluton maltôtier* 1707,[2] by Deschiens de Courtisols, dealt with the reward and subsequent adventures of Deschiens, an imaginary financier, who had died and (naturally) gone to Hell. But it was in the theatre, with the comedy of manners, that social questions were generally aired.[3] The bourgeois is still the butt of satire, and still for broadly the same reasons: lack of social style and panache, a preoccupation with making ends meet, lumpen egoism, pathetic authoritarianism. The previously unquestioned prestige of the noble is, as it were, sidetracked, and when we meet noble characters in comedy, they are usually the pretentious representatives of the country squirearchy (the *hobereaux,* traditionally a class scorned by town-dwellers like writers), or petty nobles living on expedients, or just plain counterfeits of the kind which Louis XIV's genealogical inquiries of the 1660s and 1670s had sought to identify.[4]

Of all the plays from the end of the reign in which finance and financiers are at issue,[5] the best known by far is Lesage's *Turcaret,* which received seven performances at the Théâtre Français between 14 February and 1 March 1709.

It had been read by the troupe and accepted for performance on 15 May 1708, but it is generally thought that pressure to postpone the performances was put upon the actors by the financiers, and that it was only a royal command of 13 October 1708 that finally resolved matters. Even so, the play was taken off before the house receipts fell to the level which normally justified ending a run, and was not revived until 1730.

If it displeased the financial world, it is easy to see why. The financier, Turcaret, is portrayed as an ex-lackey who, though married to the ageing daughter of a pastry cook from Normandy, has deserted her in order to pursue his career and philander in Paris. We see him courting an unscrupulous *baronne,* the widow of a recently deceased colonel. His adulterous relationships are the subject of gossip, and he makes a pass at a maid in the sight of the audience. He loses his temper and smashes mirrors and china in the *baronne's* boudoir, only to make abject apologies later. In all but financial matters, he comes across as unbelievably stupid. His crooked dealings are exposed in a scene with a shady associate, and these lead to his arrest at the end of the play, but not before his public humiliation at the hands of his wife, who arrives to collect the pension on which he has defaulted, and his sister who, as an itinerant trader of cosmetics and fashion accessories, would have been understood by contemporary audiences to be more or less a procuress. The cast is completed by a parasitic *chevalier,* who lives off gifts from the *baronne* and the profits of gambling, a dissipated marquis and two servants, Frontin and Lisette, who, by helping themselves to some of the money circulating among the other characters, put together the nest-egg which will enable them, at the end of the play, to take up where Turcaret has left off.

All the popular prejudices associated with the financiers of the period are articulated through the character of Turcaret. His origins are given as lower than modest, and the marquis recalls that he was his grandfather's lackey. This corresponds to popular calumny of the day, since in reality it would have been virtually impossible for someone from a group illiterate in all but an infinitesimal minority of cases to be able to draw up contracts and agreements and handle the complexities of *ancien régime* finance. Coarseness, lust, dubious company and crooked dealing, prodigality and plain stupidity are made the hallmark of a character whose day seems devoted to anything but actual work. In the light of other evidence, the revival of the play in 1730 suggests that, in twenty years, the broad lines if not the detail of the portrait had lost none of their appeal. Certainly, as time went on, the daughters of financiers increasingly came to be seen as an acceptable match for the sons of the nobility. Despite this, the indications are that, once the Farm was reinstituted after Law's bankruptcy of 1720,[6] the reputation of financiers among ordinary people, like theatre-goers, was still one for rapacity and callous extortion. *Turcaret* seemed to encapsulate all there was to say, or all the theatre-going public wanted to hear, about financiers, and no subsequent play was written to redress the balance of opinion until Beaumarchais's *Les Deux Amis* of 1770. In order not to fly in the face of observable fact, any play which took up the character of the financier after the 1720s would have had to attenuate the portrait, possibly to the detriment of dramatic interest. As the financiers became more closely integrated into the upper echelons of society, their manner became less crudely flamboyant, their luxury less ostentatious. Indeed, the cultural drift of the eighteenth century was away from public display and towards the enjoyment of the good things of life in both the private and the public domains. In private life, the feast and the formal park gave way to good food, taken among friends and in more moderate amounts than previously, and to exquisite private houses with rambling gardens designed to offer agreeable surprises to the wanderer. In the public arena, financiers extended their patronage to *philosophes* – like Madame d'Epinay to Rousseau – and lent their support to capitalist enterprises in which the profit motive was doubled by a concern for public welfare. The competing initiatives of the latter part of the century to supply Paris with fresh water are an example of this.

If the envious and underinformed public view of the financier had been set and fixed for the century in 1709, the merchant, for his part, fared better. The well-known opening shot in the pro-merchant propaganda campaign was fired by Voltaire in his *Lettres philosophiques* of 1734. These letters were composed in the light of his experiences in England between 1726 and 1728, when he had been obliged to leave France after an unsuccessful encounter with aristocratic solidarity.[7] In the tenth letter, he scathingly compares the relative usefulness to society of the English merchant of noble extraction and the French courtier with a powdered wig and an intimate knowledge of court protocol. Although Voltaire's understanding of the meaning of nobility in England and its relation to mercantile activity was imperfect,[8] those who managed to defeat the ban on the book and read it were generally not in a position to correct him, and the point was made: the merchant was vital to the nation's well-being. By implication, privilege and derogation were outmoded and retrograde notions. Moreover, he was to argue in his *Défense du 'Mondain'* of 1737, the benefits of industry and commerce were felt by all sections of society, both through the goods that became available and through the work provided by the process of making them available.

The theme of the usefulness of commerce in general and of the merchant in particular was echoed by other *philosophes* and developed over the next forty years. In this context, the *Encyclopédie* of Diderot and D'Alembert provides insights of capital importance. Though merchant capitalists do not themselves figure among the contributors, industrial processes are explained, and a blow is thereby struck against the monopolistic conservatism of the corporate guild system. The invention of industrial processes is praised, as in the article 'Bas', which deals with the invention of the stocking frame.[9] Véron de Forbonnais, who contributed a number of articles on economic subjects to the early volumes of the work, distances himself from the generally prevailing theories of the Physiocrats in his article 'Commerce' and insists that industry is just as essential to the prosperity of trade as agriculture is, and he praises its competitive aspects. He also points out that commercial activity brings the greatest prosperity to the greatest number of citizens through their work and hence strengthens the state. It was also on Véron de Forbonnais's *Recherches et considérations sur les finances* (published in 1758) that Jaucourt, Diderot's indefatigable collaborator in the *Encyclopédie,* drew heavily for his article 'Négoce' in which, significantly, he criticised the French state's financial system for the harm it did to trade, invoking its plethora of rules, taxes, duties, tolls, inspections, paperwork and general delay.

In the opening part of the same article, Jaucourt spoke out for the business-man, noting that in Persia even the highest nobles engaged in large-scale trade and that the king honoured international traders and chose his ambassadors from among them. (Praising foreign customs, especially Persian or Chinese, in order to imply criticism of French customs is a standard code of the *philosophes*.) The praise is reiterated by Diderot himself in his article 'Commissionnaire', where the question of derogation is taken up explicitly, and at greater length and yet more emphatically in D'Alembert's 'Fortune', where the value of commerce is contrasted with the mindless prejudice of the nobles against it, even though nobility, the writer argues, can be bought with money gained by any means, however disreputable.[10]

The philosophic party's statements of position were articulated through the volumes of the *Encyclopédie* published in the 1750s. These same years saw two other developments which are important for our purposes, one cultural, the other political. On the political side, to which we shall turn in a moment, 1756 witnessed the outbreak of the Seven Years' War. On the cultural side, 1757 and 1758 saw the performance of one of Diderot's two major dramas and, more important, the publication of two theoretical works in which he developed a new theatrical aesthetic for a new genre, the *drame: Entretiens sur le 'Fils naturel'* and *De la poésie dramatique*.[11] Over the first half of the eighteenth century, Molière's comedies and Racine's tragedies had come to be accepted as representing perfection in their respective genres. Comedies and tragedies of a traditional kind were still being written but, with the exception of Voltaire's tragedies and Marivaux's highly individual comedies, they all left a sense of disappointment. The classics themselves had achieved the status of ancient monuments, venerated, praised, but not necessarily enjoyed. Although the juxtaposition of serious and amusing elements in plays had been tried before, Diderot aimed at fusion rather than merely juxtaposition. He also put forward the (for our purposes) seminal notion that, unlike former comedies, which had focused on the protagonist's character, the *drame* should, in a serious manner, highlight the dramatic potential of people considered in relation to their social function, their *condition*, as he called it. In his third *Entretien*, he makes his imaginary interlocutor, Dorval (the hero of the play *Le Fils naturel*) argue for the portrayal, not of a character like a misanthropist or a religious hypocrite, whom the spectator could shrug off simply by saying to himself 'I'm not one', but for the portrayal of *professional* or *social types* – the writer, the *philosophe*, the trader, the judge, the, lawyer, the politician, citizen, magistrate, financier, nobleman or steward – and for the dramatic treatment of the realities of his life.[12] In other parts of his treatises, Diderot also conceives of the *drame* as an instrument in the ethical regeneration of French society, and the merchant was, in the 1760s and 1770s, to be a type specifically singled out and offered as an ethical model by practising dramatists in sympathy with the aims of the philosophic movement. As we shall see, their enthusiasms for him was to lead them into hyperbole and mythologising.

To society at large, the merchant was, if not necessarily the hero of the hour, a perfectly acceptable type at the time when Diderot was writing. While it is true that the long-term effects of the Seven Years' War were to prove financially disastrous to France because it was finances through credit rather than taxation, its short-term effects on the supply of goods were undramatic.[13] It was a war fought almost entirely away from French soil, and the French themselves therefore suffered far fewer atrocities and depredations. Supplies of goods could be maintained in the early years since international traders tended always to be on the look-out for signs of coming conflicts and increased import levels in anticipation of the interruption of supplies. (This is why the commercial gazettes of the period devote a great deal of space to political news). The supplies fed home markets well into the war, and stocks could be replenished once hostilities had ended. The merchant looked therefore to the eyes of the 1760s as if he, unlike some others, had been able to serve his country well, and he was in a position to lay claim to a patriotism to complement the cosmopolitanism which he shared with the *philosophes* who promoted him.

The *philosophes'* cosmopolitan thinking in the commercial context was doubled in the theatrical one by a lively interest in the foreign theatre, especially the English theatre. Seeing in Britain the home of modern philosophy, freedom and entrepreneurship, the *philosophes* and their supporters readily adapted modern English plays for the French stage, or incorporated Anglo-Saxon characters and settings. Two plays particularly attracted a number of dramatists, Diderot among them: George Lillo's *The London Merchant* (1731) and Edward Moore's *The Gamester* (1753), which received more attention in France than in England. Typical of the *philosophes'* eulogy of commercial activity is the kind of statement we read in Diderot's *Fils naturel,* where effort is seen as the key to justified success: 'There are other callings which lead rapidly to wealth, but commerce is almost the only one where great fortunes are proportionate to the effort, skill and risks which justify them.'[14]

The enthusiasm of the philosophical party for merchants and their activities induced them to ignore, for the purposes of propaganda designed to change the traditional French respect for titles and inherited money, the fact that no one group within the population is exempt from faults. Their merchants are all probity and humane values; bankruptcies are seen as the fault of subordinates not shown on stage or of plain bad luck, and it is never envisaged that a merchant himself may be callous, crooked or careless. The portrait is always an ideal one.

In Michel-Jean Sedaine's *Le Philosophe sans le savoir* of 1765,[15] this idealisation reaches its zenith. Monsieur Vanderk is a prosperous merchant based in the French provinces. The precise detail of his activities is left unspecified. The action of the play takes place on the day scheduled for his daughter's wedding. But, amidst the euphoria, it transpires that his son, a trainee naval officer, is engaged to fight a duel with an unknown adversary whom he had overheard denigrating merchants in a café. When the daughter's marriage contract is signed, the son notices that his father signs with noble titles. Questioned on this, the father reveals that he is in fact a noble who had been forced to flee France in his youth because he had killed in a duel an army officer who had taken umbrage at his love for the woman whom he later married. Monsieur Vanderk had apprenticed himself to a Dutch trader who, when he died some years later (having arranged his young protégé's marriage) left him his business and requested him to adopt his name. A stranger, the baron d'Esparville, comes to the house, urgently wanting cash for a bill of exchange which he is having difficulty getting cashed because, as the blue ribbon on his military decoration reveals, he is a Protestant. The son's duel goes ahead. His father had not stood in his way on the grounds that honour demanded that his son should keep his word, even although the barbarity of duelling revolted him. Antoine, a faithful family retainer, returns from spying on the duel and knocks on the door (the prearranged signal that young Vanderk had died in the encounter) at the very moment when Monsieur Vanderk is engaged in cashing d'Esparville's bill. Predictably the baron needs the cash in order to finance the escape of a son involved in a duel (with young Vanderk, of course), as he explains to Vanderk, who neither flinches nor refuses the transaction. But humanity and reflection upon his father's arguments against duelling have moved young Vanderk to fire his pistol into the air, though young d'Esparville's bullet had pierced his hat (hence Antoine's error), and the two young men have apologised to one another and become friends. The wedding ceremony goes ahead, with the d'Esparvilles as guests. In contrast to this demonstration of enlightened behaviour, Sedaine introduces into the play a ridiculous aunt, the sister of Monsieur Vanderk. She lives on the family estate in Berry (at her brother's expense) and has come up for the wedding with a retinue of insolent servants,[16] a worry about repainting the heraldic devices in the family chapel, complaints about a legal dispute with a neighbour over property boundaries and a plan to marry the nephew she has never seen to a local girl of noble rank. The aunt's old-fashioned snobbery is further underlined by her desire to pass not as a relative but as a protectress of the Vanderk family and her accusation that her brother has lost all ideas of nobility, 'his soul withered by commerce'. Clearly, Sedaine is using her as a foil, the embodiment of out-of-date preoccupations, ossified prejudice and unpleasant personal characteristics.

The eulogy of the merchant is, of course, accomplished by the contrast of Vanderk's attitudes with his sister's, but that is only one small part of it. His personal characteristics include his friendly and open relationship with his son, his gentleness towards his daughter, his patience and kindness towards Antoine (a well-meaning but irritatingly impetuous man), his fairness in his dealings with d'Esparville, his self-control when he believes his son is dead (which some contemporary critics found incredible, but so are both the protagonist and the plot) and his lack of religious prejudice (for all we know, he could be a Protestant himself). In addition to his personal qualities, we are shown the visible signs of his success. He has large sums of money at his disposal, his daughter has been provided with diamond jewellery and a dress for her wedding, and her mother has her own carriage. Over and above all this, Vanderk's behaviour implies two more general philosophical attitudes. He redefines both implicitly and explicitly the traditional concept of honour as embodied by the aunt's preoccupations and the son's duel. He denies that honour is preserved by an inward- (or backward-) looking concern with preserving and enhancing the family name and sees it instead as moral stature deriving from commercial probity and the fulfilment of one's obligations to other people. And, as a concomitant of this view, he has himself accepted the fact of withdrawal from noble status as traditionally understood and forgone the consequent social prestige and tax privileges. His path through life has been exactly the reverse of the frequently quoted stereotype, according to which the successful merchant purchased a title and retired from business in order to 'live nobly'. (As we shall see in a moment, Beaumarchais too was to express his disapproval of the idea of retiring into noble inactivity in his play, *Les Deux Amis*.)[17]

Into the ethical and material pattern, Sedaine also injects pure propaganda in favour of commerce with the intention of placing it, morally, in the fore-front of civilised activity (the sententiousness is typical of the tone of most *drames* and is designed to express their serious purpose with appropriate dignity):

I have already restored to the family all the wealth which the need to serve the king obliged our ancestors to disburse; this wealth will one day be yours, and if you think that by engaging in trade I have brought a stain on the family name, it will be your task to erase it. But in a century as enlightened as ours, that which can bring nobility cannot be the reason for losing it.

It is not a single people or a single nation that he [the merchant] serves; he serves them all and is served by them. He is the universal man.

A handful of bold individuals induce kings to take up arms, war breaks out, everything flares up, and Europe is divided. But the merchant, whether English, Dutch, Russian or Chinese, is still my closest friend. We are so many silk threads, running across the surface of the earth, linking the nations together and steering them back towards peace through the necessity of trade. That, my son, is what it is to be an honest merchant.

There are perhaps just two callings which stand above that of merchant – always supposing that there exist any distinctions between those who do their best in the station to which heaven has assigned them. I know of only these two: the magis-trate, who gives voice to the law, and the soldier, who defends the fatherland.[18]

But Vanderk's words, first uttered on stage in 1765, have a wider signifi-cance when considered in their historical context: the aftermath of the Seven Years' War, which ended in 1763. The merchant's own cosmopolitanism is emphasised, but Sedaine also voices through him praise of the modern, active nobility (the magistrate) and of the soldier who fights for the fatherland in a *defensive* war. The *philosophes'* long-standing boast of cosmopolitanism had brought upon them the accusation that they were unpatriotic. In placing the military profession *above* that of merchant in the moral hierarchy, Sedaine, through the idealised Vanderk, is approving national loyalty, patriotism, and hence incorporating it into the system of values which the *philosophes* could be seen to stand for. He is, as it were, hijacking the claim to patriotism from the anti-philosophic party, which in the 1760s was closely identified with Louis XV's government.

In the aftermath of the Seven Years' War the popularity of the government reached a new low. By the treaties of Paris and Hubertusburg of January 1763, France had given up Canada, Cape Breton Island and Grenada, recognised the Mississippi River as the easternmost boundary of its North American possessions, and then ceded then to Spain. It had also ceded Senegal. Though it retained Guadeloupe and Martinique in the treaty negotiations, its military defeats led to a crisis of confidence and increased the call for military reform. The bulk of the French fleet had been lost,[19] and under Choiseul an essential but expensive rebuilding programme was undertaken. A proportion of military and naval failure was ascribed to financial policies operated by finance ministers who had trained as lawyers, not as financial experts, and who appeared incapable of collecting and managing the revenues competently. The marquis de Mirabeau's *Théorie de l'impôt* (1760) provoked a whole series of contributions to an open debate over the steps needed to be taken towards financial reform which marked the crucial year 1763 and brought the King into conflict with the *parlementaires*. He saw the pressing need for reform but wanted also to preserve the gains for absolutism secured by his grandfather, while they sought to use the opportunity provided by the crisis to reassert ancient prerogatives.

The central *parlementaire* publication in the debate was Roussel de la Tour's *Richesse de l'état*, published in May 1763. It argued principally for a single graduated tax on wealth as the most equitable solution, since it would be calculated according to the ability to pay rather than according to status. But opposition was inevitable from the privileged sections of society and from all those who made a living from administering the many taxes then in force. La Tour's plan promised to close the vast gap between what people paid in taxes and what the Treasury received at the end of the collection process. The pamphlet provoked over forty replies, supportive and otherwise, which ended it what J.C. Riley has called 'a cacophany of visions . . . a hodge-podge of impressions, information and misinformation which revealed an ignorance so fundamental as to undermine the possibility for reform'.[20]

What the participants in the debate shared above all, though, was an awareness of the unnecessary intricacy of the existing system and a feeling of waste and peculation among those operating it. One writer, Darigrand, in his *Anti-financier*, published in Amsterdam in 1763, estimated the general loss to the Treasury as being of the order of four-fifths of its potential revenues, and, in his works and others, the tax-collectors were described in terms of 'a monstrous giant which is stifling the State', 'voracious animals which are called financiers' and a 'plague of financiers'[21] – who oppressed ordinary Frenchmen. But, in a fairly short time, the debate fizzled out, to the point where the memorialist Bachaumont wrote of it in April 1764 as a spent epidemic. It waned so quickly for several reasons. One was that the King had, in March, forbidden 'unacknowledged' writers to publish contributions to the debate. Another was that the figures on which the Finance Council worked were kept a state secret. (Financial projections were extremely unreliable in any case, thanks in large measure to the King's abuse of *acquis de comptant*. These were orders for disbursement by the Treasury of sums of money for which no justification needed to be given and for which the payee did not have to issue a receipt. No proper budget would have been conceivable under such circumstances.) And again, the one consensus that emerged – the need for equality before the tax laws – would have brought a hiatus in revenue income while it was being applied. But, perhaps most important of all, tax equality would have abolished privilege, which allowed almost total tax exemption to the richest and most influential members of society, the nobles and the ecclesiastics. The Church negotiated with the King and then voted to him an agreed lump sum, rather curiously known as the *don gratuit*, and the nobility were held to express their loyalty to the monarch not through cash payments but through service – a light, not to say illusory form of payment, since the King by this time paid for the upkeep of a standing army. In administrative terms, this debate and the continuing conflict between the King and the *parlements* led to no significant change. But the less tangible effect was to make the public acutely aware of the abuses, real and imagined, of the existing system as operated by the tax-collectors.

On 13 January 1770, Beaumarchais's *Les Deux Amis* received the first of its fourteen performances at the Théâtre Français.[22] It is a dull play with an improbable and convoluted plot. Aurelly is a rich merchant from Lyon, and Mélac *père*, his friend, is the comptroller general of the tax farm in the city. Mélac *père* owed his start in life to Aurelly's help and is now on the point of retiring. His son hopes to be appointed to succeed him in his post. Pauline, who passes for Aurelly's niece but is really his illegitimate daughter, has been brought up by Mélac *père* alongside Mélac's son, Mélac *fils*, and the two have now fallen in love. Saint-Albin, a general farmer on his rounds of inspection, is a friend of both families and also loves Pauline. Dabins, Aurelly's cashier, brings Mélac *père* news that Aurelly's correspondent in Paris, Préfort, has died and that all his assets are in the meantime frozen, which means that Aurelly will be unable to make payments of six hundred thousand *livres* on the following day. To delay payment would cause a potentially ruinous crisis of confidence among Aurelly's creditors, and he is already the object of some envy, since letters patent granting him nobility are in the processs of being issued. Mélac *père* passes the proceeds of his tax collecting over to Dabins, who is to use them to replenish Aurelly's stock of cash. This leaves Mélac *père* temporarily out of funds. He insists to Dabins that the loan is to be kept secret from Aurelly, on the flimsy grounds that Aurelly would rather risk personal collapse than expose his friend to being in temporary deficit on his tax collection. But then Saint-Albin unexpectedly asks for Mélac's proceeds to be handed over. The staunchly silent Mélac passes for an embezzler, and Aurelly speaks very harshly about him, but nonetheless offers to pass Saint-Albin a bill to cover the sum presumed to be missing. Saint-Albin, described by Beaumarchais in the *dramatis personae* as an estimable man of the world, agrees. Aurelly goes to hand over his bill, to be drawn on Préfort, and Saint-Albin informs him that his correspondent is dead. This being so, Aurelly realises that the sum which he has received that very morning cannot have been issued by Préfort. Summoned to explain, Dabins reveals all. Saint-Albin sacrifices his personal feelings for Pauline (who had also contributed to the loan for Aurelly) and provides the necessary loan from his personal funds; no breath of the affair is to be allowed to emerge in public.

Though the complexities of the plot offer little excitement, the play has considerable historical interest. Statements of the merchant's place and function within the social structure run along similar general lines to those which Sedaine made through Vanderk, but Beaumarchais, no doubt reflecting his greater grasp of financial affairs than Sedaine, includes the eulogy of the merchant's activities the more technical (and politically relevant) point that the state is the ultimate beneficiary. When Saint-Albin congratulates Aurelly on his ennoblement, he suggests that it is justified by the merchant's usefulness. The ensuing conversation includes the following reflections:

> AURELLY Useful. That's exactly the right word. A man can be enlightened, learned, sober, thrifty, or courageous, and so much the better for him. But what benefit do I personally derive from all that? I judge the value of our qualities and talents by their usefulness to our fellows [. . .] Take me as an example. Here in Lyon I keep two hundred looms moving every day. Three times as many hands as that are needed in my silk business. My mulberry plantations and my silk-worms provide work for as many again. Consignments of goods from my enterprises are distributed through every retailer in the land. They all live and make money and, because industry multiplies the price of raw materials a hundredfold, there isn't one of them – myself included – who doesn't gladly pay the State a tribute proportionate to the profits which he derives from open competition. [. . .] And who, gentlemen, brings back into the country all the gold that war sends abroad? Who would be so bold as to dispute with commerce the honour of restoring to the exhausted State the spirit and the wealth which it has lost? Every citizen is aware of the importance of this task, but only the merchant carries it out. The moment the soldier lays down his arms, the merchant has the good fortune to be, in his turn, the defender of the fatherland (II, 10).

As we can see from this extract, Beaumarchais takes the eulogy of the merchant rather further than Sedaine took it by suggesting, not that the soldier defending the fatherland was possibly superior to him, but that they were equals functioning at different times for the welfare of the state, each in his own way. Though this is no longer a live issue, it is clear that, to audiences living in the period immediately following the Seven Years' War, such questions were of immediate interest. (This view is confirmed by the fact that the play had only one successful run and that, when it was revived in 1783, it was performed only twice before being taken off for good.)

The imbroglio which Beaumarchais creates allows all the characters to engage in a potlatch of self-sacrifice and generosity. Exposed to bankruptcy and social disgrace through no fault of his own, the merchant, predictably, has all the probity, humanity and lack of pretentiousness which made up the stock character of the period. Like Vanderk, Aurelly is scornful of the snobbery that goes with titles. Whereas Vanderk had been obliged to drop his noble name (when he had killed his man in a duel and been obliged to flee France), Aurelly intends to carry on his commercial activities *after* his ennoblement. To another newly created nobleman who has expressed the expectation that he will leave commerce behind along with his common birth, Aurelly has, he tells Mélac *père*, replied that the best way of showing his appreciation of the new benefit which commerce has brought him is for him to go on practising it (I, 11). His many qualities are brought out both by his speeches and his actions. And exactly the same is true of the two financiers. Mélac *père*, exhorting his son to have regard to Pauline's reputation now that she is a young woman and no longer just a playmate, couches his homily in general terms:

> The first punishment suffered by him who falls short of the proper standards of decency is that he very soon loses the taste for it. One fault brings another in its wake. They accumulate. The heart degenerates, and one no longer feels the restraint of honour except to fight against it. One begins by being weak, only to end by being depraved. (I, 3)

He also tries to conceal his loyalty and kindness to his friend in order to preserve Aurelly's reputation and self-respect; he uses the vocative 'mon ami' to his son, an illustration of what any number of philosophical texts insisted was the *right* relationship between parents and even quite young children. (Vanderk and his son had a similar relationship.) Saint-Albin, the general farmer, gives up his love for Pauline out of consideration for her feelings for Mélac *fils*, although he was in a position to bring moral pressure to bear by having rescued her father from financial and social embarrassment, and thereupon rejoices in the spectacle of their mutual happiness. Consideration for others, an understanding of their unexpressed feelings and self-denial are for all these characters the hallmarks of moral worth, and in suggesting that it is as typical of the financiers as of the merchants, Beaumarchais is offering a direct contradiction of the popular perception of them.

Clearly, a not very successful play which attempted a hyperbolic eulogy of tax farmers in the face of a long-standing prejudice against them made little impact. It was special pleading from a literary dilettante whose highly profitable eleven-year association with the financier and businessman, Pâris-Duverney, was well-known. Beaumarchais's activities were many and varied, and inevitably he aroused mixed feelings. And although he was to survive the Revolution, it was at times a very close-run thing. His life-long involvement in financial and rather shady diplomatic affairs on behalf of the former monarch were the source of much of the distrust he encountered and were certainly behind some of the harassment he suffered. And the building of a sumptuous house opposite the Bastille on the eve of the Revolution was hardly a palliative to popular resentment either.

The last pre-revolutionary play to look at the commercial world was Mercier's *La Brouette du vinaigrier* (*The Vinegar-Seller's Wheelbarrow*) of 1775. The title itself is a challenge to the aesthetic canons of the day, a wheelbarrow being considered too vulgar to figure in a serious work of art. But Mercier's interest lay in questioning those earlier dramas which, for all their bourgeois pretensions, still involved characters drawn from the uppermost strata of society, even when they did not turn out in fact to be nobles incognito. In this play, the prestigious businessman, Delomer, who relies on paper money, is saved from ruin by the good offices of the humble

Dominique, the vinegar-seller who has prospered through hard work and thrift and is able to produce a barrow-load of specie at the crucial moment. The focus of propaganda shifts permanently from the large-scale trader-investor-speculator to the small businessman, whose future seems to lie in staying small – not a type renowned for his progressive outlook, as one recent scholar has pointed out.[23]

In the context of the development of ideas over the eighteenth century, it would be absurd to claim a great or even quantifiable influence for any of the plays we have discussed. Though *Turcaret*, for instance, was initially scandalous and subsequently well-known, it is quite impossible to say how much it contributed to stereotyping the financier for later generations of Frenchmen and how much other factors like individual personal experience contributed. Certainly he was still equally loathed on the eve of the Revolution, and the author Mercier wrote in his *Tableau de Paris (Picture of Paris)* that he could not pass by the *Hôtel des Fermes* without wanting to overturn 'this immense and infernal machine which seizes each citizen by the throat and pumps out his blood'.[24] On the other hand, we have seen that it *is* possible to arrive at a broadly accurate picture of the correlation between, on the one hand, the different allegiances of financiers and merchants and, on the other, the different public perceptions of them and the different dramatic treatments they received. And it is possible too to account for Beaumarchais's discordant attempt at rehabilitating the hated financier. In the main the theatrical portrayals reflect the public perception of the financier's rapacity and the *philosophes'* perception of the dignity of trade.

The Revolution was to set the seal on the debate as the theatre had pursued it throughout the century. The small trader, who had emerged unscathed from the debates which followed the Seven Years' War, naturally survived upheaval and the Terror much as most other groups did. The descendants of Mercier's Dominique *père* were to become the *sans-culottes*, and La *Brouette du vinaigrier* forshadows the widening gulf which was soon totally to divide the humble artisan from the cosmopolitan magnate. The *négociant* indeed became a target for hostility in the Revolution because of the obvious wealth he had earned from his large-scale commercial activities. In Lyon and Bordeaux, for example, *négociants* suffered particular persecution. Deriving their ideas from those of Rousseau, whom they read and interpreted selectively, men such as Marat and Robespierre were hostile to international trading. But in the longer term, progress was on the *negociants'* side. With their backing, the first steps were being taken towards industrialisation. There was no way in which international trading was going to be put permanently into reverse. The wider world of international cooperation was not something from which France could simply and permanently opt out. The future lay with trade and industry.

But for the financiers, the threat was more immediate, more systematic and more absolute. They had been too closely associated with the *ancien régime*, which could not have lasted so long without their backing, and from the earliest days of the Revolution they were called to account. The work of the Commission of Liquidation, composed of former general farmers and created by the Constituent Assembly on 22 July 1791, was faced with the hopeless task of sorting out the farmers' alleged debt to the Nation in a hostile economic climate and with much of the crucial paperwork dispersed or destroyed in earlier insurrections. A Commission of Surveillance, designed to hasten the Commission of Liquidation in its work, reported on 5 May 1794 that the farmers owed the state just over one hundred and thirty million *livres*. The chemist-financier, Antoine Lavoisier issued an immediate refutation, which was ignored, and the farmers' property was impounded against repayment of the sum. Three days later, on 8 May, twenty-eight general farmers were guillotined, and six more followed them within a few weeks. It was not until 1 May 1806 that the Council of State declared that, in fact, far from the farmers owing the state a hundred and thirty million *livres*, the Treasury had actually owed them eight million. And even then nobody mentioned the government's long-term debt of 68.4 millions.[25]

We have seen how, throughout the period of the Enlightenment, the merchant was a type specially singled out by the *philosophes* for promotion as the ideal modern man, productive and patriotic. He became wealthier, and public esteem for him increased at the same time. In philosophical dramas, he became the object of idealisation in the aftermath of the Seven Years' War, before paling slightly in the 1770s, when the risks inherent in his grand designs were compared unfavourably with the less prestigious incremental thrift of a lower-middle class colleague. But, since it is beyond belief that any large group of people can be uniformly and totally praiseworthy, and given that to make one's way in eighteenth-century commerce probably required more of a hard head than a generous measure of philosophical principles, the merchant was singularly fortunate in the way he was portrayed. The case of the financiers is exactly the opposite. The traditional French resistance to all taxation meant that they were loathed from the outset,[26] and they were denigrated early on by an excellent satirical play which echoed right down the century because it harmonised so well with popular prejudices.[27] Just as the merchant was idealised as all probity, so the financier was vilified as nothing but ferocious extortion and shameless peculation. The stereotype, though inevitably justified in some cases, was clearly not equally so in all, but eventually it was that stereotype that cost the financiers their lives.

NOTES

1. Derogation is a complex issue because the conditions under which it occurred varied with the activity undertaken and with the geographical region from which the noble came. A precise account of the facts of the question is given in Guy Richard, *Noblesse d'affaires au XVIIIe siècle (The Nobility and Business in the XVIIIth Century)* (Paris, A. Colin, 1974), chapter 1. Richard also discusses the nature and extent of noble involvement in commerce and industry and provides an account of the repercussions of Coyer's *La Noblesse commerçante (The Commercial Nobility)*, of 1756, which argued for abolishing derogation and thus allowing the impecunious nobility to restore its wealth and prestige through commerce, which would, in its turn, enable it to fulfil its traditional function of military service (see especially chapter 2).

2. *Maltôtier* was an insulting term for a tax-collector.

3. The debate was limited. The Théâtre Français, the official, approved theatre,

generally steered well clear of anything contentious, but the 'Italian' Theatre and the Parisian Fair Theatres were prepared to take risks with topical issues. The Italians were exiled in 1697 for performing *La Fausse Prude (The False Prude)*, a satire on Madame de Maintenon, the King's wife. Official censorship of plays was instituted between 1705 and 1709.

4. See François Bluche, *La Vie quotidienne de la noblese française au XVIIIe siècle (The Everyday Life of the French Nobility in the Eighteenth Century)* (Paris, Hachette, 1973), p.14; and A. Corvisier, *La France sous Louis XIV, 1643–1715 (France in the Reign of Louis XIV. . .)* (Paris, SEDES, 1979), pp.165–6.

5. A list of these can be found in R. Niklaus, 'The Merchant on the French Stage in the Eighteenth Century, or the Rise and Fall of an Eighteenth-century Myth', in *Studies in the French Eighteenth Century presented to John Lough*, ed. D.J. Mossop *et al.* (Durham, 1978), pp.141–56 (pp.147–48).

6. John Law's plan was to establish a central state bank whose assets were to consist of shares in a single chartered joint-stock trading company which would have the monopoly of France's overseas trade. Royal and personal debt would become national debt, and the bank would manage it. The bank was founded in May 1716. It gradually subsumed the tax gathering functions of the Farm but collapsed in a crisis of confidence by the end of 1720. See G.T. Matthews, *The Royal General Farms in Eighteenth-century France* (New York, Columbia University Press, 1958), pp.62–76.

7. The chevalier de Rohan had made a scathing reference in public to Voltaire's change of name (from Arouet), and Voltaire had replied in kind. The chevalier had Voltaire beaten up by his servants. This underlined his contempt for Voltaire, who was socially very much his inferior. Two socially equal noble opponents would have fought a duel. Voltaire found himself totally unable to obtain legal redress. He was put in the Bastille, briefly, to silence him, then temporarily exiled to beyond fifty leagues from Paris. England seemed preferable to the provinces.

8. See Norma Perry, 'French and English Merchants in the Eighteenth Century; Voltaire Revisited', in *Studies in Eighteenth-century French Literature presented to Robert Niklaus* (Exeter, 1975), pp.193–213.

9. For a translation of part of the article 'Bas' ('Stockings'), see *The Age of Enlightenment: an Anthology of Eighteenth-century Texts*, ed. Simon Eliot and Beverley Stern (London, Ward Lock Educational, 1979), vol.II, pp.155–59.

10. See John Lough, *The 'Encyclopédie'* (London, Longman, 1971), pp.354–59 and p.382.

11. The dramas are *Le Fils naturel (The Natural Son)*, which was written in 1756, printed along with the *Entretiens sur 'Le Fils naturel' (Conversations concerning. . .)* the following year, but not performed until 26 September 1771, and *Le Père de famille (The Paterfamilias)*, published along with *De la poésie dramatique (On dramatic poesy)* in 1758 and first performed on 18 February 1761. Normally, performance preceded publication.

12. See *Le Fils naturel et les Entretiens sur 'Le Fils naturel'*, ed. J.-P. Caput (Paris, Larousse, 1970), pp.171–2.

13. See James C. Riley, *The Seven Years' War and the Old Regime in France* (Princeton N.J., 1986), especially chapters 4, 5 and Conclusion.

14. Act IV, scene 5 (cf. n.9, *supra*).

15. The French title is a pun and can be translated to mean both 'the philosopher who does not know he is one' and 'the philosopher without erudition'. It is generally agreed to be the best French *drame*. Highly successful, it was first performed at the Théâtre Français on 2 December 1765 and had a first run of 28 performances, ending on 26 February 1766.

16. Her servants include a *lackey*, a type of liveried retainer whose chief function was to advertise his master's social position. They manned ante-chambers and accompanied their masters on outside business. The fact that they were seen waiting for their masters for long periods gave them a reputation for idleness. One suggestion was that they should be taught to read, another that they should be taught knitting and needlework. French lackeys tended to wear an abundance of gold braid. For further information see C. Fairchilds, *Domestic Enemies; servants and their masters in Old Regime France* (Baltimore and London, The Johns Hopkins Press, 1984), pp.31–5.

17. The stereotype represents, naturally, a simplification of the real situation. By the time a title was obtained, the bourgeois may simply have been of retirement age. Or again, to take a title, and possibly pass on the visible running of a business to a son, may simply have meant getting access, through one's new noble status, to people in a position to put commissions in one's way – a low-profile but very real commercial role. The crucial question is whether the business was passed on as a going concern, or simply closed down and the capital invested in lands.

18. These quotations are all translated from E. Feuillâtre's edition of the text (Paris, Larousse, 1936), act II, scene 4. Monsieur Vanderk also regrets that his son risks dying in a duel rather than 'pour son roi ou pour sa patrie' ('for his king or for his country') (III, 9).

19. The life of a wooden ship ranged from eight to fifteen years, depending on whether it was used in the Atlantic or the Mediterranean. About half the French fleet as it stood at the beginning of the war would have needed to be replaced anyway by 1763; see Riley, op. cit., pp.80–2. The official calculation of the average life of a ship was twelve years. This was based on estimates of ten and twenty years of service in the Atlantic and the Mediterranean respectively. Sometimes bad construction and the use of green timber reduced the life of a vessel to as little as four years, pending a rebuild; see J. Pritchard, *Louis XV's Navy, 1748–1762* (Kingston and Montreal, McGill-Queen's University Press, 1987), p.126 ff.

20. op. cit., p.202.

21. ibid., p.204.

22. It received twelve performances in its first run, which ended on 4 March, and two more in its revival (12 and 14 February 1783), before being dropped from the repertoire.

23. R. Niklaus, op. cit., p.155.

24. *Tableau de Paris* (Hambourg, Virchaux et Cie., 1781), vol.II, pp.53–4; also quoted by G.T. Matthews, op. cit., p.277. Matthews examines in detail the end of the Farm in chapter 9.

25. ibid., p.282 n.33, and p.283.

26. Evidence of this stereotype was published by F. Gaiffe in his *L'Envers du Grand Siècle (The Dark Side of the Glorious Century)* (Paris, Albin Michel, 1924), pp.117–33. Gaiffe took most, though not quite all of his material from fictional sources but clearly believed that it represented the unvarnished truth. Matthews (quoting M. Marion's *Histoire financière (Financial History)* (Paris, Rousseau, 1914–31)) also states that, at the end of Louis XIV's reign 'it was believed, with much justice, that the *traitants* [financiers] had made enormous profits at the government's expense (pp.61–2).

27. Popular prejudice in France went against anyone who suddenly became rich. In the Revolutionary period this prejudice is reflected in the number of plays which satirise or denigrate people who had made money in the sale of *biens nationaux*; see H. Welschinger, *Le Théâtre de la Révolution, 1789–1799* (Paris,Charavay frères, 1880), pp.288–94.

8

1688 AND 1788: WILLIAM ROBERTSON ON REVOLUTION IN BRITAIN AND FRANCE

Richard B. Sher

At the conclusion of the celebrated *History of Scotland* that he published in 1759, William Robertson offered an interpretation of early modern Scottish history that reflected the complacency and optimism of the Presbyterian-Whig establishment around the middle of the eighteenth century. Scotland, argued Robertson, had traditionally been a nation of weak kings and overbearing nobles. While not entirely obliterating this older tradition of local aristocratic domination, the union of the English and Scottish crowns in 1603 had fostered royal absolutism emanating from London. For most of the seventeenth century, therefore, Scotland had endured the worst features of aristocracy and monarchy: 'subjected at once to the absolute will of a monarch, and to the oppressive jurisdiction of an aristocracy, it suffered all the miseries peculiar to both these forms of government.' Relief from this predicament had come in two stages. First, the Revolution of 1688 had secured the 'liberties' of the people and opened their minds to the prospect of improvement. And then the parliamentary union of 1707 had 'completed what the Revolution had begun' by weakening the power of the reactionary nobility, encouraging further cultural and economic development, and increasing the rights and enhancing the 'dignity' of non-noble members of Scottish society. By the middle of the eighteenth century the inhabitants of Scotland and England had become, in Robertson's words, 'one people' enjoying unprecedented political and religious liberty as well as economic prosperity and cultural refinement.[1]

Robertson's Whiggish support for the Revolution of 1688 and the Union of 1707, couched in terms of the progress of liberty and refinement, can be considered one major reason for the great success of his *History of Scotland*. As a self-proclaimed 'Revolution Whig' and man of the Enlightenment, Robertson was inclined to view the seventeenth century as a dark age in the Scottish past – an age that featured an unwholesome mixture of political absolutism, lingering feudalism, religious fanaticism and unrest, and cultural confusion. The Revolution was seen as the first critical step towards fashioning the new world of liberty, stability, and politeness from which the Scottish Enlightenment would emerge. Yet the *History of Scotland* contains few details about the precise contributions of the Revolution. Apart from passing references to a few of the Revolution's beneficial consequences, such as the 'claim of right' that restored Presbyterianism as the established religion of Scotland, the growing parliamentary influence of commoners, and the rise of 'freedom of debate' in the Scots Parliament, the book reveals little about the significance of the Revolution for an 'enlightened' Scottish Presbyterian Whig like Robertson.

Fortunately, Robertson left behind a handwritten sermon that provides some insight into his views on the significance of the Revolution. The occasion was the centennial celebration of the Revolution on 5 November 1788, which the General Assembly of the Church of Scotland had declared 'a Day of Solemn Thanksgiving to Almighty God' to commemorate 'that happy and illustrious event.' Ministers were called upon to remind their congregations of 'this special interposition of Divine Providence in their favour', which had established 'Civil and Religious Advantages' far beyond those granted 'to any other Nation'.[2] Many of the sermons preached by Scottish Presbyterian clergymen on that occasion were eventually published,[3] though 'Calvinianus Presbyter' (the anti-burgher seceder Archibald Bruce) produced a long work maintaining that such ecclesiastically sanctioned celebrations of secular events violated true Presbyterian principles.[4]

Bruce's position, however, was far from the mainstream. For most Presbyterian Whigs in Scotland the centennial celebration was an occasion of considerable importance. 'The Churches were all remarkably crowded, more so perhaps than on any former holiday', the *Caledonian Mercury* reported the following day.[5] Several months later, the excitement of the day was strongly conveyed in a letter from Robertson's colleague at Old Greyfriars and long-time rival for leadership in the Kirk, the Reverend John Erskine, to the former Popular party minister Charles Nisbet in Pennsylvania:

> It has been an exciting and remarkable time in Britain since the beginning of November. On the 5th of that month, by appointment of the last General Assembly, a Thanksgiving was observed through Scotland, for the Revolution in 1688. Most, or rather all of your old friends were hearty in the measure; as was Dr. [Hugh] Blair, on the other side, and many more.[6]

The thanksgiving day found William Robertson in the twilight of his illustrious career. He was sixty-seven years of age and internationally renowned as the author of histories of Scotland (1759), Charles V (1769), and America (1777). Though still serving as principal of the University of Edinburgh, he had retired eight years earlier from his unofficial position as leader of the dominant Moderate party in the kirk. During his long academic and ecclesiastical career he had fought hard to institutionalise the principles of freedom of expression and religious toleration that were such vital components of the Enlightenment throughout the Western world.

It is therefore not surprising to find him exalting these two principles as among the most valuable benefits of the Revolution of 1688. The first part of his sermon stressed the importance of freedom of expression – particularly in its uniquely modern form of 'freedom of the press' – for securing and maintaining political liberty. Owing to the Revolution, Robertson stated, 'the principles of liberty, the knowledge of the natural rights of man, and of the true end of civil government are more universally diffused, and more perfectly understood'.[7] During the seventeenth century people had forgotten that they had originally founded societies to protect their rights and secure their happiness. 'Illiberal' ideas of subservience to rulers were taught by clergymen, lawyers, and teachers. When at length men were incited to take up arms against 'a deluded monarch',

> . . . new maxims with respect to government were introduced, and more enlarged ideas began to spread. . . . The acknowledgement of the rights and privileges of the subject were incorporated into the constitution as essential parts of its frame. The sceptre was placed in the hands of sovereigns who had no title to sway it, but what they derived from the people. They were considered, and they considered themselves, as the chosen Guardians of those liberties and laws which they had contributed to preserve.

Gradually, men began to rejoice in their new-found liberty and to acquire 'liberal sentiments', which were spread 'by the labours of several learned and ingenious men, who investigated the principles of civil policy with freedom and discernment, and being now permitted to publish the result of their inquiries without disguise or restraint, they diffused the light of liberty and of truth throughout the nation'. As a result of this development, Robertson believed, it was possible to identify, discuss, and reform 'every defect in the Constitution'.

Aided by the technology of printing, the practice of freely exchanging liberal ideas had raised modern Britain far above the ancients:

> Even in the Republicks of Greece, those boasted mansions of liberty, I question whether the natural rights of men were so generally understood as they are now among us. In those times, there was no mode of communicating the instructions of wise and learned men but in writing; they were, of course, confined within a narrow sphere, and enlightened only a few, whereas among us, by the happy invention of printing, and our noble privilege of the liberty of the press, information reaches unto all.

Robertson was describing a kind of information revolution that gave birth to, and was in turn sustained by, the public, in something like the modern sense of that term:

> There never was any extensive society in which knowledge was so generally diffused and in which so great a number of men are in the habit of reasoning and inquiring concerning what is best and most beneficial to the society. Every measure that can affect the publick happiness is examined and discussed not only by the legislators who are the representatives of the people but by the people themselves. They judge, they decide, they publish their sentiments boldly, they defend them with zeal, and their concurring voice is a formidable restraint upon the exercise of power, warning kings and their ministers how dangerous it is to run counter to the general sentiments of the people.

In the second part of the sermon Robertson emphasised the equally important role of freedom of conscience and religious tolerance. For 'another consequence of the great transaction we are celebrating, was the establishment of more just notions with respect to the religious rights of men'. Religious rights, like political ones, were all but lost during the seventeenth century, as British subjects were kept from worshipping God according to the dictates of their consciences and 'compelled by the exertions of authority equally violent, to conform to the rites of a service which they considered as superstitious, and inconsistent with the simplicity of the Gospel'. Reference is made to the heroic days of the Scottish covenanters, who took to the mountains to worship God with 'the holy work' in one hand and 'the sword in the other'. The Revolution changed all this by establishing the principle of religious 'toleration', which in turn led to a lessening of 'alienation and rancour' among all denominations of Christians.

Once intellectual and religious freedom have been established, Robertson argues, truth inevitably follows, for 'the sceptres of night . . . disappear at the approach of light, whereas the more fully truth is exposed to view, and the more closely it is in inspected, it shines with greater splendour and strength'. By establishing freedom of expression and religion, then, the Revolution liberated the British people from the dual tyranny of ignorance and superstition and spawned an enlightened age of prosperity and progress. This is the language and vision of the Scottish Enlightenment, powerfully expressed by one of its leading voices. But Robertson's sermon can also be read as an example of what Duncan Forbes has called 'vulgar' Whiggism,[8] meaning a crude sort of Whig apologetics that identifies the later Stuart kings and the Roman Catholic religion with the apex of political and religious tyranny, defends the Revolution on the basis of historical 'fictions' such as the social contract, and regards Great Britain as, in Robertson's words, 'the only mansion of liberty in any extensive community' and 'the last station among the kingdoms of Europe of a free constitution and equal laws.' Robertson's 'vulgar' Whiggism, however, was tempered by his enlightened sensibilities, which led him to hope that the nations of Europe would one day emulate the model of Britain by possessing 'civil and religious liberty':

> No sooner did men whose minds were enlightened and enlarged by science begin to study the British constitution, than they perceived that it was by the possession of our civil and religious liberty that we were distinguished from other nations. They admired and celebrated the fabric of our government as the most perfect production of political wisdom, and recommended it as a model for the imitation of mankind . . . .
> Nor were these new ideas long confined to the wise and the learned; they spread on the Continent among the people in general, and in various countries we see men claiming rights and privileges of which they were not formerly conscious, and to which they did not pretend to aspire.

Robertson realised that his desire to export the fundamental principles of Britain's success was in a sense unpatriotic, since it entailed supporting changes that would lead Britain's Continental rivals to 'rise in strength and power'. Though a staunch British patriot, he had no doubt that in this case the spirit of 'benevolence' and a humane religion 'which teaches us to consider all men as our Brethren' must take precedence over 'that narrow spirit of jealousy which prevails between rival nations'. The triumph of the cosmopolitan ideal over 'vulgar' Whiggism is clearly shown by the following lines:

> Nor is it within the limits of the British dominions that the salutary effects of this great change in civil and religious opinion is confined. A view more enlarged and more noble opens to us. All the civilised nations of Europe may be considered as forming one extensive community. The intercourse among them is great, and every improvement in science, in arts, in commerce, in government introduced into any of them is soon known in the others, and in time is adopted and imitated. Hence arises . . . the great resemblance among all the people of Europe, and their great superiority over the rest of mankind.

The European Enlightenment, in other words, came first.

Robertson's attempt to demonstrate the contemporary relevance of the Revolution of 1688 for the nations of Europe constitutes the sermon's most interesting, and at the same time most controversial, feature. In the previously cited letter that John Erskine sent to Charles Nisbet in April 1789, Robertson is presented as an opponent of the centennial thanksgiving day: 'But my colleague [Robertson] was, throughout, cold, or rather unfriendly to the scheme, perhaps from the fear that on such an occasion, whig principles would be zealously inculcated. In fact they were so by Mr. Kemp, Mr. Jones, and several others in our Presbytery.' This assessment of Robertson seems surprising in light of the strong Whig principles that Erskine well knew his colleague had actually preached on this occasion.[9] At least one young member of the congregation at Old Greyfriars Church on 5 November 1788, Robertson's grandnephew Henry Brougham, was profoundly moved by the Whiggish zeal of Robertson's sermon. In his sketch of Robertson in *Lives of Men of Letters Who Flourished in the Reign of George III* (1845), and again in his posthumously published memoirs (1871), Brougham devoted nearly two pages to the powerful impression this sermon had made on him. He had been overwhelmed by 'the extreme earnestness, the youthful fervour' of its delivery and by its seemingly prophetic content, which appeared to anticipate the events of 1789. It touched in some passages, Brougham wrote,

> . . . upon a revolution which he expected and saw approaching, if not begun, as well as the one which was long past, and almost faded from the memory in the more absorbing interest of present affairs. I well remember his referring to the events then passing on the Continent, as the forerunners of far greater ones which he saw casting their shadows before. He certainly had no apprehensions of mischief, but he was full of hope for the future, and his exultation was boundless in contemplating the deliverance of 'so many millions of so great a nation from the fetters of arbitrary government'.[10]

Brougham proceeded to say that he and Robertson's sister (Brougham's great grandmother) had 'often afterwards reflected on this extraordinary discourse with wonder', but he had been prevented from examining the manuscript by Robertson's eldest son, Lord Robertson of the Court of Session, for fear that 'the author of it would be set down for a Jacobin' in the charged atmosphere of the 1790s and early 1800s. In a triumphant footnote to his life of Robertson, Brougham stated that following Lord Robertson's death he had finally managed to obtain the handwritten copy of this sermon, which clearly revealed where the author had 'added remarks made on the inspiration of the moment, particularly the one above cited'.[11] Add to this Alexander Carlyle's remark about Robertson being 'so much dazzled by the splendours of the French Revolution' that he could not listen to 'the ravings of Burke, as he called them',[12] and a picture of Robertson emerges that is diametrically opposed to the reactionary one painted by John Erskine.

But William Robertson was no radical, certainly no Jacobin. Like Adam Ferguson and his other friends affiliated with the Moderate party, he was a conservative, albeit 'enlightened', Whig who deeply respected the political and religious establishment of eighteenth-century Britain.[13] If Robertson initially disliked Burke's *Reflections on the Revolution in France*, this was presumably because he was willing, as Burke was not, to interpret French events of 1789–90 in terms of the Whig mythology of 1688 and the French political rhetoric of 1788, as a blow against despotic tyranny in the name of ordered liberty and constitutional monarchy. When it became clear that the Revolution was something more, Robertson, along with Ferguson and many other early sympathisers, turned emphatically against it.[14]

It is interesting to note that Carlyle, the conservative Whig, and Brougham, the liberal one, each had a strong motive for exaggerating Robertson's radicalism: the former to gloat over his old friend's failure to condemn the French Revolution from the outset, and the latter to portray his famous relation as a spokesman for the progressive political ideals that he himself held dear. Brougham did much the same thing in regard to the American Revolution, to which he said Robertson was a 'warm friend' when in fact he was a pretty warm enemy.[15] Other aspects of Brougham's account of Robertson's sermon are equally suspicious. In the extant manuscript one finds occasional corrections and revisions in the margin but no trace of the line about contemplating the deliverance of 'so many millions of so great a nation from the fetters of arbitrary government', even though Brougham claimed to have located it in the copy of the text that he saw. Furthermore, Brougham was only ten years-old when he heard Robertson preach his sermon, and his childhood impressions of it were 'confirmed', as he put it, by subsequent conversations with Robertson's sister (a warm Whig) and, at the opposite extreme, by the 'apprehensions' of Robertson's son, whom Brougham labelled a member of the 'strong alarmist party' during the era of the French Revolution. The question is whether Robertson's meaning can be properly understood when interpreted by alarmists like Carlyle and Lord Robertson on the one hand or by their liberal Whig opponents like Brougham on the other.

I submit they cannot be. To understand the meaning of Robertson's allusions to Continental affairs in his sermon of 1788, it is necessary to put aside Brougham, Lord Robertson, Carlyle, Erskine, and others whose views were coloured by the Reign of Terror or (in Erskine's case) by ecclesiastical and

religious differences, and to consider first Robertson's own beliefs about
French political history and then the specific context of the sermon in
question. Robertson discussed the constitutional history of France in the
widely-acclaimed Introduction to his *History of Charles V* (1769), 'A View
of the Progress of Society in Europe'.[16] There he traced the rise of French
monarchical absolutism since the Middle Ages in a manner that left no doubt
about where his own sympathies lay. In feudal times, Robertson observed,
French kings had been exceedingly weak, but by the end of the Middle Ages
'the gradual increase of the royal authority' had virtually destroyed all ves-
tiges of 'the ancient mixed government' of the nation. Fortunately, however,
the 'constitution of France' had been protected from 'mere despotism' by two
forces. The first was the nobility, which formed an 'intermediate order . . .
between the Monarch and his other subjects'. Though stripped of political
power, this class possessed honorific privileges that served as a check on the
king's authority. 'Thus a species of government was established in France',
Robertson wrote, 'unknown in the ancient world, that of a monarchy, in
which the power of the sovereign, though unconfined by any legal or
constitutional restraint, has certain bounds set to it by the ideas which one
class of his subjects entertain concerning their own dignity'.[17]

This was, of course, pure Montesquieu. In a footnote to this discussion
Robertson acknowledged his debt by citing the famous chapter in the *Spirit
of the Laws* where similar ideas are expressed (Book 1, chapter 4) as well
as the chapter in his friend Adam Ferguson's *Essay on the History of Civil
Society* where 'President Montesquieu' is eulogised in the strongest terms.[18]
The use of Montesquieu's judicial title by Robertson and other Scots (he was
Président à Mortier of the parlement at Bordeaux) is revealing: to the proud
inhabitants of a nation that had lost its court and its courts, a nation where the
legal profession and aristocracy were closely intermingled and every judge
bore the title 'lord', Montesquieu's brand of enlightened provincial elitism
must have looked familiar and appealing. In the Introduction to *Charles V*
Robertson contended, again à la Montesquieu, that the second barrier to
French royal despotism was 'the jurisdiction of the Parliaments of France,
particularly that of Paris', which he believed had come to establish principles
of justice and forms of proceeding

> . . . which were considered as so sacred, that even the sovereign power of the
> Monarch durst not venture to disregard or to violate them. The members of
> this illustrious body, though they neither possess legislative authority, nor can
> be considered as the representatives of the people, have availed themselves of the
> reputation and influence which they had acquired among their countrymen, in
> order to make a stand to the utmost of their abilities against every unprecedented
> and exorbitant exertion of the prerogative. In every period of French history, they
> have merited the praise of being the virtuous but feeble guardians of the rights and
> privileges of the nation.[19]

In a word, or rather two, Robertson believed that 'robe' and 'sword'
constituted the twin bulwarks against the triumph of despotism in France.
Robertson's support for a version of the *thèse nobiliare* in the introduction
to *Charles V* must be seen against the background of what has been called the

'quasi-revolution of the 1760s'.[20] During that critical decade the *parlements* of France, and particularly the Parlement of Paris, had begun asserting – some would have said inventing – their historical role as 'guardians of the rights and privileges of the nation'. Not even the infamous *séance de la flagellation* of 1766, in which the King had reminded them in no uncertain terms of his absolute supremacy, had been enough to silence them. As he prepared *Charles V* for the press in 1768, Robertson could not have known where the crisis was headed – the abrupt abolition of the *parlements* by Maupeou in 1771 and their triumphal recall following the ascension of Louis XVI in 1774. But he recognised a lively topic when he saw one and was not afraid to take an unequivocal stand on the side of liberty as he understood it.

Though *Charles V* consisted mainly of a dry narrative account of sixteenth-century political and diplomatic history, the book's wide-ranging, controversial Introduction was primarily responsible for making it one of the major publishing events of the eighteenth century. Robertson received by far and away the most advance royalty yet paid to any author (£3,500 outright and at least another £500 upon publication of later editions), and a popular French translation by J.-B.-A. Suard, undertaken before the English edition was published, did more than anything else to establish the translator's literary reputation and earn him membership in that most aristocratic of intellectual societies, the French Academy.[21] But not everyone in France was happy with the book. The royalist radical Mably, for example, wrote of his profound disappointment at reading the translation of Robertson's highly touted introduction, where he was especially dismayed to find, in what concerned the history of France, 'all the prejudices and all the errors' of French historians whose works had been superficially understood.[22]

The point is that Robertson did not come to French affairs cold in November 1788: he was already a keen observer, and in a sense a participant, in the prolonged constitutional crisis of the second half of the eighteenth century. The seemingly radical rhetoric that Robertson employed in his sermon of 1788 must be read in the spirit of that continuing crisis, especially as it developed in 1787–88. The *révolte nobiliare* of that time was much like the 'quasi-revolution' of the 1760s, only on this occasion the defeat of the King by the *parlements* and aristocracy was more decisive, and the prospects for lasting constitutional reform, personal liberties, and by the end of 1788 greater involvement in public affairs by a broader segment of the public began to seem much more likely. No one has ever captured the momentary thrill of this apparent triumph better than Tocqueville:

> In reading the writings of authors before the end of 1788, one is astonished to find them speaking of a great revolution already accomplished before 1789. Yet if one considers the history of 1788 one sees that the changes which occurred during that year were greater than those of previous centuries. This was truly a very great revolution but one destined to be obscured by history, lost as it was in the immensity of the revolution about to follow.[23]

Strong words, to be sure. Brougham probably would not have been able to make much of them, and even today we often obscure their meaning by using loaded terms like 'pre-revolution' to describe the events of 1787–88.

Looking at matters in France as Robertson would have seen them in the autumn of 1788, however, one can readily appreciate the incisiveness of Tocqueville's point.[24] In November 1787 the French government passed the Edict Concerning Those Who Do Not Profess the Catholic Religion, which granted limited freedom to Protestants. After more than two months of debate and a few modifications the Parlement of Paris registered this law in late January 1788. Four months later it issued the famous *arrêté* (decree) of 3 May that listed the 'fundamental laws' of France, including the right of all citizens accused of a crime to due process before the law. Another of Robertson's basic principles of British 'civil and religious liberty', freedom of the press, was in effect implemented on 5 July 1788, when the government invited all Frenchmen to give opinions on the proper way to constitute the Estates General that the King now spoke of convening. A month later the date of the Estates General was set for the following May, and late in September the Parlement of Paris, which the government had suspended following its decree of 3 May 1788, was recalled in response to intense public pressure. By the time Robertson preached his sermon in November, there was mounting opposition to the Parlement of Paris's ruling of 25 September that the Estates General of 1789 should follow the precedent of 1614, and claims for the right of the Third Estate to equal representation were being voice. Perhaps these first stirrings of political activism by the Third Estate in France were among the factors that Robertson had in mind when he spoke admiringly of 'men claiming rights and privileges of which they were not formerly conscious, and to which they did not pretend to aspire'.

The reasons for Robertson's optimism and excitement about events across the English Channel should now be clearer. As one who considered freedom of the press and freedom of religion to be among the most important consequences of the Revolution of 1688, he was happy to see those freedoms established in France a century later. As one who loathed monarchical absolutism and regarded the nobility and *parlements* as the fundamental bulwarks against it, he could only have been pleased to observe the victory of the *révolte nobiliaire* over 'despotism'. And as one who cherished the political rights of commoners secured by the Revolution of 1688 – and who no doubt remembered well the lessons of Scottish history in the century before that Revolution – he was hopeful that the upper echelons of the Third Estate would have an important role to play in the nascent constitutional monarchy of France. Preaching before the differences between the interests of the aristocracy and Third Estate began to appear irreconcilable, Robertson was encouraged by the belief that the basic principles of British liberty were being adopted by France. Details remained to be worked out, of course, but they might have seemed rather insignificant in light of what looked to him like a broad consensus about the need for fundamental reforms modelled on the British example.

France was not the only country undergoing revolutionary ferment in 1788. In this context it is important to remember that Robertson's allusions to the spread of British principles of civil and religious liberty were meant to refer to Europe as a whole. Unfortunately, the allusions are usually too vague to indicate precisely which countries and which movements Robertson had in mind. Only in the case of an indirect reference to the Austrian Patent of Toleration, which granted limited relief to Protestants in 1781, can the reader be sure of Robertson's meaning. That example, however, raises one of the most serious difficulties with Robertson's position, for the Patent of Toleration was the product of the very same monarchical absolutism that Robertson so detested. So, for that matter, was the French Protestant relief law mentioned earlier. Armed only with a 'vulgar' Whig model that assumed a necessary correlation between constitutional limitations on the powers of kings and the growth of personal liberty, Robertson could not easily explain the 'enlightened' despotism of a Joseph II.

If the elderly Robertson was not quite the radical Whig that Brougham wished and Carlyle feared him to be, and was far from the thoroughgoing Tory that Erskine considered him, he was every inch a man of the Enlightenment. The dominant terminology of Robertson's thanksgiving day sermon is Enlightenment rhetoric in its classical form: 'reason', 'science', 'progress', 'mutual forbearance and toleration', 'natural rights of man', 'publick happiness', 'general welfare', 'truth', 'liberty', 'light'. The concepts of the social contract, sovereignty of the people, brotherhood of man, and government by law rather than by royal will are all articulated or clearly implied, and attention is drawn to the importance of the process by which enlightened ideas are 'diffused' throughout society and mankind. Robertson's sermon is a marvellous expression of the humane, cosmopolitan, optimistic spirit of the Whig-Presbyterian Enlightenment in eighteenth-century Scotland, pronounced, ironically, just as the Enlightenment in Scotland and elsewhere was about to be torn asunder by monumental social, political and economic changes.

Because both of Robertson's surviving sermons were preached on special occasions and devoted to world-historical themes – in this case a theme of an explicitly secular nature – they do not provide much guidance for discovering what Robertson was really like as a Presbyterian preacher and pastor.[25] Yet here and there, especially in the closing passages of his sermon on the Revolution, one catches glimpses of the omnipotent God of Calvin lurking in the distance, determining human affairs in ways that appear 'marvellous' – though often incomprehensible – to mankind. In answer to the question of why Britain had been chosen to be 'the only mansion of liberty in any extensive community', Robertson asked his congregation to 'join wise and good men of every age in considering this as the work of God and not of man' and quoted Deuteronomy 4: on the need for nations to 'keep thy soul diligently, lest thou forget the things which thine eyes have seen, and lest they depart from thy heart all the days of thy life'. It would be presumptuous of us to assume that these references were mere window-dressing, especially considering the testimony of the pious John Erskine about the orthodoxy of Robertson's doctrine in the weekly sermons and lectures he delivered at Old Greyfriars.[26] For Robertson, the Revolution of 1688 and its glorious consequences were ultimately 'the work of God and not of man', and Whig ideology was grounded in Presbyterian faith in the goodness and justice of 'that super-intending providence, in whose hand it is to lift up nations and to cast them down'.

Notes

1. *The works of William Robertson*, 8 vols. (Oxford, 1825), II, p. 246.
2. 'Act appointing a National Thanksgiving in Commemoration of the Revolution of 1688', in *The Principal Acts of the General Assembly of the Church of Scotland* (1788), pp. 32–3.
3. William Peebles, *The Great Things which the Lord Hath Done for this Nation, Illustrated and Improved* (Kilmarnock, 1788); John Robertson, *Britain the Chosen Nation* (Kilmarnock, 1788); Alexander Ranken, *A Discourse on the Advantages of the Revolution of 1688* (Glasgow, 1788); *A Sermon on the Centennial Day of the Revolution in Great Britain* (Dundee, 1788); *Secular Anniversary of the Revolution* (Glasgow, 1788); William M'Gill, *The Benefits of the Revolution* (Kilmarnock, 1789); James Peddie, *The Revolution the Work of God, and Cause of Joy* (Edinburgh, 1789). John Adamson, *A Sermon Preached on the 5th Day of November 1788* (Edinburgh, 1789). To these may be added a sermon preached by Henry Hunter before the Scots Presbytery in London on the English thanksgiving day (4 November): *The Universal and Everlasting Dominion of God, a Perpetual Source of Joy and Praise* (London, 1788).
4. *Annus Secularis; or the British Jubilee: or a Review of the Act of the General Assembly, Appointing the 5th of November 1788, As an Anniversary – Thanksgiving, in commemoration of the Revolution in 1688* (Edinburgh, 1788).
5. Quoted in John D. Brims, 'The Scottish Democratic Movement in the Age of the French Revolution' (Edinburgh Univ. Ph.D. thesis, 1983), p. 63.
6. Erskine to Nisbet, 21 April 1789, in Samuel Miller, *Memoir of the Rev. Charles Nisbet, D.D.* (New York, 1840), pp. 195–6.
7. All quotations from Robertson's sermon are taken from the manuscript in Robertson's own hand in the Robertson-Macdonald papers, Nat. Lib. Of Scotland, MS. 3979, fos. 11–21, and are reproduced with permission of that library's trustees. I wish to acknowledge the assistance of Dr T.I. Rae, keeper of manuscripts at the National Library, and Professor Doris Sher, who managed to decipher Robertson's messiest marginal scrawl when I was unable to do so.
8. Duncan Forbes, *Hume's Philosophical Politics* (Cambridge, 1975), ch. 5, and 'Sceptical Whiggism, Commerce and Liberty', in Andrew S. Skinner and Thomas Wilson (eds.), *Essays on Adam Smith* (Oxford, 1975), pp. 179–201, esp. p. 180.
9. The explanation for this mystery almost certainly lies in the way Erskine used the term 'Whig'. In the letter to Nisbet mentioned earlier (Miller, *Charles Nisbet*, p. 196), he stated that his own thanksgiving day sermon had 'chiefly considered the evils of Popery, the imminent danger of these evils, and the remarkable deliverance', and that, of all the Scottish thanksgiving day sermons published to commemorate the Revolution, he had liked only James Peddie's – which attacked 'Popery' with a degree of hostility and an urgency that Robertson would have found reprehensible (Peddie, *Revolution the Work of God*, pp. 7, 11, 25–30). The latter was no lover of Roman Catholicism but placed a much greater value on the principle of toleration, which Erskine viewed with disdain where Catholics were concerned. Thus, Erskine probably viewed Robertson as insufficiently anti-Catholic to be considered a good Whig.
10. Henry, Lord Brougham, *Lives of Men of Letters and Science who Flourished in the Time of George III*, 2 vols. (London, 1845), I, p. 270.
11. ibid., p. 271. This footnote was integrated into the text of the almost identical account of Robertson's sermon in Brougham's memoirs, *The Life and Times of Henry, Lord Brougham*, 3 vols. (New York, 1871), I, p. 31.

12. Alexander Carlyle, 'A comparison of Two Eminent characters Attempted after the Manner of Plutarch', in *Anecdotes and Characters of the Times*, ed. James Kinsley (London, 1973), p. 281.

13. Richard B. Sher, *Church and University in the Scottish Enlightenment: The Moderate Literati of Edinburgh* (Princeton and Edinburgh, 1985), pp. 187–212, 262–76.

14. See, for example Robertson to John Douglas, Bishop of Salisbury, 15 February 1793, Brit. Lib., Egerton MS. 2182, fos. 78–9.

15. 'Of American independence he was the warm friend', Brougham wrote of Robertson in *Lives of Men of Letters* (I, p. 315). That the opposite was in fact the case is shown in Sher, *Church and University*, pp. 263–76. For a fuller account of Robertson's thoughts on America, see Jeffrey Smitten, 'Moderatism and History: William Robertson's unfinished History of British America', in Richard B. Sher and Jeffrey Smitten (eds), *Scotland and America in the Age of the Enlightenment* (Edinburgh and Princeton, forthcoming).

16. William Robertson, *The Progress of Society in Europe*, ed. Felix Gilbert (Chicago, 1971). This introduction was also published separately in the eighteenth century.

17. ibid., pp. 131–2.

18. Adam Ferguson, *An Essay on the History of Civil Society*, ed. Duncan Forbes (Edinburgh, 1966), pt. 1, sect. 10 (esp. p. 65).

19. Robertson, *Progress of Society*, pp. 132–3.

20. R. R. Palmer, *The Age of the Democratic Revolution*, 2 vols. (Princeton, 1959), II, pp. 86–99, 449.

21. R. B. Sher and M. A. Stewart, 'William Robertson and David Hume: Three Letters', *Hume Studies: 10th Anniversary Issue* (1985), pp. 69–86, especially notes 33 and 34; Alan Kors, *D'Holbach's Coterie: An Enlightenment in Paris* (Princeton, 1976), p. 191.

22. 'De la manière d'écrire l'histoire', in *Collection complète des oeuvres de l'abbé de Mably*, ed. Guillaume Arnoux, 15 vols. (Paris, 1794–5), XII, p. 446. I am indebted to Keith Baker for this reference.

23. Alexis de Tocqueville, *The European Revolution and Correspondence with Gobineau*, ed. and trans. John Lukacs (Garden City, N.Y., 1959), pp. 61–2.

24. For what follows, see Jean Egret, *The French Pre-Revolution, 1787–1788*, trans. Wesley D. Camp (Chicago, 1977), and Bailey Stone, *The Parlements of Paris, 1774–1789* (Chapel Hill, N.C., 1981), ch. 6.

25. Cf. William Robertson, *The Situation of the World at the Time of Christ's Appearance, and Its Connection with the Success of His Religion Considered* (Edinburgh, 1755). In 1909 Peter Hume Brown incorrectly asserted that 'no sermons of Robertson have been preserved' besides this one, which was preached before the Scottish S.P.C.K., Brown, *History of Scotland*, 3 vols. (1900–9), III, p. 365.

26. John Erskine, 'The Agency of God in Human Greatness,' in *Discourses Preached on Several Occasions*, 2nd edn. 2 vols. (Edinburgh, 1801–4), I, p. 274.

9

THE BRITISH PRESS AND EIGHTEENTH-CENTURY REVOLUTION: THE FRENCH CASE

Jeremy Black

The Frenchman acknowledged that they had been miserable and wretched, but pleased himself with the prospect of what was to come; he said that 'the States General . . . were forming a constitution preferable in many respects to that of England . . . that the Tiers Etat-': Here the Englishman interrupted with 'D-n your Tiers Etat! Where is your Magna Carta and your Bill of Rights!'

London Chronicle 2 March 1790.

The English Civil Wars, the Glorious Revolution and the Jacobite risings helped to produce considerable ambivalence in eighteenth-century British attitudes to rebellions. This can be seen not only in the discussion of violent disturbances and rebellions within Britain, but also in the consideration of disturbances abroad, a subject that has received relatively little scholarly attention, with the conspicuous exceptions of the American Revolution and, to a lesser extent, the French Revolution.[1] However, as the British press devoted much space to foreign news,[2] it was scarcely surprising that rebellions abroad attracted considerable interest. They did so for a number of reasons. Foreign news could serve to comment on British developments.[3] Indeed the uniqueness that some modern historians lay claim to for eighteenth-century Britain in their rebuttal of claims that it was an *ancien régime* society or can be profitably compared with them is seriously compromised by the willingness, indeed eagerness, of contemporaries to discuss British developments in terms of the situation in foreign countries and to consider the latter in the light of British circumstances. The extent to which the consequent discussion can be regarded as informed will vary. Arguably, many British commentators were insufficiently sensitive to the particular constitutional and political traditions in foreign countries and to the nature of political and governmental activity in them. In particular, there was only a limited awareness of the process of compromise and the realities of consensus and cooperation that lay behind the political façades of the continental states whose governmental system have been described subsequently as absolutism, a term with misleading connotations. Misleading or not, the reporting of foreign news could serve as the basis for points about British developments and it was never more thus focused that in the discussion of dramatic political events abroad that involved mass activity. It was at that point that the usual political world perceived abroad, one of courts and 'private' politics, became public and appeared most similar to the British political world.

In addition, dramatic foreign political events provided not only points of reference in terms of public activity that could serve to explain, or rather provide an explanation for these developments, but also types of political activity that produced material for those who wished to report them. By their very nature, rebellions and other violent disturbances involved an appeal to a public wider than that involved in political activity. This appeal had to be striking and dramatic, comprehensive and swift. The central means for making such an appeal involved the use of print. The extent to which print was used in continental Europe in the period prior to the French Revolution for political statements associated with disturbances is insufficiently stressed. It was obviously the case with those states that possessed powerful representative institutions, such as Poland, Sweden and the United Provinces. A serious riot in Amsterdam in January 1754 was associated with printed criticism of the government:

> . . . many libels have been dispersed at Amsterdam, reflecting upon the present Government.[. . .] This country is still over-run with anonymous papers upon the late tumults at Amsterdam.[. . .] I do not know whether replying to libels is the surest way to get to the root of the evil complained of, or to maintain the present form of government, unless they are supported by measures of a different nature.[4]

However, it was not only in states with powerful representative institutions that printed criticism of the government appeared. It was also published, even if illegal, in states where the 'public' world of politics was more limited.[5] In 1768 Paris was affected by a rise in the price of grain, leading Robert Walpole, the British envoy, to report:

> . . . this misfortune either by itself or mixed with other distresses, draws out the ill humour of the People, which shows itself in threatening papers stuck up in the most public parts of this City, pointing out the Duke of Choiseul by name and menacing attempts upon his life. The consequence of this is, what can be safely done by the Ministry in this country, that many persons are taken up, and sent to prison, right or wrong.[6]

Such mechanisms of control were rarely effective. In the mid-1770s, Breteuil, the minister responsible for the control of printers and publishers in Paris, was driven to conclude that existing French regulations for the suppression of critical material had failed.[7] Their failure was even more apparent at times of serious disturbances. The resultant discussions in print then provided foreign newspapers with their prime source for reports. They were crucially important because the newspapers of the period rarely used what is today understood by the term foreign correspondents. This reflected the undercapitalised nature of the press of the period, but it was also due to an absence of any tradition of employing such individuals. Rather than sending reporters abroad, newspapers preferred to rely on plagiarism from foreign and British newspapers and newsletters and sometimes on individuals resident abroad who were prepared to provide material. As important events could occur anywhere in Europe, it is understandable that no network of reporters abroad developed. Indeed, the first moves towards such reporting occurred in the early 1790s in the case of Paris, at a time when the primary importance of reliable news from one particular place was obvious. James Perry of the *Morning Chronicle* went to Paris in 1791 in order to send back reports that could give the paper the edge in its coverage of the Revolution:

> Although Perry's summary of events at Paris had only one day's priority, his reports of the proceedings of the National Assembly consistently had two days' priority; they were published on Tuesday, and gave the debates up to the preceding Friday evening, whereas other papers gave the proceedings up to Wednesday, and had to reprint the *Chronicle's* accounts next day.[8]

Thus the breakdown of authority in foreign countries both excited interest in Britain and helped to provide the press with material with which they could satisfy this interest. Interest and the availability of information with which to satisfy it, however, varied greatly. It was far harder to obtain information about disturbances in rural Europe even if, as in Bohemia and Russia in the 1770s[9] or Transylvania in the 1780s, these were on a vast scale. In contrast, it was relatively easy to obtain material concerning disturbances in major cities, particularly if the cities were linked to Britain by regular and relatively good communications and if the disorders produced at least some printed material in English or French. Partly as a result, the impression created by the British press of disorder and rebellion in the last three decades of the century was very much that of an Atlantic Revolution. Disturbances in the Habsburg territories, other than in the Austrian Netherlands, received relatively little attention.

The relationship between the demand for news and opinion and the role played by the press is far from clear. Mention of the reporting difficulties facing the British press serves to qualify any impression of the newspapers simply seeking to satisfy the demands of readers. However, the scanty nature of the surviving evidence concerning the finances, organisation and intentions of British newspapers in this period makes it very difficult to assess the autonomous nature of their role. This has commonly been underrated because of the tendency to discuss their political relationships in terms of political subsidies.[10] There is a danger that, as a result, these relationships have been simplified. Clearly they varied by newspaper, but there is no reason to believe that because a newspaper received a subsidy this explains its attitude. As with parliamentarians, payments may have reflected, as much as they created, loyalties.

Irrespective of their political opinions, newspapers required news. Rebellions provide this when they led to the creation or growth of the mechanisms and habits of eighteenth-century public politics, specifically representative institutions and the printed accounts of their proceedings, public societies, newspapers, petitions, addresses and instructions. All of these struck echoes in Britain, where the apparent similarity in the methods of political discussion could hamper awareness of differences in their content. In the case of foreign rebellions, this was possibly encouraged by the fact that the violent nature of the Glorious Revolution made it possible to argue that violence was not incompatible with what was regarded as progressive development and thus not an indicator that a particular rebellion would necessarily turn out to be harmful. This can be seen in the forbearance that many who did not welcome the French Revolution initially extended to it.

The two revolutions outside Britain that were most discussed were those not only about which it was easiest to obtain a large amount of information, but also those which most influenced domestic British politics, the American and the French Revolutions. America should not be regarded as a foreign country. Until it became independent, it was subject to the British Crown, and the American Revolution was, as a civil war within the British Empire, understandably followed closely in Britain. The French Revolution, in contrast, appeared at least initially to be of little consequence for Britain. Professor Read recently claimed that 'the storming of the Bastille on July 14, 1789, was immediately recognised as a turning point'.[11] This was not in fact the case. France's failure to act decisively during the Dutch crisis of 1787 and the political disputes of that year had constituted a turning point in terms of foreign attitudes towards France, and from then on press portrayal of the country had stressed domestic disaffection and the weakness of her government. In January 1788 the *Newcastle Courant* reprinted a report from London stating that war with France was unlikely, 'for the best of reasons, because of the national poverty – and general embarrassment in every interior circumstance of government. Excepting in a civil war, the confidence and attachment of a whole people, never were more apparently alienated, than at present in France'.[12]

That year brought reports of disturbances in France:

> According to all the accounts we can gain from the Continent, it appears that the affairs of France exhibit no appearance of a pacific tendency. On the contrary the King seems determined to persevere in his present measures, and even to take more violent steps, if he meets with opposition; while the people, apprehensive that they may sink yet lower into misery, slavery, and disgrace, unless they show a strong conviction of their rights, and a determination to maintain them, seem absolutely determined to hazard all, rather than submit to what they deem oppression and injustice.[13]

The centenary in 1788 of the Glorious Revolution provided an opportunity for a restatement of the value of that episode, a restatement that events in France were soon to make controversial. The use which reformers could make of the Glorious Revolution was already apparent before the discussion of developments in France became controversial. A local item printed in the *Leeds Mercury* in November 1788 urged the abolition of the slave trade and praised the events of 1688:

> In order to know the true value of that glorious and important event, which has just been commemorated throughout this island, we should contrast our present

state with what it would inevitably have been, had not that triumphant change
produced by the Revolution been effected. Bigotry and superstition, despotism
and tyranny, would, long ere this, have defaced this fair flourishing Isle, and
have so contracted and damped the noble and emulous spirit of Britons, that they
would, compared with what they now are, scarce have seemed like men. With
liberty, the source and course of every human good would have fled, commerce,
industry, every ornamental and useful art, that polish and refine our manners, give
pleasure in our social and solitary hours, and bread to thousands. Instead of that
free communication we now enjoy, we must have conversed by nods and shrugs,
with doubtful and ambiguous looks.[14]

Given such attitudes, it is not surprising both that many could praise the
events of 1789 in France and that the violence that accompanied them could
be seen as an obvious aspect of necessary changes.[15] *The Times* reported in
July 1789 that developments in France 'must afford sincere pleasure to every
citizen of the world and every friend of the rights of mankind', and it ascribed
them to the experience of revolution, the experience of supporting the cause
of liberty in America: 'a people who have once fought for the emancipation
of another nation can afterwards but ill relish the slavery in their own'.[16]

Thus, the experience of one revolution could be held to have led France to a
second, while the ideological legacy of the Revolution of 1688 influenced the
manner in which this was regarded in Britain. Many Foxite Whigs claimed
to discern a growing parallelism in the development of the two countries,
and similar views were expressed in print: 'France and England looking
up to the same standard for happiness will probably prevent all national
hostilities'.[17] If a growing parallelism in political circumstances was apparent
to some politicians the obvious weakness of the French government made it
unlikely that the two states would come into conflict. This permitted both
Foxite enthusiasm and a wider habit of regarding French developments with
interest, but without concern. British enthusiasts could be seen by others as
foolish, but not, as yet, dangerous fools. *The Times* ridiculed the Revolution
Society in July 1790: 'My Lordship, it is true, has ever been a warm friend to
high flown principles of democracy: yet we are apt to think that he would
not joyfully part with his two titles and hereditary honours, to make the mob
happy by levelling all distinction.'

The same month the *Leeds Intelligencer* published a letter from 'Old Noll'
mocking, but in a light-hearted fashion, the French abolition of titles and
discussing what this would produce in Britain. The House of Lords would
become the House of Monsieurs and parliamentary reports would refer to
Ned Thurlow and Davy Murray.[18] Attitudes hardened that autumn. As is
well known, this owed much to the appearance of Burke's *Reflections* on 1
November and to the subsequent controversy. However, political circumstances were possibly also partly responsible. The general election of the
summer having been fought, the political nation was prepared to address
new topics. Moreover, the attitude of France during the Anglo-Spanish
Nootka Sound crisis had not been satisfactory from the British point of
view. France was clearly not powerful, but the crisis had revealed that the
Revolution had not removed anti-British attitudes. On 26 August 1790 the
National Assembly had ordered the preparation of a fleet of 45 ships of the

line in order, if necessary, to lend weight to any confrontation with Britain. The British ministry and British public opinion were sceptical, with reason, of France's ability to wage war or prepare a major fleet, but there was little doubt of French hostility. *The Times* observed in October 1790, that 'the annihilation of royalty and of nobility, the plundering of the clergy and the total destruction of the ancient monarchy have caused no alteration of the political sentiments in the rulers of France to this country.' A month later the *Public Advertiser* noted that there were reports in the City, 'that a majority of the National Assembly had determined to lay a duty on British goods, amounting nearly to a prohibition, and that a resolution to this effect was to be proposed without delay. It is certain that the Assembly, in several of its late decisions, has not shown itself amicable to this nation'.[19]

It was against this background that Burke's attempt to redefine revolution so that a contrast appeared between events in contemporary France and in Britain in 1688 was received. Some of the newspapers were more than willing to propagate this view. Eight days after the *Reflections* appeared, the *Public Advertiser* observed: 'The spirit of Anarchy, misnamed Liberty, has migrated from France, and appeared in Martinique and Guadaloupe with as direful an aspect as molested the seat of empire in the summer of 1789.' Burke focused attention on the ambiguities in contemporary British political thought. The issues at stake were far broader than that of representation around which much of the debate over the American Revolution had revolved. Now the purposes of social organisation and the relationship between change and stability were under discussion. Seeking to woo him, the pro-ministerial *Times* informed its readers that 'Mr. Burke, while he has excited the vengeance of the Paris mob by his late publication, has ggained the reverence and admiration of every thinking man who esteems a well ordered Government, which is the best bond of civil society'.[20]

In addition, the activity of British radicals appeared to justify a frequent theme of the pre-revolutionary press, namely that events abroad could prefigure developments at home. The radicals appeared to many to be evidence not only of such a link, but also of the means by which it might take effect. *The World*, a London newspaper subsidised by the ministry to the tune of £600 a year, reported in June 1791:

> The panegyrists of the intended celebration of the anniversary of the French Revolution, seem to be sore at any observations made upon the approaching event, and say, 'it is hard that a few persons cannot celebrate the *freedom of their neighbours*, without reproach or remark'. No doubt it would be so, was that freedom established on the principles of reciprocity and good government – but when we find a country professing to boast of a King, and at the same time whittling him down to a cypher – when we find a nobility degraded, an army without order and discipline, a clergy disgraced, and a legislature conscious of its errors and its vices, only making laws to screen themselves from the consequences of both, they should form no examples of triumph or commemoration.[. . .] Therefore it is to meet this intended Reformation in the bud, that remarks and observations are made on this unnatural fete, and which we trust will be followed up by the prudence and foresight of government as well as of the public at large.[21]

The Times announced a month later: 'Mr. Burke's book has been the means of disuniting the Revolution Society from all its respectable members. Sensible men, and persons of property now plainly perceived that to celebrate the anniversary of Rebellion is now to sow the seeds of a revolution in England'.[22]

Many who sympathised with certain aspects of the Revolution were careful, nevertheless, to stress the purity of their motives and their loyalty. A Leeds report in the *Leeds Intelligencer* of May 1791 reveals Quaker caution about their reputation:

A paragraph having been copied from the Evening Mail into our last week's papers, in which the address from the people called the Quakers to the National Assembly of France was mentioned as being in secret circulation, and containing matter of an inflammatory nature we feel ourselves bound to mention that the translation of the original paper which many of our readers no doubt have seen, and which hath been very openly disseminated, contains nothing contrary to the established principles and uniform practise of that well known and pacific people. If anything of a rebellious purpose is published under their name, that very circumstance is the strongest possible proof of a forgery.

A Derby item in the *Derby Mercury* two months later noted:

On Thursday the 14th instant several gentlemen, desirous of expressing their satisfaction at the delivery of many millions of the human race from the oppression of an arbitrary government, dined together at the George inn in this town, in commemoration of the Revolution in France. The day was spent in great harmony and decorum, and the following loyal and constitutional toasts were drunk . . .'[23]

Such attempts to present support for Revolution as 'loyal and constitutional' became increasingly difficult. As the French Revolution was redefined for British observers in more radical terms it became progressively harder to present it with reference to the Glorious Revolution, as then perceived. Furthermore, British radicals who had little time for conventional definitions of 'loyal and constitutional' attitudes saw little reason to refer for justification to the events of 1688. Burke was correct in arguing that the modern revolutionaries and their sympathisers had little interest in historical continuity or in justification in terms of past traditions and events.

The Glorious Revolution was commonly presented in late-eighteenth century Britain as an essentially peaceful act. Such a presentation was made possible by a concentration on English events, rather than Scottish and Irish consequences. It served as an obvious basis from which to condemn the violence of modern revolutionaries. A profound sense of disquiet about mob violence was readily apparent in much of the press by the late summer of 1791 when the flight to Varennes made it likely that constitutional monarchy would only have a precarious future in France, while the disturbances in Birmingham suggested that the British debate over the Revolution would no longer be non-violent. 'Quidam', in a letter to the *London Chronicle* suggested that:

The recent *popular* transaction at Birmingham call for the most serious attention, as both the *cause* and *effect* were the spontaneous proceedings of the *Tiers Etats*.

There are men enough ready at all times and in all countries, ambitious to raise themselves into consequence upon the shoulders of the people; and, being daring where they have little to risk, are watchful of all opportunities to stir up confusion, in the hope during a scramble to snatch something for themselves.

Thus, on the event of the French Revolution (a good measure perverted by such men, by extending it to be absurdity of speculative extremes) we see associations formed in this country, who are suspected to be ready, were the humour to spread, to begin the like operations here. But may God in his mercy give the good people of Britain sense enough to know the due value of a constitution, that has long been the admiration of the whole world; and to be warned by the horrors of the perilous experiment of refining systems of Government above the standard of humanity, and then with stern despotism exacting conformity to them! We have had occasional specimens among ourselves of the government of mobs, when they take it in their heads to burst loose from the restraint of laws, which fit as easy upon them here, as laws ought to do: and the arbitrary acts of their majesty the People are infinitely more intolerable and dreadful, than those of any individual majesty whatever!

The writer then returned to the Birmingham riot, arguing that it was:

a fortunate circumstance that it was a Church of England mob . . . they showed discrimination in their fury in favour of the established Government, in opposition to those who, as least in their opinion, manifested a disposition to tear up the constitution by the roots. Had it been a Revolution mob, influenced by Revolution meetings, it might have acted only as a prelude to more extensive ruin.[24]

The following year was to add disquiet about the conduct abroad of the French government, as opposed to that simply of their foreign supporters. Whereas 1688 could be located in a favourable international context, that of opposition to an allegedly aggressive Louis XIV, the international context against which revolutionary France was judged was by 1792 less sympathetic to its cause. Attempts by supporters to present its case in a favourable light appear to have had little success. France was not in general seen as a victim, but as an aggressive force. The *Public Advertiser* claimed in March 1792, that 'a new system is now opening to the view of the world; the European courts are plotting to counteract it'.[25] Supporters of France drew attention to the situation in Poland where Catherine II of Russia wished to reverse the constitutional and political developments of 1791, the so-called Polish 'Revolution'. The pro-ministerial *St James's Chronicle* claimed in June 1792: 'The friends of sedition in this country, are extremely solicitous to confound the *Polish* with the *French* Revolution. Nothing can be more unjust, as they very essentially differ both in principle and effect.'[26]

Whatever the parallels or differences, the comparison was of limited value, because British opinion was concerned with France, not Poland. The situation echoed that of the early 1730s. Then British newspapers had followed the dispute between the Parlement of Paris and the Fleury ministry closely and some had expressed support for the Parlement. In contrast, when Poland was invaded by Russia in 1733, little sympathy was voiced for the Poles. The availability of news clearly played a major role, but so also did the range of public attention. There were, of course, several 'publics'. The mercantile public, for example, had distinct interests. In recent years much attention has been devoted to Anglo-Russian links in the eighteenth century. This may have diverted attention from the continued dominance of Western European concerns. The striking feature of any examination of the press in 1791–93 is the contrast between the reporting of French and of Polish developments. Reports of events in Poland and comments upon them were relatively scanty. Thus, the comparative revolutionary dimension was not really presented at any length. The press reflected and sustained a notion of Europe and of Britain in relation to Europe that placed Eastern Europe in an almost intermediate category between the rest of Europe and the non-European world. Revolutions in this area did not receive the attention devoted to the disturbances in the Austrian Netherlands and the United Provinces in the 1780s, let alone to the French Revolution. They could not therefore serve successfully as a basis for comparison with events in France.

The suggestion that there were in the 1780s essentially three foreign zones, Western Europe and North America, Eastern Europe and the rest of the world, as far as the British press was concerned, reflects a contrast with the situation earlier in the century when 'North Africa, Persia, the Ottoman Empire, Russia, and, to a certain extent, the Carpathian Principalities, provided news that was recognizably different in type from that of lands nearer to Britain'.[27] This was due to the more obvious westernisation of the states and élites of eastern Europe, especially Russia. There was no longer an element of the exotic and mysterious.

Clearly these suggestions reflect personal impressions. One of the great problems affecting the study of newspaper history is the absence of a methodology that is of value to the political historian. Statistical analysis, though exacting in its demands for resources, can shed light only on a few topics. It can serve for content analysis and is particularly value for a study of advertisements. However, at present it has not been used for qualitative content, especially comment. This is but part of the wider problem affecting work on the eighteenth-century British press. There is no agreement as to how its impact should be assessed, nor of the relationship between content, both by type and in the form of comment, and the views of readers. These problems make it difficult to know what should be made of what is one of the most impressive and readily accessible sources to survive from the period, a source moreover that is more extensive than the contemporary press of other European states. Even if circulation figures can be gauged and readerships guessed at, it is by no means clear that a reader of the *Morning Chronicle* or *The Times* was interested, let alone influenced, by the arguments advanced in the paper. This essay has relied upon impressions created by a thorough reading of the surviving papers from the period, but it does not pretend that other interpretations could not be advanced.

Assessment of the sources is clearly a central problem for those who work on literature and history. It is certainly a central concern for those who would seek to use the press. At a time when Burke, Paine and Wordsworth would probably be most cited as examples of contemporary British views on the

French Revolution and on eighteenth-century revolutions in general, it is worth remembering that they were not alone and that the press offers a vast quantity of readily available material. How it should be assessed and used, is, however, far from clear.

Notes

1. S. Lutnick, *The American Revolution and the British Press 1775–1783* (Columbia, Missouri, 1967).

2. D.B. Horn, *British Public Opinion and the First Partition of Poland* (Edinburgh, 1945); M. Schlenke, *England und das friderizianische Preussen 1740–1763* (Munich, 1963); G.C. Gibbs, 'Newspapers and Foreign Policy in the Age of Stanhope and Walpole', *Mélanges offerts à G. Jacquemyns* (Brussels, 1968); J. Black, 'The Press, Party and Foreign Policy in the Reign of George I', *Publishing History* 13 (1983), pp. 23–40; J. Black, *The English Press in the Eighteenth Century* (London, 1987), pp. 197–243.

3. J. Black, 'The Challenge of Autocracy: The British Press in the 1730s', *Studi Settecenteschi* 3–4 (1982–3), pp. 107–18.

4. Joseph Yorke, envoy at The Hague, to the Duke of Newcastle, Secretary of State for the Northern Department, 18 Jan., 19 Feb. 1754, London, Public Record Office, State Papers (hereafter PRO.) 84/466.

5. H.F. Schulte, *The Spanish Press 1470–1966. Print, Power and Politics* (London, 1968) pp 88–9; D. Coward, 'The Fortunes of a Newspaper: *The Nouvelles ecclésiastiques* (1728–1803)', *The British Journal for Eighteenth-Century Studies* 4 (1981), pp. 1–27; J.R. Censer and J.D. Popkin (eds.), *Press and Politics in Pre-Revolutionary France* (Berkeley, 1987).

6. Walpole to the Earl of Shelburne, 28 Sept. 1768, PRO. 78/27; Stephen Poyntz, envoy in Paris, to Charles Delafaye, Under-Secretary in the Southern Department, 10 Jan. 1730, PRO. 78/194; Delafaye to Earl Waldegrave, envoy in Paris, 18 Aug. (o.s.) 1732, Chewton Mendip, Chewton Hall, papers of James 1st Earl Waldegrave.

7. Breteuil, 'Réflexions . . .', edited by P.M. Conlon, *Studies on Voltaire* 1 (1955), pp. 125–31; D. Echeverria, *The Maupeou Revolution* (Baton Rouge, 1985), p. 23.

8. I.S. Asquith, 'James Perry and the *Morning Chronicle* 1790–1821', (unpublished Ph.D. thesis, London, 1973), pp. 18–19.

9. J.T. Alexander, *Autocratic Politics in a National Crisis* (Bloomington, Indiana, 1969), p. 183.

10. A. Aspinall, *Politics and the Press c.1780–1850* (London, 1949).

11. D. Read, 'Taking history on the turn', *The Times*, 31 Aug. 1987.

12. *Newcastle Courant*, 19 Jan. 1788.

13. *Newcastle Courant*, 31 May, 26 Ap. 1788.

14. *Leeds Mercury*, 11 Nov. 1788.

15. *Oracle*, 6 Aug. 1789.

16. *The Times*, 17, 22 July 1789.

17. *The Times*, 3 Aug. 1789.

18. *The Times*, 9 July 1790; *Leeds Intelligencer* 13 July 1790.

19. *The Times*, 4 Oct. 1790; *Public Advertiser*, 12 Nov. 1790; Anon., *A Letter from a Magistrate to Mr. William Rose, of Whitehall, on Mr. Paine's Rights of Men* [sic] (London, 1791), p. 7; *Newcastle Courant*, 5 Feb. 1791.

20. *The Times*, 25 Nov. 1790.

21. *The World*, 8 June 1791.
22. *The Times*, 18 July 1791.
23. *Leeds Intelligencer*, 24 May 1791; *Derby Mercury* 21 July 1791.
24. *London Chronicle*, 26 July 1791.
25. *Public Advertiser*, 10 Mar. 1792; *St James's Chronicle*, 1, 8 May 1792; *The Times*, 7 May 1792.
26. *St James's Chronicle*, 16 June 1792.
27. J. Black, 'The British Press and Europe in the Early Eighteenth Century' in M. Harris and A. Lee (eds.), *The Press in English Society from the Seventeenth to Nineteenth Centuries* (Cranbury, New Jersey, 1986), p. 71.

10

WRITING HISTORIES OF THE FRENCH REVOLUTION: ROMANTIC OR RATIONALIST

Noel Parker

This chapter illustrates a movement in the style and theoretical apparatus employed in French nineteenth-century histories of the Revolution. The first histories envisaged long-term rational benefits arising as if by accident from an *ir*rational content. But by situating the Revolution in a long-term historical process and by embracing wider conceptions of the principles that may guide comprehensible human action, histories moved towards an intuition (albeit flawed) that the Revolution expressed the dimly-felt purpose of the people as historical actors: rational self-liberation.

The first, 'rationalist' histories saw the motivation of the people as passion, which it was the business of government and culture to constrain, and the forces of the Revolution as destructive; though their destructive energy might be a necessary preliminary to later rational liberty. The developing romantic sensibility and idealist conceptual apparatus, however, reached out to embrace what is irrational in human motivation – notably in the deeds of the people – and what is distant in time. The high point of this development, Michelet, offered *rational* unity, justice and liberty as the people's unique underlying motivation. But in the very texture of his account, the actions of individual opponents of rational unity, etc. appear to possess a coherence lacking in the doings of its advocates.

Limited Rationality

Madame de Staël's *Considérations sur la Révolution française* (1818)[1] is not exactly a history, though it set an agenda for historical writing. It begins with a memoir of events in which de Staël's father, Necker, had been a leading participant, and ends with a lengthy section discussing the political system in England, and whether the French by comparison can be regarded as capable of freedom. Her affirmative answer is founded upon the hope that the cultural leadership of courageous people of good sense will prevail as it has at times in the past, rather than upon the expression of broad historical tendencies. In the consequent agenda, liberty could not have been achieved as the rational purpose of the Revolution. Collective action is irrational; and individual action has little scope in the liberty that has been achieved or will be achieved in the future.

De Staël's cautious optimism is rooted in a basically rationalist suspicion of the ability of the mass of humankind to escape from its passions and achieve a rational sense of liberty and justice. De Staël expressed this in her *De l'Influence des passions sur le bonheur des individus et des nations* of 1796, where human passions are presented as a 'stimulus which drives man independently of his will'. Because human beings are subject to passion, the state can neither regiment the people nor leave government in their hands. 'The sole problem of constitutions is, then, to what degree passions can be aroused or repressed without compromising public welfare.'[2] Though Mme de Staël managed greater optimism by 1818, the same structure of thought is in operation. The social order is at best an irrational product of rational skills and fortuitous circumstances, assisted by a noble, but unstable collective will. Her affectionate respect for the stirrings of national consciousness is balanced by caution: '14 July had greatness: the movement was national; a whole people aroused always holds true and natural feelings . . . there was still only good in the souls [of men], and the victors had not had time to be infected with boastful passions.'[3]

However, de Staël is surprisingly optimistic in believing that the fundamental irrationality of passion in society need not overwhelm political liberty. This is partly the fruit of a notion of liberty which, she can claim, has already existed in France for a long time. It follows that the eclipse of liberty is a recent phenomenon and may be a temporary one. For liberty in the sense of independence from the king, has, she argues, been pursued by various social strata, such as the nobility or the Church, throughout French history. Liberty had, then, already made real progress before 1789 (vol. 1, pt 1, ch. 2). Hence she is able to discuss at length 'Did France have a constitution before the Revolution?' (the title of chapter 11 of Part 1), arguing that liberty on the basis of that tradition might have been sustained if abuses of royal power had been brought to an end.

The idea of a traditional French constitution, the need to reform royal abuses and admiration for the English model had, of course, been prominent reforming currents in the late 1780s. They suggested a route to reform built upon and likely to preserve the position of some of the privileged elites. The tactical advantage of this position just after the restoration of the monarchy is evident: it allows advocacy of 'liberty' to be dissociated from loyalty to the 'revolutionary' regime. Thus de Staël claims, for the benefit of the newly restored nobility of France, that the knights of the past were not supporters of absolutism (vol. 3, pt 6, ch. 12, pp. 377ff.).

But there are more than merely tactical implications. The liberty from the monarchy that various groups were said to have sought cannot be the kind of thing that the revolutionaries themselves often had in mind: a society-wide, positive value guiding the nation and initiating a new historical start. It cannot be inserted into history in that way. For it is an absence of something, namely of power. Liberty exists more or less as the impact of the king or the state is limited by a diversity of factors – including insufficiencies in the potential centres of power. As the mere obverse of power, it cannot be the motor of history.

The major popular history of the 1820s and 1830s was that of Thiers, which began to appear in 1823. Thiers's style of historical thought and writing matches the shrewd, pragmatic politician that he in due course became. As a politician, he protected limited liberal, constitutional government, rather than democratic republicanism, and pursued an aggressive nationalist foreign policy.[4] This statement at the close of his enormous history nicely reflects his political values through his view of the Revolution:

> The Revolution, which was to give us liberty, and which prepared everything for us to have it one day . . . was to be a great struggle against the old order of things. . . . the new society would be consolidated in the shelter of its sword, and liberty could come one day. It has not come, it will come.[5]

Like de Staël, Thiers situates the Revolution in the longer term: here a long-term purpose which is yet to be realised. The assurance of political advance to come licenses in Thiers a tolerant view of events in the Revolution. He has spoken, he says, 'without hatred, pitying error, respecting virtue, admiring greatness, endeavouring to grasp the grand designs'.[6] But it is also a view that is rather sceptical of the power of human beings over events.

The structure and tone of the work mirror that agnosticism. The book consists mostly of detailed accounts of events in the political and military centres, put together with some care from records and recollections. Of itself, this tends to confine the motive force to the conscious, political centres, and emphasise the importance of the plane of relations with other states, possessing comparable centres of power – as against a relatively inarticulate mass of the people. Overlaying this narrative approach, the book is divided into periods for each different constitutional regime. But the long-term and the international planes are especially important because liberty will not be possible until the Europe-wide struggle against the past is complete. This was the justification for Thiers's aggressive foreign policy when he was in power. But it refers the reader implicitly to a realm of long-term historical necessity, where obstacles to liberal rationality in politics are destroyed *not* by rational action, but merely by the passage of time. In his conclusion, Thiers claims that by the time the Revolution and the revolutionary wars were over, the destruction of the old order both in France and in Europe had created the conditions for liberty at last. In this long-term realm, history works its destructive processes, opening the way to liberty by means of non-rational, unintentional action outside the control of the agents caught up in it. 'A chance combination of various circumstances brought the catastrophe, whose day could be postponed, but whose arrival sooner or later was inevitable.'[7] Given the realm of the irrational in history and the people, what, then, is the scope and nature of liberty for Thiers? The long-term historical movement is towards liberty; but within the Revolution, the people's secular passions have a threatening, irrational character. Rationality and intention are limited even when found in the centres of power and are not to be found in collective action at all.

Looking back over the work of de Staël and Thiers, one can see a definite movement governed by that opposition, identified first in de Staël, between passion and rationality. It reproduces the classical abstraction of liberty, by counterposing it to Nature and to the Public. The people are a more or less menacing breeding-ground of natural passion, and hence the enemy of conscious, rational freedom. Implicit in de Staël's view there is a causal plane beyond the Revolution and its chaos of passion. The idea is made more explicit in the work of Thiers. Counterposing the people and reason removes the content of the Revolution from history. In a real sense, it removes freedom from history, too. For freedom does not evolve within the history lived by those promoting liberty. The important movement of history, of which freedom will be a by-product, is largely displaced to a plane outside the Revolution. The public as an entity is not, as it was in the Revolution's own self-image, the conscious bearer of a universal value of freedom. The public is Nature; and Nature is opposed to rational progress towards freedom in history. Rationality is a virtue found in individuals, though sometimes it can be seen translated in a limited fashion into the public arena.

Romantics and Republicans: Thierry and Guizot

Two elements may be envisaged in order to move from the position of those historians who contrasted rationality with the public of the Revolution and to make liberty a more feasible goal of action by historical agents: a new attitude to those things which are not rational (one thinks of religious belief, private emotion and ideology); and a more fully worked-out account of those long trends that lead up to the Revolution. Both can be found in the nascent romantic taste for diversity in history, as it emerged in the first decades of the nineteenth century.

In different ways, Thierry and Guizot, the next historians I wish to consider, provided the conceptual apparatus, and the style and sensibility to encompass the Revolution in a more fully worked-out long-term evolution than de Staël had offered. Both gave accounts of French history which traced an early development of liberty in France from the fall of Rome. Thus, they situated the Revolution towards the end of a long-standing causal sequence, embracing the events of the Revolution itself, which was bound to lead to the realisation of liberty in due course. In different ways, they (like de Staël) postulated the suppression of liberty by royal government. But they interpreted the Revolution as the *revival*, by the provincial bourgeoisie of the Third Estate, of that liberty which de Staël had imagined. In the context of the restored monarchy, this was clearly a thesis of some political force. Yet, it was also a matter of sensibility – of the way history could be viewed and felt about – as well as a matter of explanatory concepts. Though Guizot was the more theoretically sophisticated, both Thierry and he made the past and its pains seem more attractive and more purposeful.

If a writer was to put flesh on the liberty that returned in a longer time-scale via the Revolution, it required a definite affection for the forgotten components of French history, and a certain vision capable of embracing the

diversity of a long history in a broad, coherent sequence. The necessary confi-
dent, visionary interest and affection for diversity which, I have suggested,
may be found in romanticism were most evidently present in Augustin
Thierry. In 1817 Thierry began publishing what was to become his *Lettres
sur l'histoire de France*,[8] re-assessing the writing of French history, calling for
a new vision and reshaping the overall view. He continued in over forty years
as an historian and journalist to mine an evocation of the lives and activities
of France's long-dead forebears. He aimed, he said, to '. . . penetrate to the
hearts of men across the distance of the centuries . . . represent them living
and acting . . . . They have been dead for . . . hundreds of years, . . . but what
does that matter to the imagination?'.[9]

Thierry's thesis in the *Lettres* casts the idea of a long-term evolution neatly
into romantic views and preferences. For he attributes the suppressed tradition of liberty to an exotic racial diversity such as attracted the romantic taste;
and he presents its suppression as the dead hand of uniformity imposed by
absolutism. The heroes of the struggle of the French people for justice and
liberty as Thierry describes them are humble people full of 'patriotism and
energy' (p. 18), doubly disregarded in that to date even the historians have
passed over them. By arguing that the historian should by the nature of his
trade be looking rather for diversity than uniformity (pp. 32–3), Thierry then
nails the historian's duty to the romantic drift of his historical investigation.

According to Thierry, the Frankish invaders of Gaul began a long tradition of oppression from Paris (Letters II, VI and VII). But by the time
it happened, the suppression of the remaining local autonomy was, like
the Revolution itself, a blessing. For its slow decline had shown the need
for a national constitution instead (p. 413). The Revolution emerges from
Thierry's long historical story, therefore, as the necessity pursued by 'opinion and the public will' at the moment 'when the mass of the nation felt the
hollowness . . . of restoring ancient rights'.[10]

Thierry's deployment of romantic colour to evoke the living nature of the
French in the past effects a remarkable combination of a sense of participation
in the reader and a sense of the long causal necessity guiding history. For the
complex of strands that motivate the longer history consists of elements in
the identity of the French reader. As well as constituting the substance of
a long-term causal process, the slow fusion of racially peculiar culture and
manners, lovingly described, goes to make up the modern nations. Yet this
racial inheritance, like inherited family resemblances, can appear as their free
property to its contemporary bearers. It can, for example, be counterposed
to climatic givens in the manner of Montesquieu.[11] Accordingly, 1789 is at
one and the same time a reliable necessity, which was inevitable and its effects of which cannot be long reversed by reaction, and a *free* act expressing
something which belongs to Thierry's intended reader. Hence, the tone of
Thierry's closing remarks:

> . . . and thus there came about that immense gathering of men, possessing civil
> liberty but lacking political rights, which undertook in 1789, for the sake of France
> as a whole, what their ancestors had done in simple towns in the Middle Ages. We
> who still look upon it, that society for modern times, struggling with the debris

of the past, of conquest, of feudal obligations and absolute royalty, let us not worry ourselves for it. . . . it has conquered all the powers that have been vainly recalled.[12]

An imaginative identification after the manner of Romanticism adds a sense of involvement to the reassurance in the inevitable long-term historical process.

Though a much more austere and intellectual figure, Thierry's friend Guizot was performing a similar reorientation of attitude and of overarching causal structure in writing his history. He, too, attributed vigour and nascent political liberty to the bourgeoisie of medieval France, and, hence, regarded 1789 as the *revival*, in a new form, of the earlier spirit and precedent of civic freedom. In Guizot's case, the topic of the long-term course of history and his two enormously successful series of public lectures as professor of history at the Sorbonne[13] was the growth and evolution of 'civilisation'. Guizot's concept of civilisation has a romantic tinge. Running in parallel with Thierry's romantic predisposition, Guizot held that diversity was the source of progress in civilisation.[14] However, his major theoretical sources were, via French intermediaries, German idealist thinkers,[15] from whom he learnt the idea that the different manners constituting civilisation in different places and times (what he calls its 'moral state') might be versions of underlying forms – resembling Kantian categories – within the social character of human beings.

Guizot's account of the main flow of French history resembles Thierry's to a degree: a rich diversity unites to form feudal society following the fall of Rome, generates first the feudal system and then the political liberties of the towns which are suppressed by the monarchy but revived in 1789. On the other hand, the historical currents Guizot identifies entwined in French history are of a different character. The role of racial heritage is taken over by the state of the law, culture, social relations and private attitudes, all drawn out from legal records and other documents. By analysis and comparison Guizot attempts to establish speculatively how principles and practices of civilisation were articulated in the reality of social life. The result is a historical critique to show how commune society was already decadent by the fourteenth century (vol. IV, Lesson 19), and how the moral state left by the suppression of feudalism in 1789 could not sustain and govern the social order. Therein lay the source of the difficulties of the Revolution.

In fact, the very notion of civilisation, with which Guizot binds his long-term causal structure, implies that society cannot survive if it neglects people's internal feelings. For civilisation, as Guizot's own approach to examining it had implied, is a fusion of external with internal. 'Civilisation consists in essence of two things: the development of the social and the intellectual condition; the development of the exterior and general, and of the internal and personal nature of man; in a word, the perfection of society and of humanity.'[16]

But by the time of the Enlightenment, civilisation in Europe had, in Guizot's view, got out of phase with itself. Though less in France than elsewhere, the different elements that were needed had grown out of proportion. History as Guizot was writing it had; then, a particular role to play in generating the understanding necessary for civilisation to get back on the rails. On the one hand, it brought fact and principle together by showing how the broad elements of the moral state of a society were articulated. On the other hand, by taking a renewed interest in the Middle Ages, it may allow us to 'understand the role that the imagination plays in the life of man and of society' (vol. III, Lesson 1, p. 235).

Guizot, like Thierry, offers not only a particular interpretation of the past but also an attitude to it which facilitates participation in completing the aims of the long-term causality he identifies. The more sophisticated conceptual apparatus he deploys incorporates an idealist, even a Hegelian idea of a world in which history is made by the interaction of human agency and human thought with objective given.

> We are thrown into a world that we have neither created nor invented; we find it, we look upon it; we study it; we have no choice but to take it as a fact. . . . As agents, we do otherwise: when we have observed external facts, knowing them generates in us ideas of something better; we feel duty-bound to reform, to perfect, to regulate what there is; we feel able to act upon the world, to extend the glorious empire of reason. That is the mission of humankind . . .[17]

Guizot's causal structure for civilisation implies how the past, with its diversity and its setbacks, had to reach the point it did. But, by interlocking conscious change within the imagination and thought of both individuals and societies, he encouraged his readers to complete consciously the direction he found in the long historical roots of the Revolution. Such change would, as he says, contribute to the 'permanent, regular, peaceful character of the social condition that is being established and appearing on all sides,' founded on 'convictions common to all'.[18] Guizot's manner of understanding history is not, therefore, merely intended to describe the deep-rooted reasons for the course of the Revolution, but also to advance the free, conscious realisation of its aims.

Michelet

Michelet, the last historian I want to consider, addresses explicitly the issue of how to represent the nation *to itself*, both for political reasons and for reasons of historical accuracy. Michelet applied an idealist perspective and a romantic sensibility to the representation of national unity both to be extrapolated from historical sources and to be felt by writer and by readership. This underlying unity would both account for the past and help to constitute the people. Yet it was intended to do so in such a fashion as to leave them capable of seizing hold of their own identity and exercising their own freedom.

This task calls for personal sentiment as well as scholarly technique. To advance beyond the conventional historians, Michelet writes, one must consult the heart: in history 'Thierry saw a *narration* and Monsieur Guizot *an analysis*. I have called it *resurrection*.'[19] To interpret historical events is, for Michelet, to lay out the principles running through the diverse currents in the past. He narrates and analyses, just like Thierry and Guizot, using the same sources. But, in writing his own history he himself brings a still more romantic empathy into play. Though he finds much that was wrong in romanticism as such, Michelet openly supplements Thierry's and Guizot's technical procedure with an emotional reconstruction of the sentiments that motivate ordinary people past and present. He made no secret of the positively intimate relationship which he sought with France.

Yet the human sentiments that Michelet uncovers at play in history by means of this romantic approach express *rational* values, in the sense that history for him is a realm in which humans freely *develop themselves* from out of Nature. He took up Vico's phrase, 'Humanity is its own Prometheus'.[20] Where humanity self-consciously executes principles that it has itself invented and validated, it reaches the pinnacle of human evolution: rational freedom realised in history. Michelet therefore opposes those theories of human unsociability which in fact underpin the liberal fear of popular passion and disorder. He advocates instead a more 'Aristotelian' view in which society is harmonised by the mutual *affection* of diverse individuals and groups: the nation is 'the great friendship', and the people can possess the necessary combination of instinct and reflection.[21]

His *Histoire de la Revolution Française*[22] is constructed around the key moments of the Revolution – the Bastille, the invasions of the legislature, the flight to Varennes and so forth. But the build-up to each moment emphasises the *principles* that are going to be at play when the climax is reached. For those moments which Michelet finds most important, it is the Republic, the people itself, that pursues *its own* principle of action.

So, before he begins the history proper, Michelet 'defines' the Revolution (Intro. S1, p. 20). The Revolution is: 'The advent of Law, the ressurrection of Right, and the reaction of Justice' (Intro. S1, p. 17). The key principle of the monarchy is Grace: the dependence of man, the purported author of evil, upon an arbitrary higher power for salvation and for whatever is good. The justice created by man for man is fundamentally opposed to this view. Under the old monarchy, men were divided from each other instead of united by justice and mutual love (Intro. Part 2, SS3 and 9). The Revolution, on the other hand, 'founds fraternity on the love of man for man, on mutual duty – on Right and Justice. This base is fundamental, and no other is necessary. (Intro. Part 1, S2, p. 22). The principle operating in the Revolution equates justice with collective unity and freedom in action. Michelet then goes on to introduce particular moments in the history as instances of conflicting principles subsidiary to the battle between Grace and Justice.

In the interplay of these principles, the people hold a peculiar position. For the emerging principle of Justice is that of the people's own self-organisation. So, even though they are too ill-educated to be able consciously to spell out or practise their own principle, they display, according to Michelet, a compensating ability to sense on their own initiative what is right and necessary. And once they have sensed what is right in terms of justice, the people are able to *create* it. For justice consists precisely in the self-organisation which may create an active, self-conscious community out of a merely intuitive unit. Acts by the people are, therefore, able to transcend the creative limitations felt by other actors. 'The attack on the Bastille was by no means reasonable. It was an act of faith.' (Bk 1, ch. 7, p. 162.)

In Michelet's view, if they act autonomously, the people follow their own inherent principle. For only a nation creates itself by the principle of independent self-regulation, that is Sovereign Justice. For Michelet, therefore, 'the essential basis of history is in the thinking of the people. Without doubt the republic was floating in this thinking'.(Vol. 3, Bk 5, ch. 4, p. 69.) The storming of the Bastille was not promoted by orators or electors, then; it was carried out by those 'who had also the devotion and the strength to accomplish their faith. Who? Why, the people – everybody' (Bk 1, ch. 7). The participants sensed the direction of the conflicting principles of past and future, and intuitively pursued their own logic.

On the other hand, the situation of individuals, given this way of identifying the historical agent, shows the point of breakdown in Michelet's manner of accounting for the Revolution. They become either the spokespersons or the bearers of the evolving, conflicting principles of motivation. Yet, almost without exception, individuals in Michelet's account do not manage to embody motivations happily and successfully. On the other hand, if it is hard to be successful and well-intentioned, it seems easy to be a successful, ill-intentioned conspirator. With those who are *against* the Revolution, one always seems to find a terrible coherence of action compared with the benighted individuals on the side of right. Take the Church, for example: 'This was clear, simple and vigorous; the clerical party knew very well what they wanted. The Assembly knew it not.' Bk 3, ch. 9, p. 415.)

It appears that in Michelet's writing, coherence and fixity of purpose are confined to inspired action of the people, and the pursuit of evil. For Michelet, history is fundamentally motivated by the spiritual growth of the principles of the people's action. But the people's principles have to be intuited, whereas those of their *opponents* do not. The deeds of narrowly self-interested actors are understandable precisely because they are narrow and self-interested, related to a clearly identifiable focus, the specific individual and his advantage. The deeds that transcend that level and serve the higher order of the sovereign people have no such specifiable focus. But once principles are specified in identified individuals, they become limited by the specific social structure in which those individuals move and circumscribed by the interests of those individuals: hence something less than the self-creating unity of the people as a totality. The union of rationality and freedom, of nature and history can only be maintained so long as the will that miraculously combines these contradictions is not specified.

Conclusion

The 'republican' historians I have considered sought to construct histories of the Revolution in which the public held a central role in the action – as it had done in principle for the revolutionaries themselves. The injection of idealism into their view of social reality and of romantic taste into their interests enabled them to pay attention to the people in a new way, portraying anonymous, 'irrational' masses as historical actors. They did this by identifying the historical actors *through* ideal entities of which they or their actions were instances: race, legal or institutional forms, social organisation and mores peculiar to their culture, shared emotions, higher principles motivating their deeds. These elements extended the range of the historians' chronology, and broadened their subject matter with a larger range of historical actors. Hence, they moved progressively away from the juxtaposition that opposed reason to the people-public, which had characterised the earlier histories. Reason, passion and the people came to be conceived of together in a historical movement such as the Revolution.

Notes

1. All references are to volumes, parts and pages of the 2nd edition, Paris, 1818.
2. 'Le seul problème des constitutions est donc de connaître jusqu'à quel degré on peut exciter ou comprimer les passions, sans compromettre le bonheur public.' (*De l'Influence des passions etc*, introduction, quoted in *Madame de Staël: Choix de textes*, ed. G. Solovieff (Paris, Klinksieck 1974), pp. 197–9.
3. '. . . la journée du 14 juillet avait de la grandeur: le mouvement était national; . . . l'émotion de tout un peuple tient toujours à des sentiments vrais et naturels . . . il n'y avait encore que de bon dans les âmes, et les vainqueurs n'avaient pas eu le temps de contracter les passions orgueilleuses . . .' (vol. 1, pt 1, ch. 22, p 241).
4. J.P.T. Bury and R.P. Tombs *Thiers: 1797–1877: a Political Life* (London, Allen and Unwin, 1986)
5. 'La Révolution, qui devait nous donner la liberté, et qui a tout préparé pour que nous l'avons un jour . . . devait être une grande lutte contre l'ancien ordre des choses . . . la nouvelle société allait se consolider à l'abri de son épée, et la liberté devait venir un jour. Elle n'est pas venue, elle viendra'. (A. Thiers, *Histoire de la Révolution française* (22nd edn., Brussels, 1844), vol. 2, ch. 33, pp. 585–6)
6. 'sans haine, plaignant l'erreur, révérant la vertu, admirant la grandeur, tâchant de saisir les grands desseins.' (ibid.).
7. 'un concours fortuit de diverses circonstances amèneront la catastrophe, dont l'époque pouvait être différée, mais dont l'accomplissement était tôt ou tard infaillible.' (vol. 1, ch. 1, p. 14)
8. Published in book form, 1820–27. References are to the edition of 1935, (Paris, Garnier).
9. '. . . pénétrer jusqu'aux hommes à travers la distance des siècles; il faut se les représenter vivants et agissants . . . Il y a sept cents ans que ces hommes sont morts, . . . mais qu'importe à l'imagination?' (*Histoire de la conquête de l'Angleterre par les Normands* (Paris, 1825), quoted in Pierre Moreau *Le Romantisme* (Paris, Gigard, 1932), p. 137
10. 'ce travail nouveau de l'opinion et de la volonté publique. . . . la masse nationale eût senti à fond le néant pour elle d'une restauration de droits historiques.' (*Essais sur l'histoire du Tiers Etat* (1850) (Paris, Furne Jouvet, 1866), p. 259.)
11. 'La constitution physique et morale des peuples dépend bien plus de leur descendance et de la race primitive à laquelle ils appartiennent que de l'influence du climat sous lequel le hasard les a placés.' (1824); quoted in P. Moreau, op. cit., p. 146.
12. '. . . et ainsi se trouva formée cette immense réunion d'hommes civilement libres, mais sans droits politiques, qui en 1789 entreprit, pour la France entière, ce

qu'avaient exécuté, dans de simples villes, ses ancêtres du moyen âge. Nous qui la voyons encore, cette société des temps modernes, en lutte avec les débris du passé, débris de conquête, de seigneurie féodale et de royauté absolue, soyons sans inquiétude sur elle. . . . elle a vaincu toutes les puissances dont on évoque en vain les ombres.' (*Lettres*, p. 431.)

13. Delivered in 1828–30 and published as *Histoire de la civilisation en Europe* (Paris, 1828) and *Histoire de la civilisation en France* (Paris, 1829–32; references in my text are to the Paris, Didier edition of 1843).

14. See Douglas Johnson, *Guizot: Aspects of French History* (London, Routledge & Kegan Paul, Toronto, University of Toronto Press, 1963) pp. 337–40.

15. See ibid. p. 334.

16. 'La civilisation consiste essentiellement dans deux faits: le développement de l'état social, et celui de l'état intellectuel; le développement de la condition extérieure et générale; et celui de la nature intérieure et personnelle de l'homme; en un mot, le perfectionnement de la société et de l'humanité.' (vol. I, Lesson 1, p. 6).

17. 'Nous sommes jetés dans un monde que nous n'avons point créé ni inventé; nous le trouvons, nous le regardons; nous l'étudions: if faut bien que nous le prenions comme un fait. . . . Comme acteurs, nous faisons autre chose: quand nous avons observé les faits extérieurs, leur connaissance développe en nous des idées qui leur sont supérieures; nous nous sentons appelés à réformer, à perfectionner, à régler ce qui est; nous nous sentons capables d'agir sur le monde, d'y étendre le glorieux empire de la raison. C'est là la mission de l'homme . . .' (vol. I, pp. 25–7).

18. '. . . le caractère permanent, regulier, paisible, de l'état social qui se fonde et s'annonce de toutes parts' (vol. I, Lesson 1, p. 23).

19. *Le Peuple* ed. P. Viallaneix (Paris, Flammarion, 1974) p. 73.

20. 1868 Introduction, p. 150. See also Pugh, op. cit. pp. 69–72.

21. *Le Peuple*, pp. 19–205 and 147.

22. First published 1847–53. References in my text give volume, part and chapter with page numbers from the Flammarion Edition, Paris, no date in the case of the French text, or the translation by C. Cocks, ed. G. Wright (University of Chicago, 1967).

11

RUSSIAN REVOLUTIONARY CULTURE: ITS PLACE IN THE HISTORY OF CULTURAL REVOLUTIONS

Richard Stites

I pose a very simple but important question in this chapter: what was new or unique in the culture-changing movements that accompanied the Russian Revolution? By 'new' I mean: how different were they, if at all, from those of previous great social and ideological revolutions (especially the English and the French)? Since my focus is on culture-building or culture-changing movements – which I will explain presently – a few remarks about high culture are in order here if only by way of contrast.

The neoclassical rejection of the art of Watteau and Fragonard and 'republican' drama's displacement of eighteenth-century theatrical styles in the French Revolution, for example, were hardly more violent than similar generational revolts created in non-revolutionary times by the very dynamics of the art history. Furthermore, after the restoration in France, all historical periods were given due respect. In Russia, the great avant-garde movement in the arts and literature began a decade or so before the Revolution and, with only minimal friction, flowed into it. Some figures emigrated; some were drafted into the work of revolutionary adornment; others joined with great enthusiasm. But after a decade of experimentation, this movement gave way – via orders from above and pressure from below – to a more conservative cultural configuration. This was not a restoration in the French sense – one that would have allowed free flourishing of all styles; it was rather a peculiar system of ideological and aesthetic controls which has characterised the life of art and letters from Stalin's time until the very recent past.

I wish to deal here with culture in the broad, anthropological sense. The Revolution was intent not only on adjusting *belles-lettres*, theatre, music, and the fine arts to its needs; it wanted to change the culture of the Russian people – their sense of self, their myths and symbols, their beliefs and rituals, their style of work and of life. This must be held up against the mirror of the past, especially the French revolutionary experience, in order to make some meaningful comparisons. A big part of the massive effort at cultural innovation was of course education, literacy campaigns, and propaganda; but since these have been studied in some depth, I will not dwell upon them.[1] I will try to show that in the realm of festival, symbol, myth, ritual, and egalitarianism, the Russian Revolution bears marked similarities to those of the past. This was, I think, inevitable in that the Russian events were preceded by over a hundred years of self-conscious revolutionary tradition, much of it inspired by French radical forms (real or imagined); and in that the Bolsheviks were themselves a Europeanised elite, many of whom had dwelt psychologically and physically in the capitals of Western Europe. Beyond this lay what seems to be a deeply-felt need in any large-scale revolution for self-asserting statements of identity through emphasised novelty.

The Reordering and Adornment of Revolutionary Space

A common feature of great revolutions is the occupation and reordering of space and the artifacts and structures that repose upon it. Vandalism, a word coined during the French Revolution, loomed up menacingly in the Russian Revolution. *Jacqueries* of all sorts had studded Russian agrarian history from early modern times, but nothing on the scale of what arose in 1917 and 1918: hundreds, perhaps thousands, of manor houses put to the torch, the deliberate destruction of what the peasants saw as alien luxury items – books, musical instruments, *objets d'art*, bedding, furniture, tapestries, windows, porcelain, sheet music – anything that smacked of elite culture and all emblems of inequality and remembered oppression. The peasantry cleared the land of unwanted people – landowners, teachers, officials – and thus liberated the space around them of foreign elements. The houses were rarely occupied; they were burned or left to rot. When peasants destroyed signs of any sort, they never erected new ones to replace them. When the Soviet regime finally made its presence felt in the countryside, it planted its symbols of culture and authority in every village. Bolshevik cultural stations were islands of signs in a signless world.[2]

In cities, the desolation possessed a consciously symbolic character. The erasing of wicked remainders seems to be an unavoidable feature in revolutionary cities. The French announced their hatred of the arrogance and the power-imagery of the *ancien régime* monuments as they dismantled them. The urban space had to be desacralised and purged of the memory of the despicable Capets. In Russia, 'deromanovisation' was invoked to describe the process of removing graven and sculpted images of tsars and generals of the old order, imperial regalia and emblems, edifices, and names. The pictures and emblems presented no problem: they were both odious and dispensable. The statues, however, were heavy bronze ensembles encased in concrete pedestals and very hard to pull down rapidly. During parades, statues still up had to be covered with cloths (as had been that of Louis XV in the 1790s). Another obstacle to iconoclasm were the preservers who thought that some monuments possessed artistic value. Some buildings, especially jails, had been stormed and gutted in the first days of the February Revolution. The Schlüsselburg Fortress – called the Russian Bastille – was the best known example. But authorities in both revolutionary regimes of 1917, the Provisional Government, March to October, and the Bolsheviks after October, stepped in to save buildings on grounds at once historical, aesthetic and utilitarian.[3]

In both great cultural revolutions, art itself fell under the scrutiny of republican virtue or proletarian sensibility. An anti-art movement in Paris linked all of the cultural production of the *ancien régime* to the poisonous social miasma of privilege and effete indolence. In the Russian Revolution, the nihilistic critique was launched by two movements: an artistic avant-garde determined to outlaw all previous art, to cast out the 'museum junk' (the term is Vladimir Mayakovsky's) of the past to make way for a Futurist culture of machines, energy, metal, and speed; and a Proletarian Culture movement, nominally composed of workers but led by proletaroid intellectuals in blue shirts, also exalting the machine but insisting on its own exclusive monopoly in building a new culture.[4]

Vandalism, iconoclasm, and cultural nihilism threatened to annihilate the entire past of a great civilisation. But from the very outset, the Bolshevik authorities led by Lenin at the political centre and by Anatoly Lunacharsky as Commissar of Enlightenment, fought against vandalism, curbed iconoclasm by selective preservation, and wrested cultural hegemony from the hands of the Futurists and the Proletcult. Exactly as in the French Revolution, preservation teams were sent into the countryside to collect and protect valuables; buildings were locked and guarded; and museums were established to display the treasures of the past both as the creation of a great people and as shameful relics of injustice. Bolsheviks echoed the sentiments of the French revolutionaries who asserted that an 'enlightened' revolution should preserve the arts of the past and exhibit them in museums.[5]

Names are an intimate part of culture. Revolutionaries feel compelled to rename things and places – not only political institutions or administrative units (including the nation itself), but also the space they have occupied and desacralised – streets, squares, and buildings. Nowhere is the depth of a cultural revolution better revealed than as in what Crane Brinton called 'the little things'. Even before the Russian Revolution, wartime anti-German sentiment had led to the renaming of the capital from St Petersburg to Petrograd. After 1917, Soviet Russia became studded with towns like Stalingrad, Leningrad, Trotsk, Zinovievsk, and Kalinin. Streets, squares, and cinemas were baptised as Revolution, Insurrection, or Barricade. 'October' and 'Red' were two of the favourite adjectives employed in this way. Sometimes linguistic common sense won out and the Avenue of the Twenty-Fifth of October (the date of the Bolshevik takeover) had to revert to is old familiar name – Nevsky Prospect.[6]

Revolutionised space became the natural venue for the festivities that always attend major social upheavals. Russian festival style incorporated traditions of the church processions and dynastic ritual – now properly secularised and democratised; of the military parade; and of the protest march and demonstration. The last, with its radical songs and red banners, predominated. After the fall of the Tsar, 'revolutionary days' – clearly invoking the *journées* of 1789 – erupted spontaneously in many cities: victory parades of workers and soldiers, joyful celebrations of kinglessness, and solemn funeral rites for the martyrs of the street fighting. When the Bolsheviks came to power, they codified the celebratory process. Lunacharsky, as the equivalent to a minister of culture, was the key figure in Bolshevik festival – analogous in the way to Jacques-Louis David, the pageant-master and artistic impressario of the French Revolution. The Russian possessed a loftier title than had David, but the latter possessed almost undiminished authority in his realm whereas Lenin often dictated to Lunacharsky. David also enjoyed a major reputation as an artist of the first rank whereas Lunacharsky, though immensely learned, was at best a mediocre dramatist. Most interesting of all, David drew directly and unambiguously from the ancient culture of Greece and Rome, whereas Lunacharsky was surrounded by competing aesthetic systems and styles.[7]

There were two other striking contrasts in the cultural-festive styles of France and Russia. In Russia, public executions mounted as theatrical and educational events played no role: and the Russian ambiguity about the 'real capital' produced a divergence of styles. Moscow, the official Bolshevik capital from 1918 onward, was the site of Lenin's 'monumental propaganda' scheme which replaced the old statues with those of revolutionary heroes – Russian and European. Almost one hundred such monuments were planned (and about half of them realised), including such figures from the European revolutionary tradition as Voltaire, Rousseau, Danton, Robespierre, Marat, Babeuf, and an array of French utopian socialists.[8]

In Petrograd, the old capital (where Lunacharsky remained for a time), a different genre of festival developed, very much influenced and dominated by the artistic and theatrical community who also remained there: outdoor theatre. These were extravagant spectacles with casts of hundreds and audiences of thousands, mounted hundreds of times in this magnificent city, criss-crossed by rivers and canals and adorned by spacious squares. Like David's Parisian outdoor shows, they were carefully deployed according to elaborate scenarios, featuring multiple orchestras, military personnel as actors, searchlights, fireworks, and a generally carnival atmosphere. Their content was the historical mythology of the revolution, legitimised by a genealogy that tied the Bolshevik Revolution to revolutions of the past, vividly illustrated by the playing of Henry Litolphe's *Robespierre Overture*, waves of *sansculottes* storming the gates of the forbidden land of freedom, and the execution of the Paris communards of 1871, with a kind of *translatio revolutiae* effected when an actor spirited away the fallen red banner of the Paris commune to Russia.[9]

The revolutionary renaming, the monuments, and the spectacles thus served to establish for the October Revolution a two-line family tree: a native one arising from the great peasant upheavals through the revolutionary tradition; the other stretching from Spartacus through the early modern revolutions and through the fathers of European Marxism up to the momentous present. It was a visual, plastic, and kinetic rewriting of Russian history, denying virtue or legitimacy to all previous regimes and graphically asserting a new identity for the new state. It was, in many ways, reminiscent of a large-scale attempt at religious conversion.

Symbolic and Ritual Reordering

Since the hastily built plaster statues soon crumbled and the outdoor theatricals were abandoned after the Civil War, the process of image-making and myth-making had to be deepened and made permanent. Two realms of culture-building helped to provide this: new symbols of community; and invented rituals. The importance in the French Revolution of the Tricoleur, the Marseillaise, and Marianne are well known – and they resonated through French politics at least up to 1945.[10] Their Bolshevik equivalents have remained in place and largely unchallenged (except during the Civil War and the Second World War) ever since. After the disappearance of the monarchy, the Provisional Government blandly adopted the two-headed eagle of the Romanovs – tamed and de-imperialised – and took as its anthem the 'Marseillaise' which was both that of its ally in the war and, in adapted form, a Russian workers' song. It also retained the old flag of Peter the Great – a tricolour.

The Bolsheviks were determined to innovate completely in the symbolic sphere and they mounted a contest soon after their revolution for new symbols. The winner was a crossed hammer and sickle over a looming sword. Lenin had the sword removed and the new design, representing the workers and peasants, became the national emblem, seal, and coat of arms as well as the main ornament of the new red flag – another product of European radical traditions. The red star – inspiration unknown – was taken as the insignia of the Red Army. Lenin disliked the 'Marseillaise' because of its association with bourgeois belligerents and insisted on the 'Internationale', the rallying song of European social democracy. The Kremlin bells were tuned to its melody and it was sung ceaselessly at every revolutionary occasion. It remained the Soviet national hymn until the time of Stalin who preferred something more distinctively Russian.[11]

The Bolshevik war against religion was deeper and more thoroughgoing than the French dechristianisation movement. The Bolsheviks attacked all religions and the very notion of God itself. In doing so, they rearranged the calendar, as had the French republicans, and fought against any kind of public religious ceremony, including feast days and ecclesiastical baptism, wedding, and funeral services. What did they offer to replace them? During the 1920s, a number of Red rituals emerged designed to provide the joy and solemnity of religious rituals but without clerical or theological associations. Workers' clubs mounted politicised ceremonies, with speeches, the adornment of red bunting, and theatricalised assaults against religion, superstition, poor work habits, folk medicine, and unsanitary customs. But these lacked the drama, the art, the depth, and the emotionalism of the magnificent Orthodox rituals they were trying to displace. Counterfeasts were also invented to parallel and compete with the old Church holidays, a form of social mimicry in which Electric Day coincided with Elijah Day (the feast of St Ilya). On these days, young people trumpeted the virtues of cleanliness, energy, and electric power as new objects of reverence.[12]

On the more intimate level of family cycle ritual, the Bolsheviks introduced revolutionary modes of baptism, wedding ceremony, and funeral. 'Octobering' was a secular service for newborn babies and their parents where the child was dedicated to the building of communism by a Party official in the presence of fellow workers. To deepen the act, 'revolutionary' names were given to the infants in order to ward off the Orthodox associations of traditional saints' names. Giving names (or adaptations of names) of revolutionary heroes such as Spartak (Spartacus), Marks (Marx), Rosa (as in Luxemburg), Mara (Marat), Robesper (Robespierre), Stalina, or Vladlen was a custom that predated the Russian Revolution in the european socialist movement. But this repertoire was rather limited. Since the Russians eschewed the French revolutionary practice of going back to Rome and Greece for babies' names, they exalted the lexicon of revolution itself with such names as Barricade, Guillotine, Bastille, Commune, Proletarian, October, Sickle, Freedom, Dynamite, Atheist, and Marseillaise, with a nod also to the technological ethos of Bolshevism in the names Textile, Dynamo, Industry, Tractor, and Electrification.[13]

Since women were equal by law in the new Soviet state, the wedding ceremony was made to reflect that announced equality. The couple were treated identically, the wife was allowed to retain her maiden name, and the 'Red wedding' itself was hardly more than a club event, like Octobering, with ample yardage of red cloth, songs, and speeches. The reorientation of funerals caused more problems. Bolshevik heroes were put to rest amid great ritual splendour and public attendance: Lenin's interment in a mausoleum was a landmark in the cult of worship of his immortal memory. But ordinary people received no such funereal magnificence. The secular funerals were politicised, arid, unemotional and thus unsatisfying to a people accustomed to lavish lamentation, religious feeling freely exhibited, and the food and drink that went with it.[14]

For some Bolsheviks, the ritual movement of the 1920s was a way of turning Bolshevism into a religion without god, a surrogate spiritual system based on martyrology, political dedication, and a commitment to 'modern' consciousness. But these were few in number and not very influential. The Bolshevik movement itself, though bathed in revolutionary emotionalism, was hostile to anything that smacked of religion; and its revered leader, Lenin, despised what was called 'God-building' or the construction of a socialist religion. Nor did the masses in Russia take fondly to the new-fangled invented rituals. They flourished mainly among the urban, politically conscious working class, but declined and were discounted after Stalin came to power.

Egalité and Levelling

Both the Puritan Revolution and the French Revolution offered certain central concepts of equality whose limitations were vividly displayed when the revolutionary 'left' – the Levellers and the conspiracy of Babeuf rose up to broaden that concept. This fact, among others, led the Bolsheviks rather patronisingly to label these revolutions 'bourgeois.' But the Bolshevik Revolution produced its own tension between the preachers of egalitarianism and the practitioners of equality in everyday life. Levelling took many forms in the Russian Revolution – division of the land, confiscation of valuables, the redistribution of living space, and the refashioning of attitudes in dress, language and deferential gesture. The dispossession of the propertied classes – landowners, capitalists, clergy, urban landlords – and the reassortment of wealth, land, and property were the most dramatic and best known aspects of the egalitarian policies of that revolution. There can be no question that their impulse was as popular as it was officially inspired. The peasants rose immediately to take all of the land away from their gentry neighbours and distribute it equitably according to peasant custom. Workers seized factory assets and divided up funds among themselves in equal portions. People and regime combined in Soviet towns to relocate affluent occupiers of huge flats into one room to make space for incoming workers.

The fight against deference and deeply-rooted outward signs and postures of inequality had been less studied – and is known chiefly from the lamentation of the dispossessed émigrés, later popularised in Western movies such as *Tovarich, Ninotchka,* and *Dr Zhivago.* Ranks, titles, classes and estates were immediately abolished and the Russian equivalents of aristos were persecuted. Symbolic retribution and angry spite accompanied the expropriation of the expropriators. But there was a positive, culture-building side to levelling as well. Language and personal appearance were the two main vehicles for this. Some posed a global solution to human communication by suggesting Esperanto as the language of the Revolution and then of all mankind. But in the practical world of everyday Russian speech there was plenty of innovation. Along with grandiose titles, certain words were abolished: Mr and Mrs were replaced by 'citizen' among the populace and by 'comrade' (*tovarishch*) among Communist Party members. Humiliating gestures and speech styles in the armed services were discarded and officers became 'Comrade Commanders'. All people were to address each other by the polite or formal 'you' (*vy*) and its related verb forms instead of the demeaning or intimate *ty* formerly used by 'superiors' to 'inferiors' (in rank, age, gender, occupation, social prominence, or power). The most powerful Bolshevik Commissars (a generic name for officials) were to speak to cleaning ladies (who continued to exist!) as Comrade So-and-so.[15]

Ball gowns and officers' epaulets joined the imperial emblems and crowns in the symbolic junk-pile of the Revolution. It was even dangerous in some situations to wear spectacles – to say nothing of top-hats, furs, tiaras, or waistcoats – because of the heavy anti-intellectual streak that emerged with levelling. Everyone knew what not to wear and what not to say – but it was not clear what one *should* wear as a badge of radicalism or proletarian sensibility. By 1917 in Europe, trousers were trousers and there was thus no discarding of breeches and no parading of *sansculottes* as such. Workers and peasants needed no sartorial revolution, and most Bolshevik leaders, including Lenin, dressed in the old bourgeois uniform of three-piece suit and tie – topped with a vestimentary nod to the workers: a proletarian peaked cap. But in the army a visible revolution was enacted: in addition to certain humiliating deferential gestures (such as the salute), epaulets and other distinguishing embellishments of the officer corps were outlawed for a time and a new uniform was designed. Some intellectuals and commissars affected workers' clothes, the peasant blouse, or black leather jackets. In the 1920s, avant-garde artists began planning a new wardrobe of socialist costume – for work, sport, and play – functional and egalitarian and sometimes unisex. The most extreme effort to equalise the dress was the 'Down with Shame' movement which taught and practised nudity as the only sensible form of socialist appearance.[16]

How did the Bolshevik leaders feel about egalitarianism? They favoured it when directed against the 'old classes' and they employed egalitarian rhetoric and symbols everywhere. They saw the Soviet state as a Republic of Equals. But in certain essential matters, they drew the line, as had the leaders of past revolutions. They opposed wage levelling, invoking the Marxist slogan for the socialist period of history: (from each according to his or her ability and to each according to his or her work) thus allowing unequal remuneration for varying quantities and qualities of 'work'. Lenin insisted on meting out high wages to managers, officers, government officials, technicians, specialists of all kinds, artists, and foreign employees, justifying this on the grounds of the Marxist canon and on revolutionary expediency. Yet egalitarian ideals, experiments, and slogans were allowed to float freely in the revolutionary breezes until the 1930s when Stalin introduced an openly harsh attitude toward the very idea of equality and to any critique of hierarchy and privilege.[17]

It is not my purpose here to make sweeping comparisons of vast, complex, and very different revolutions. But the brief outline I have given not only shows certain common features of culture building that are probably found in all great revolutions, but might even serve as a shorthand measure of the psychological depth of a revolution. Many influential leaders and apologists and ideologues, and many followers as well among the masses – though certainly not all the people – made serious, visible, palpable, and audible efforts to remake their consciousness as well as remaking the social or economic system. It may very well be that Crane Brinton's 'little things' are really the big things in a revolutionary process. These 'little things' are the products of mass experiments and popular culture, phenomena replete with emotional content and thus possessing greater explanatory power than does the fate of high culture in a revolution – however important that is in its own right.

Notes

1. For thorough introductions to these matters, see Sheila Fitzpatrick, *Commissar of Enlightenment* (Cambridge, 1970); Roger Pethybridge, *The Social Prelude to Stalinism* (London, 1974); and Peter Kenez, *The Birth of the Propaganda State* (Cambridge, 1985). Many of the themes of this chapter are treated in greater detail, but with less comparative emphasis, in my *Revolutionary Dreams: Utopian Vision and Experimental Life in the Russian Revolution* (New York, 1989).
2. For the major sources, see Richard Stites, 'Iconoclastic Currents in the Russian Revolution', in A. Gleason, *et al.*, (eds.), *Bolshevik Culture: Experiment and Order in the Russian Revolution* (Bloomington, 1985), pp. 1–20.
3. Stanley Idzerda, 'Iconoclasm During the French Revolution.' *American Historical Review*, vol. LX, no. 1 (Oct. 1954); David L. Dowd, *Pageant-Master of the Republic: Jacques-Louis David and the French Revolution* (Lincoln, Nebraska, 1948), P. 40; G.I. Ilina, *Kulturnoe stroitelstvo v Petrograde: Oktyabr 1917–1920 gg.* (Culture Building in Petrograd, October 1917–1920) (Leningrad, 1982); T. Hasegawa, *The February Revolution: Petrograd, 1917* (Seattle, 1981), pp. 212, 224, 248, 299, 303.
4. Idzerda, 'Iconoclasm' for France. For aspects of cultural nihilism in the Russian Revolution, see Anna Lawton (ed.), *Russian Futurists Through their Manifestoes* (Ithaca, 1988); Richard Lorenz, *Proletarische Kulturrevolution in Sowjetrussland, 1917–1921* (Munich, 1969).
5. I.E. Grabar, *Moya Zhizn* (My Life) (Moscow, 1937), pp. 274–6; N. Pomerantsev, 'Revolyutsionnyi narod khranit pamyatniki kultury' (A Revolutionary People Preserves its Monuments of Culture) *Iskusstvo* (Art), no. 5 (1960), 38; Stanley Mellon, 'Alexandre Lenoir: the Museum vs. the Revolution,' *Proceedings of the Conference on Revolutionary Europe* (1979), pp. 75–88; Emmet Kennedy, 'Vandalism and Conservation,' in *The Culture of the French Revolution* (New Haven, 1989).
6. A.M. Selishchev, *Yazyk revolyutsionnoi epokhi* (The Language of the Revolutionary Epoch) (Moscow, 1928), p. 189; L. Uspensky, *Zapiski starogo Peterburzhtsa* (Notes of an Old St. Petersburger) (Leningrad, 1970), pp. 510–11; Yury Lotman and Boris Uspensky, 'Myth-Name-Culture', in Daniel Lucid (ed.), *Soviet Semiotics* (Baltimore, 1977), p. 251.
7. Stites, 'The Origins of Soviet Festival and Ritual Style', in *Symbols of Power*, ed. C. Arvidsson and L.E. Blomqvist (Stockholm, 1987). There is no adequate study of Lunacharsky in any language. Fitzpatrick, *Commissar*, is still the best introduction. For David, see Dowd, *Pageant-Master* and Mona Ozouf, *Festivals of the French Revolution* (Cambridge, Mass., 1987).
8. John Bowlt, 'Russian Sculpture and Lenin's Plan of Monumental Propaganda', in H.A. Millon and L. Nochlin (eds.), *Art and Architecture in the Service of Politics* (Cambridge, Mass., 1978), pp. 182–193, A. Mikhailov, 'Programma monumentalnoi propagandy' (The Programme of Monumental Propaganda) *Iskusstvo*, no. 4 (1968), p. 31–4 and no. 5 (1968), p. 39–42.
9. A.I. Mazaev, *Prazdnik kak sotsialno-khudozhestvennoe yavlenie* (Festival as a Social and Artistic Phenomenon) (Moscow, 1978), pp. 306–42; N.A. Gorchakov, *Istoriya Sovetskogo teatra* (A History of Soviet theatre) (New York, 1956), pp. 77–93, a frankly hostile account. Julien Tierseau's *Les Fêtes et les chansons de la Révolution française* was translated into Russian in 1917.
10. Maurice Aghulon, *Marianne into Battle* (Cambridge, 1979).
11. S. Dreiden, *Muzyka-revolyutsii* (The Music of the Revolution) (Moscow, 1970), pp. 137–44; G.F. Kiselëv and V.A. Lyubisheva, 'V.I. Lenin i rozhdenie

gosudarstvennoi pechati i gerba RSFSR' (Lenin and the Birth of the State Seal and Emblem of the RSFSR), *Istoriya SSSR* (History of the USSR), no. 5 (Sep.-Oct. 1966), p. 21–6.; M. Yu. Lyashchenko, *Rasskazy o Sovetskom gerbe* (Tales about the Soviet Emblem) (Moscow, 1963), pp. 29–40, 82–3.

12. V.V. Veresaev. *Ob obryadakh starykh i novykh* (On Old and New Rituals) (Moscow, 1926), pp. 5–8; V.E. Khazanova (ed.), *Iz istorii Sovetskoi arkhitektury* (From the History of Soviet Architecture), 2 vols. (Moscow, 1963–70), I, pp. 134–43, 150–5, II, p. 7; M. Danilevsky, *Prazdnik obshchestvennogo byta* (Celebrations of Community Life), (Moscow, 1927), pp. 3–13.

13. Hendrik de Man, *The Psychology of Socialism* (London, 1928), pp. 156–64; Ivan Sukhoplyuev, *Oktyabriny* (Octobering) (Kharkov, 1925), pp. 20–30; Selishchev, *Yazyk,* pp. 179–80, 190.

14. Veresaev, *Ob obryadakh*; Khazanova, *Iz istorii*, I, pp. 214–15 (on crematoria); Nina Tumarkin, *Lenin Lives! the Cult of Lenin in the Soviet Union* (Cambridge, Mass., 1983).

15. B. Comrie and G. Stone, *The Russian Language* (Oxford, 1978), pp. 142, 193–7, 173–4, 156; Selishchev, *Yazyk,* pp. 74, 193, 214.

16. Tatyana Strizhenova, *Iz istorii sovetskogo kostyuma* (From the History of Soviet Dress) (Moscow, 1972), pp. 24–6, 81–110; John Bowlt, 'Constructivism and Early Soviet Fashion Design',, in Gleason, *Bolshevik Culture*, pp. 203–19.

17. Mervyn Matthews, *Privilege in the Soviet Union* (London, 1978), pp. 60–90; David Dallin, 'The Return to Inequality', in Robert V. Daniels (ed.), *The Stalin Revolution*, 2nd edn. (Lexington, Mass., 1972).

12

CULTURAL HISTORY AND REVOLUTIONARY THEORY: THE EXAMPLES OF JACQUES BARZUN AND LEON TROTSKY[1]

Terry Brotherstone

What is the relationship between cultural history and a view of culture based on historical materialism – the pre-eminent method of approaching the understanding of the past which has the concept of revolution at its centre? An answer to this would surely assist with two other questions which must have occurred to the reader of this book, as they have, of course, to the readers – and writers – of many other books: what is revolution? and, what is culture? In addition, the elaboration of such an answer would take readers concerned with such matters some way along the road signposted 'Marxism,' which is often today very variously drawn on the intellectual map. Alas, the task would require a whole volume at least.

This essay attempts something much more modest. It takes two statements, one on the nature of cultural history, one on the way in which a revolutionary society should relate to the history of culture; and it tries to examine them in relationship to each other.[2] At the cultural history conference which has generated this book a pragmatic method was successfully employed; papers on apparently very diverse topics were brought together without obligation on the authors to define a methodological or theoretical common ground. I have followed this approach here hoping that the subtitle of this essay will be sufficient to allay any disappointment for those for whom the main title might arouse expectations of a discourse on theories, modernism or post modernism. It is not that I consider it unimportant to grapple with such theories but rather that it seems to me worthwhile to establish some basis from which to approach such a task historically. This chapter therefore outlines some ideas about the history of culture which were propagated as questions of practical concern at two key moments earlier in the twentieth century and asks if, amidst the mass of more recent theorising available today, they remain relevant to defining tasks of cultural history.

The humanist historian and critic, Jacques Barzun, told the American Historical Association in December 1954 that, in the mid-1920s:

> ... cultural history meant little or nothing outside professional circles ... [where] the phrase, taken as a literal translation of the German *Kulturgeschichte,* carried a taint of fraud ... [Most] solid historians feared that a dangerous kind of philosophy lurked behind any professed history of culture. How could it deal with tested and tangible facts? And if did not, it must dabble in ideas and 'forms'; it must talk of the spirit of an age; and it must reduce the past to essences and pursue the *Zeitgeist* by means which, strictly considered, would prove incommunicable.[3]

About the same time as, according to Barzun's retrospective, Western historical orthodoxy viewed culture with such suspicion, Leon Trotsky was telling a Soviet audience:

> Culture is everything that has been created, built, learned, conquered by man in the course of his entire history, in distinction from what nature had given, including the natural history of man himself as a species of animal. The science which studies man as a product of animal evolution is called anthropology. But from the moment that man separated himself from the animal kingdom ... began the creation and the accumulation of culture, that is, of all kinds of knowledge and skill in the struggle with nature and the subjugation of nature.[4]

The first point of interest, from the standpoint of cultural historians considering how and why to study 'culture and revolution', seems to me to lie in how much Trotsky's approach and Barzun's have in common. For both, as will emerge, the study of culture is an important matter, and not just for personal satisfaction. For both it presents definite theoretical problems which must be confronted for that study purposefully to proceed. For neither are these problems insuperable, although they resolve them quite differently. For neither is there some absolute contradiction between 'high' (intellectual, aesthetic) culture and 'low' (popular, socio-anthropological) culture; nor therefore a mutually exclusive choice to be made as to which is the more important to study historically.[5]

When we turn to consider the situations in which Trotsky and Barzun were speaking, the purpose of their respective lectures, and the theoretical foundations on which they were based, it is of course necessary to highlight the difference between the Marxist revolutionary and the humanist historian. We do not need, however, to lose sight of any points of contact.

As to the circumstances, Trotsky's lectures were delivered in conditions dominated by the aftermath of the first of the twentieth century's catastrophic world wars, by jeremiads on the 'decline of the West', and by the problems being confronted by the Bolshevik Revolution. Barzun spoke to American academics at the end of the decade following the Second World War, at a time when hopes for a renewed development of capitalist civilisation had come to rest firmly on the economic strength of the USA; when national liberation movements were striking further blows at the prestige of the West; but when images of communism – and indeed ideas about Marxist theory in general – had become blurred and confused as a consequence of three decades of Stalinism in the Soviet Union.

Their purpose were certainly different. For Trotsky an understanding of the history of human culture – material and spiritual, and the relationship between the two – was a necessary element in the journey forward to communism: 'Mastery of the art of the past is . . . a necessary precondition not only for the creation of new art but also for the building of the new society, for communism needs people with highly developed minds . . .'[6] For Barzun, during his thirty years or so as a historian, the 'maelstrom' of war, the philistinism of the American business ethos, the economic crisis of the West and the rise of the East, has forced 'anyone who thinks at all' to be 'something of a cultural historian':

> He thinks with the notions of cultural force, cultural crisis, cultural trend perpetually in mind. Newspapers and magazines are one mass of cultural 'analysis', and books of every kind . . . make a large place for 'the cultural context' as something far more intimate and compelling than the old economic base, the physical environment, or the still older 'manners and morals'.[7]

On the question of the philosophical underpinnings of the two statements, Trotsky was of course a Marxist, and Marxism, for him, could be a living doctrine only if it were seen as the constantly developing outlook and guiding method of the revolution itself. He warned that the basic elements of Marxism, dialectics and materialism, could not 'be applied to any sphere of knowledge, like an ever-ready master key. Dialectics cannot be imposed upon facts, it has to be deduced from facts, from their nature and development . . .'. Marx's historical writings, Trotsky insisted for example, were constructed through 'painstaking work on a vast mass of material', and 'even his newspaper articles likewise'. Science and art differed as forms of cognition of the world, in that the former seeks to uncover 'a system of laws', the later to present 'a group of images'. But neither could be approached by the genuine Marxist 'with sweeping criticisms or bald commands': 'Learning and application [in science] go hand in hand with critical reworking. We have the method, but there is work enough for generations to do . . .'. And the art of the past can 'enrich us with an artistic knowledge of the world . . . because it is able to give nourishment to our feeling and to educate them. If we were groundlessly to repudiate the art of the past, we should become at once the poorer spiritually'.[8]

Trotsky's views on method have been noted here in part because they are so strikingly different from those which have often been presented as Marxist since the 1930s; but primarily to compare them to Barzun's. For the latter, from his humanist standpoint, was very conscious of the impact of Marxism on the study of history in general, and cultural history in particular.

In the 1920s, Barzun observed, traditions of historical study were limited. The 'political' tradition he dated from the early nineteenth century, whence it had evolved into a more scientific phase, during which E.A. Freeman had designated history 'past politics'. Its adjuncts and supports lay in military and diplomatic history. However:

... a second, newer tradition proclaimed the shallowness of those state-ridden histories and regarded its events as being but the surface manifestations of underlying economic forces. The influence of Karl Marx was at work in this departure from 'standard' history, but he himself had in fact been jolted out of his Hegelian historical philosophy by the writings of the Saint-Simonians and other socialists, as well as by the histories of Sismondi, Guizot, and Louis Blanc; so that he was not the sole cause of the new departure.[9]

In so observing Barzun, in part, simply echoed Marx himself who, in a well-known letter to Joseph Weydemeyer, dated 5 March 1852, wrote:

... no credit is due to me for discovering the existence of classes in modern society or the struggle between them. Long before me bourgeois historians had described the historical development of this class struggle and bourgeois economists the economic anatomy of the classes , ...

But what *was* new in historical method, Marx insisted, was its demonstration

1) that the *existence of classes* is only bound up with *particular historical phases in the development of production*, 2) that the class struggle necessarily leads to the *dictatorship of the proletariat*, [and] 3) that this dictatorship itself only constitutes the transition to the *abolition of all classes* and to a *classless society* , , , .[10]

And it was this 'aspect' of historical materialism that lay at the centre of the theory and practice for which Trotsky saw himself as fighting when he spoke about culture in the mid-1920s. Barzun, the professional historian concerned for the future of Western culture in the period of the Cold War and the immediate aftermath of Stalin's death, had a very different conception of Marxism. It was, he had argued, elsewhere, merely one of several powerful nineteenth century 'faiths. . . . [which] disregarded the pluralism of the world of experience, or called it chaos so that some order – imposed, not fitted – could make all things fixed and convenient forever after'.[11] He recognised its significance but passed on, evidently assuming that there was no need, for his purposes, to engage in a serious confrontation with it.
    Barzun went on:

It had taken a century for the acknowledged economic element in human affairs to generate a specialised form of research and writing. We can judge of its unfamiliarity to American readers when we remember the hostile reception given Beard's *An Economic Interpretation of the Constitution* in 1913.[12]

In his view, however, 'the economic interpretation' which 'made earlier histories seem narrow', had, within a generation, been vitiated by what he described as 'the post-depression cult of "Marxist Science"'. However he felt that the episode left 'a valuable residue of economic studies free from doctrine'. A comparable view of the relationship between Marxism and economic history may be inferred from Sir John Clapham's inaugural lecture at Cambridge in 1929. 'Marxism', said Clapham, 'by attraction and repulsion has done more to make men think about economic history and inquire into it than any other teaching – especially in Germany, Italy and Russia'.[13]

If Barzun saw no need to differentiate between the 'Marxist Science' of the Stalin era and any other species of Marxism, the distinction did impress itself unobtrusively – and in a manner particularly relevant to the present chapter – on another historian writing not so long before Barzun's lecture. G.P. Gooch – an English liberal (not of course quite the same thing as a Franco–American one) – in an addendum to the second edition of his *History and Historians in the Nineteenth Century* (first published 1913), remarked that 'In Russia the Marxist blight has paralysed disinterested research . . . [but that] Trotsky's *History of the Russian Revolution* is a Marxist classic . . .'.[14]

Returning to Barzun's analytical recollections, the First World War, he suggested, led many writers to the belief 'that such catastrophes, were the work of bankers, cartels, and munition makers'. Serious historians were influenced by the idea that 'men and nations were "pawns" in perpetual struggle of "interests". Imperialism, which so regularly brought about wars, was the product of that same capitalist greed to which every other movement in society was but a "cloak"'. This tendency temporarily enhanced the prestige of Marxism, but in a manner which also undermined Marxism (as Barzun understood it) even before its degeneration into the 'cult'. During the war many Americans discovered Europe and some returned there in the 1920s, finding in Marxism a basis from which 'through novels or plays' to satirise their native land. But, in doing so 'they consciously or unconsciously denied the first premise of economic causation: the capitalist systems of Europe and America might be identical in form and purpose, the two cultures *felt* different'.

Returning home during the depression years, many of the American literati were driven into Marxist discussion circles. Their central concern tended to be with ideology. Barzun recognised this as a Marxist question, but held nonetheless that this emphasis told against what he regarded as historical materialism. The influence both of foreign culture and a Marxism concerned primarily with ideology, he held, tended to lead the mind 'away from the tangible elements of society expressible in laws, battles, statistics, and toward the imponderable influence of habits, assumptions and beliefs'.
The possibility of studying the latter, and thereby developing cultural history, was progressively enhanced by the assimilation of the new disciplines of the twentieth century such as 'the cultural anthropology of Franz Boas, the sociology of Durkheim, and the psychiatry of Freud'.[15]

At this point Barzun's argument became, on my reading, a little obscure. But he seems to have been saying that these tools provided the means by which the 'civilised goals' of 'leisure for sensation and the fine arts' could be intellectually justified by those who were revolted by 'practical and business life' and its ideological reflections, on the one hand, and alienated by the forms of Marxism they had encountered on the other. The dynamic for this type of study came from the sense that civilisation itself was in crisis:

Spengler's *Decline of the West* appeared in 1918 and inspired critics and imitators
. . . Thoughtful readers were taken back to earlier prophets of doom or decay . . .
and without abandoning their interest in the local and contemporary, came to feel
that mere events, however great or striking, were trivial compared with the rise
and fall of great cultures.[16]

For Barzun, then, the context within which modern cultural history
developed was specifically connected with a perceived crisis of civilisation, and with a rejection of the Marxist method of confronting that crisis,
theoretically and in practice. Professional historians, however, had still to deal
with the problems which had made their predecessors of the 1920s suspicious.
The 'chief obstacles' for the cultural historian were 'the indefiniteness of
"ideas" when considered as historical agents and the apparent remoteness of
the arts from mainstream of history'.

Yet there could be no cultural history which did not 'embrace art and
thought', 'without them, we might as well content ourselves with politico-
economic history, seasoned with a dash of "social history" whenever some
powerful movement of feeling disturbs familiar customs'.[17]

The remainder of Barzun's lecture, which was in part intellectual autobiography, in part general analysis, concerned the evolution of cultural
history and the further definition of its proper business. Scepticism as to
its worth, he thought, had been overcome not so much theoretically, more
by a practical 'combination of boldness with intelligent trial-and-error'. The
interdisciplinary instinct to explore 'the possibility of uniting some parts at
least of philosophy, history and the arts in an intelligible account of our past
as thinking beings', was central. In part this involved a return to the ideal
of imparting knowledge of 'the elements of *general literature and universal
history*', an ideal lost sight of 'when men gave up omnicompetence for
specialization'. Cultural history was a way to fulfil the pragmatic ideal
of giving humanistic integrity even to the most technical departments of
specialised knowledge. It would heed the warnings of philosophers who had
long before seen 'the danger of atomized knowledge', without subordinating
the empirical standards, by virtue of which history now claimed 'the status of
science', to the 'sponsorship of philosophy'. Cultural history, it was implied,
would play its part in educating a humane elite (Barzun might have said
humane citizenry) which would be philosophically literate yet secure against
the overarching epistemological ambitions or positivistic false-certainties to
which post-Enlightenment philosophy had given rise.[18]

It remains to see what, so far as the practice of research is concerned,
Barzun meant by cultural history, and, in counterpoint, to summarise
Trotsky's conception of the importance of the history of culture.

Barzun's working definition of the cultural historian was that he or she
should:

> . . . Steer a middle course between total description (which is possible only to the
> anthropologist working on a limited tribal culture) and circumscribed narrative
> (which is the task of the specialist in the institutionalized products of culture:
> poetry or metaphysics or old silver) . . . [The] cultural historian selects his
> material not by fixed rule but by the *esprit de finesse* that Pascal speaks of,

the gift, namely, of seeing a quantity of fine points in a given relation without ever being able to demonstrate it. The historian . . . can only show, not prove; persuade, not convince; and the cultural historian more than any other occupies that characteristic position.[19]

Cultural history was an activity to be justified by results.

Yet it need not be apologetic, it need not be any vaguer than any other sort of history. The continuities in human culture were sufficient for the scholar capable of recognising the essentials of the culture of his or her own time, with proper historical training and imagination, to describe that of the past. Nor was the charge of elitism relevant, since the work of artists and philosophers, however remote it might be from the life of the masses, drew on and embraced, however abstractly, the experiences of the society in which it was carried out:

> The example of a work such as Hegel's *Philosophy of History* shows how unimportant can be the gap between rarefied thought and its raw material – in this instance the philosopher's difficult vision encompassing the dumb travail of Europe's millions during the Napoleonic Wars. It is the same miracle which in Goya's drawings of the same period turns the casual disasters of war . . . into spiritual treasure. The unrecordable comes to exist for history through a cultural product of the most deliberate and elevated kind.

In its examination of the 'reciprocal dependence of the articulate and the inarticulate in life', cultural history separated itself from 'intellectual history or the history of ideas narrowly defined'. The latter activities, on the other hand, had to pay attention to the logical or aesthetic merits of a philosophy or a work of art, and to making as exact as possible their categories and definitions:

> . . . the outstanding characteristics of history as of life is indefiniteness; which is why, again, the *esprit de finesse* is required to grasp it . . . . [The historian should seek to] make an apparently hopeless confusion graspable . . . but the moment the picture begins to look like a checkerboard, he had overshot the mark . . .[20]

A number of reasons seem to me to justify quoting Barzun at some length. The first is how contemporary his lecture of 1954 sounds. I am neither qualified, not would I wish, to play down the extent to which the theoretical work germane to cultural history of the last thirty years has inspired particular contributions in this field, added to the general grasp of its overall importance, or helped to provide critical criteria to put dialogue between culture historians on a surer basis. But, unless the essays in this book have been greatly altered since their delivery as conference papers, Barzun's account of the basis on which cultural historians do what they do seems still reasonably accurate. Most of the authors would, I think, take it as a compliment to be regarded as having triumphed in a display of *esprit de finesse*.

Secondly, unlike some, more fashionable, commentators on method – or at least those who take up their ideas – Barzun was concerned to trace the evolution of the *concept* of cultural history. It is this quality, alongside that of seeking to justify the concept in terms of the needs of contemporary society (and not merely its benefits to academic research as such) that makes possible a comparison with Marxism, and, in particular, with the way Trotsky confronted the problem of culture. Barzun's short history of cultural history, in part admittedly for personal reasons, took off, as we saw, in the 1920s, at about the same time as Trotsky, from the point of view of the practical revolutionary, was urging his audience to study culture and its evolution. Barzun sought to justify cultural history from the angle of its capacity to enrich the present by explaining the past in a way that avoided the narrowness of traditional history, the dogma of what he called 'Marxist Science', and the indefinable realms of the *Zeitgeist*. For Trotsky, the theory and methodology with which to overcome narrowness, dogma and misplaced speculation were already to hand in the concepts of historical materialism, dialectically understood and empirically explored.

A brief counterfactual exercise may be useful here. If we may permit Trotsky to survive not only the efforts of the assassin sent by Stalin, but also Stalin himself, one might imagine him responding to Barzun along the following lines. We Marxists appreciate your humane goals. But to achieve them we see the necessity to address ourselves to the specific task of this historical epoch, which you do not really confront. Given the horrors of the 1930s and 1940s, this is intellectually understandable, but still not permissible. If what you call the inarticulate mass is indeed in 'reciprocal dependence' with 'elevated' and 'deliberate' cultural products, how, in 'the age of the masses', are the masses to become the articulate possessors of what is therefore their cultural inheritance? Is this to be the act of the masses themselves, guided by a theory which includes humanism, but which, given the social and scientific developments since humanism came on the scene of history, must also supersede it? Or is it to be done for the masses, by the sort of enlightened elite you seek to train in your universities, dependent as they are on the continued prosperity and tolerance of that same capitalist system which, as you acknowledged, many in the 1920s identified as the very source of the inhumanities to which your 'cultural history', in its own scholarly way, is clearly opposed?

Of course that question cannot be answered in this essay, and some may object even to its being posed in such a context. It may be argued that it is what did happen that counts in historical discourse, and that the facts of Soviet history under Stalin disqualify Trotsky's views on culture because they did not influence policies or the mainstream of events. They were, as one might say, proposed for E.H. Carr's famous 'select club' of historical facts, maybe even seconded: but they were blackballed by Stalin and Zhdanov.[21] It may also be objected that the capitalism which Barzun assumed to be compatible with the forward march of humane learning and teaching in the 1950s, was fundamentally different from that of the 1920s and 1930s.

But, in cultural terms at least, this latter objection had less force today than in the 1950s and 1960s when the very word 'capitalism' appeared to have been mothballed by orthodox theorists. Now, not only are the systems' virtues once again militantly proclaimed in some quarters, but its capacity to sponsor humane learning – at least in the forms established in Britain in the quarter century after the Second World War – are being called in question by political decisions about the allocation of resources. At the conference on which this book is based this was exemplified in a small way by the fact that one of the liveliest sessions was a discussion on the 'crisis in the humanities' in the British universities. Of course this phrase has been used before, but never perhaps with the same sense that the potentially democratic role of humane education as it was widely perceived by the post-Second World War generation is being called in question. If the existence of this crisis is set beside the possibility of reconstructing a serious discourse on the history of Marxism which is being opened up by events since the mid-1980s in the Soviet Union – and more recently in China – the potentiality for a re-examination of the real relationship between Marxism and liberal humanism, free of residual Cold War prejudices, must surely be apparent.

Barzun, while he disclaimed for cultural history the philosophical function of deciding on the merits of a particular idea, clearly felt that *esprit de finesse* could sometimes lead one to consider the importance of ideas which did not, in their own times, succeed in making history, or at least in guiding its mainstream. He said that by

> tracing an idea to its source . . . we . . . see it at work, meeting a problem . . ., misunderstood, struggling for life like a newborn infant – not as we shall see it later, washed and dressed up for the photographer . . . [We see the thinker and the idea] *in history* [which is] pragmatically moving toward an unknown future, instead of as an event already classified – pioneer, or a sad case, or an imperfect product of [the] time . . .[22]

The orthodox historian, always, despite disclaimers, a prey to the magisterial authority of hindsight, will usually see Trotsky's fight in the 1920s for the revolution to assimilate the gains of past culture, not to reject them as, at best, a 'sad case'. For the cultural historian, seeking Barzun's substitute for the *Zeitgeist*, Trotsky's remarks on literature and art, and on culture in its widest sense, may lead to a much more profound grasp of the spirit of those times and their meaning for today. If I have understood Barzun, even if he might not find my particular example congenial, he was saying that the fact that there was a struggle for ideas that did not win at the time and that those ideas in some form thereby entered the record from which the historian of the future could rescue them, opens up the possibility of finding something *for us*, for the cultural historians today, in a rounded understanding of the past which has been denied to us by the orthodoxies of the victors.

I lapsed into the use of the term 'spirit of the times' as though, in its Anglo-Saxon down-to-earthness it might lack the Germanic dangers of *Zeitgeist*. It was a deliberate slip, because Barzun's argument, I think, left the door open for such a mental trick, although he is too subtle a thinker to have made use of it. We cannot, he again insisted 'believe in a *Zeitgeist* invisibly at work like Ariel on Prospero's isle'.[23] Yet cultural historians must find ways of describing particular cultural periods, or giving conventional definitions of such periods real meaning. Barzun's answer was the concept of 'style', which was to define the content of a particular time, not merely 'the outward marks of fashion'; and which was to encompass 'the diverse tendencies and warring schools of one age which [the cultural historian] knows belong together', and 'the internal unity of cultural periods that . . . come not from the ideas and forms themselves but from the problems to which these ideas and forms offered answers'.

Understood in this way, style could be said to define a particular period or a particular society's approach not so much to 'formulated problems as to felt difficulties of an emotional kind'. Once again Barzun returned to the problem of the relationship between high culture and the societies in which it is created. A hypothesis about the overall style of a period, said Barzun, 'makes genuine at last the connection between style in cultural products and the oft-invoked 'existing conditions' . . . [which] ceases to be vague and begins to yield to analysis only when we see them as nameable facts arousing the emotions reflected in style'.[24]

Barzun ended with two caveats. Cultural historians, while they would clearly be working with evidence going beyond words, would still very substantially be using written sources. The closest attention to the meaning of words in their particular cultural context was essential. Nor should they neglect 'the radically unlike which co-exists with the dominant forms, though submerged by them or subdued'. 'Every period has minority interests, which the discerning eye must note even when the minority does not enlarge into the majority of the next generation'.[25]

Here Barzun seemed close in his exposition to including a theory of, or at least a way of approaching, conflict as the mechanism of transition from one period to another; but he quickly shied away, declaring that the purpose of such discernment was to be able 'to say what the dissonant note contributed to the harmony, how it came to be part of it, and what fresh, unexpected general problem its resolution would imply'.

Flirting perilously once again with the *Zeitgeist*, Barzun more clearly than before showed his own way out of the problem: professional objectives informed by the special qualities of imagination and sensitivity – the *esprit de finesse* – of the talented professional. The questions raised in the 1920s could never be decisively answered theoretically; only continually dealt with through the practice of humane research and teaching. The cultural historian 'will be able to answer them only by the application of such finesse as he is gifted with. Intelligibility being his goal, he cannot escape the effort to understand; he cannot ask somebody else to explain nor shut his eyes and count'.[26]

If Barzun is not much referred to by practising cultural historians today, it is perhaps because in the last analysis his lecture on their subject offered a philosophical rather than a methodological approach to it. He sought to inspire faith in cultural history as indispensable to a humane society, rather than to provide guidelines as to how it should be practised. His criteria for evaluating the worth of the subject were subjective in that their final court of appeal was the individual judgment of the talented practitioner; and his criteria were social in the sense that he advocated cultural history as a humanising educational discipline. They did not involve rules or especially sophisticated methodological guidelines internal to the discipline itself. Trotsky's comments on culture are also relatively neglected, although some historians of art and literary critics pay attention to them.[27] This may seem less surprising than in the case of Barzun, since no one would expect Trotsky's criteria or purpose to be identical with those of the cultural historian as such. Moreover, there can be no complete appreciation of, or argument about, Trotsky's ideas on culture, which does not set them in the context of a discussion of his philosophy as a whole and his role in the making of, and the struggle to preserve what he saw as the principles of, the October Revolution. This clearly poses practical problems for academic discourse. In the specific context of cultural history, however, and of the comparison with Barzun, it is important to see how Trotsky, having urged the importance of grasping the cultural gains of the past, dealt with – or, rather, did not have to deal with – the problem of the *Zeitgeist*.

Looking first at culture in its material form, Trotsky observed that this was 'the tools, machinery, buildings, monuments, and so on', which created 'on the basis provided by nature, the fundamental setting of our lives . . . our creative work'. But the most important thing about this aspect of culture was 'its deposit in the consciousness of man himself – those methods, habits, skills, acquired abilities of ours which have developed out of the whole pre-existing material culture and which . . . also improve upon it'.[28]

But if culture had grown out of the human struggle for existence and improvement, so also had 'a complex organisation of classes'. It was a basic precept of historical materialism that the 'class structure of society had determined to a decisive degree the content and form of human history'. Therefore, argued Trotsky, culture historically itself 'possessed a class character'. And since society in history 'has been an organisation for the exploitation of man by man', clearly culture had 'served the class organisation of society'. Here was 'a profound contradiction':

> Everything that has been conquered, created, built by man's efforts and which serves to enhance man's power is culture. But since it is not a matter of individual man but of social man, since culture is a social-historical phenomenon in its very essence, and since historical society has been and continues to be class society, culture is found to be the basis instrument of class oppression. Marx said: 'The ruling ideas of an epoch are essentially the ideas of the ruling class of that epoch'.[29] This also applies to culture as a whole. And yet we say to the working class: master all the culture of the past, otherwise you will not build socialism. How is this to be understood?[30]

The answer, stated Trotsky, was that the level of development of technique and of the productive forces in general was more fundamental than the class organisation to which it gave rise. Technique, is not *only* 'an instrument of class oppression'. It is also 'the fundamental conquest of mankind':

> The machine [today] strangles the wage slave in its grip. But he can free himself only through the machine. Therein is the root of the entire question . . . the problem that needs to master the sum total of knowledge and skill worked out by humanity in the course of its history, in order to raise itself up and rebuild life on principles of solidarity . . .[31]

As to 'spiritual culture' the same basic principles applied:

Spiritual culture is as contradictory as material culture. And just as from the arsenals and storehouses of material culture we take and put into circulation not bows and arrows, not stone tools or the tools of the Bronze Age, but the most improved tools available, of the most up-to-date technique, in this way also must we approach spiritual culture as well . . .

   Art is one of the ways in which man finds his bearings in the world; in this sense the heritage of art is not distinguished from the heritage of science and technique – and it is no less contradictory than they.[32]

There could be no question for Trotsky of a one-sided rejection of the art of the past because it had been the preserve of, and helped to provide ideological sustenance for the ruling class.

Nor should art be seen purely as spiritual inspiration. Here Trotsky turned to something which sounded very like 'cultural history', understood from the standpoint of the proletarian revolution:

The significance of art as a means of cognition – including for the mass of the people, and in particular for them – is not at all less than its 'sentimental' significance. The ancient epic, the fable, the song, the traditional saying, the folk rhyme provide knowledge in graphic form, they throw light on the past, they generalize experience, they widen the horizon, and only in connection with them and thanks to this connection is it possible to 'tune in'. This applies to all literature generally, not only to epic poetry but to lyric poetry as well. It applies to painting and to sculpture. The only exception, to a certain degree, is music . . .[33]

Trotsky then turned to another important concern of cultural historians – one to which, in a slightly different way, Barzun was also to allude: language. Because culture is a social phenomenon, said Trotsky:

. . . language, as the organ of intercourse between men, is its most important instrument. The culture of language itself is the most important condition for the growth of all branches of culture, especially science and art. Just as technique is not satisfied with the old measuring apparatus but is creating new ones, micrometers, voltameters, and so on, striving for and attaining ever greater accuracy, so in the matter of language, of skill in choosing the appropriate words and combining them in the appropriate ways, constant, systematic, painstaking work is necessary in order to achieve the highest degree of accuracy, clarity and vividness. The foundation for this work must be the fight against illiteracy, semi-literacy and near-illiteracy. The next stage of this work is the mastering of Russian classical literature.[34]

Not so many years later, Barzun – in the context where basic illiteracy was not a problem – was to be promoting a humanist educational programme based on mastering the great works of Western literature.[35]

In the rest of his lecture Trotsky went on to deal with the specific contradictions of Soviet culture arising from the occurrence of social revolution not in the most advanced capitalist countries but 'at the point where the capitalist West and the colonial-peasant East meet'. This is not perhaps directly relevant to the immediate concerns of this essay. Lest the impression be left, however, that in adumbrating the humane goals of the revolution Trotsky was some sort of utopian dreamer, his views on priorities must be quoted:

Having accomplished the proletarian revolution we say: the development of the social forms is pressing against the development of the productive forces, that is technique. The big link by seizing which we can carry through the cultural revolution is the link of industrialization, and not literature or philosophy at all. I hope that these words will not be understood in the sense of an unfriendly or disrespectful attitude to philosophy and poetry. Without generalizing thought and without art, man's life would be bare and beggarly. But that is just what the life of millions of people is to an enormous extent at the present time. The cultural revolution must consist in opening up to them the possibility or real access to culture and not only to its wretched fag ends. But this is impossible without creating very big material preconditions. That is why a machine which automatically manufactures bottles is at the present time a first-rate factor in the cultural revolution, while a heroic poem is only a tenth-rate factor.[36]

Or, put more sharply, it 'is good when poets sing of the revolution and the proletariat, but a powerful turbine sings even better'. It should not be inferred from this that 'mediocre verses hinder the appearance of turbines', only that

... an understanding of the real relationship between phenomena, the how and why of things, is absolutely necessary ... It is a question of changing the conditions of life, the methods of work and the everyday habits of a great nation, of a whole family of nations ... [Tractors, machinery, turbines, aeroplanes, and so forth:] only all these things together will ensure the cultural revolution, not for a minority but for all ... Only on that basis will a new philosophy and a new art come to flower.[37]

Trotsky in 1926 and Barzun in 1954 confronted, of course, quite different situations. The former was a social revolutionary in an economically backward country, for whom the interconnection between material and spiritual culture presented itself as a real, practical problem; the latter was a professional intellectual in the most advanced capitalist nation, for whom the issue of the deprived masses in the USA, who would not be touched by his cultural programmes, was not an immediate practical concern. Each, I am however arguing, engaged with vital questions concerning interconnection and purpose which need to be confronted again today if the current wave of interest in cultural history is to contribute to the qualitative task of advancing meaningful understanding of the past, on a philosophically coherent basis. The evidence that today's cultural historians can provide the history-reading public with more information about unconventional things in excitingly new ways is strong indeed. Allusion to the work of a scholar such as Simon Schama[38] – demonstrating as it does a fair share of *esprit de finesse* – is sufficient to make the point. Cultural history from this point of view may perhaps be seen as a continuation of, and an addition to, the work that the *Annales* school of historians has been doing since the 1920s.

But the unearthing of new facts about the past, and their ever more ingenious and elegant arrangement into stimulating patterns, do not necessarily take forward the great enterprise of showing how consciousness of history

– in the sense of what is known about the past – plays a crucial role in determining how men and women today fight to make their own history. Many will continue to write brilliant 'cultural history' without addressing this problem, or even believing it to be a real problem at all. Yet men and women will continue to struggle for a just and rational social future and to invoke history, and try to learn from the past, as they do so – whether professional historians like it or not. Cultural history, with its aspiration to break free of fixed categories, hackneyed questions and stifling disciplinary boundaries, could be an arena on which the theoretical issues arising from this contradiction might be more clearly identified and fought out, without speculation being allowed to break free from the empirical base which historical scholarship uniquely provides. If this aspect of cultural history is to be coherently developed, I would contend, attention to the sort of issues raised both by Jacques Barzun in the 1950s (and indeed throughout his scholarly career) *and* by Leon Trotsky in the 1920s (and throughout his revolutionary career) will be prominently on its agenda.

Notes

1. This little essay is an elaboration of one aspect of the talk I gave at the conference 'Culture and Revolution', which I attended out of an interest in discovering in what essential ways 'cultural history' differs from other sorts of history. Starting from the assumption that such differences must lie not only in the nature of the phenomena the cultural historian studies, but also in the way that she/he studies them, I hoped to raise some questions about certain interconnections which seemed relevant to a discussion on 'culture and revolution' taking place in a Scottish university which has pioneered the study of 'cultural history', at any rate as an undergraduate programme, in the United Kingdom. The principal connections I had in mind were, methodologically, that between cultural history and historical materialism; and, in terms of content, that between the revolutionary socialist – or Marxist – tradition in the Scottish labour movement and what has been called (by, amongst others, the noted philosopher-historian George Elder Davie) 'the culture-crisis of modern Scotland'. My project was too ambitious for a short conference-session, although Professor Stites – more, I suspect, out of personal relief than intellectual objectivity – remarked that it performed the function of bridging the gap between the Jacobite rebellions and the Russian Revolutions, something he had not seen how to do easily in a single day! Other aspects of the project I was adumbrating at the conference have now begun to be developed in my essays 'Internationalism in the Twentieth Century: comments on John Maclean', and 'In lieu of a conclusion', in T. Brotherstone (ed.), *Covenant, Charter and Party: traditions of revolt and protest in modern Scotland* (Aberdeen, 1989); and 'Proletarian Revolution and Culture: aspects of the intellectual impact of the Russian Revolution in Scotland', forthcoming in the proceedings of the conference 'Turning Points in History' held under the auspices of the International Society for the Study of European Ideas in Amsterdam, September 1988. See also my review article, 'The Poetry and Politics of the Scottish Question', *Workers Press*, 26 Nov. 1988, p. 7.
2. The two statements are (i) an essay by Leon Trotsky, published under the title 'Culture and Socialism', which was based on a number of lectures delivered in

the mid-1920s, particularly one at a Moscow club on 3 Feb. 1926; and (ii) an
article by Jacques Barzun, 'Cultural History as a Synthesis', the substance of
which was given as a lecture to the European History Section of the American
Historical Association on 29 Dec. 1954. Trotsky's essay was first published
in *Krasnaya Nov*, 6 (1926), and reprinted in *Novy Mir*, 1 (1927) and in
L. Trotsky, *Sochinenya* (Moscow, 1925–27), XXI. It was first translated into
English by Brian Pearce and appeared in *Labour Review*, VII (3) (Autumn
1962), pp. 101–13. The extracts used here all appear in *Leon Trotsky on Literature and Art*, ed. Paul N. Siegel (2nd edn., New York, 1972), pp. 83–91, which is
hereafter cited simply as 'Trotsky'. Barzun's article appears in Fritz Stern (ed.),
The Varieties of History from Voltaire to the Present (2nd edn., London and
Basingstoke, 1970), pp. 287–403, hereafter cited as 'Barzun.'

3. Barzun, p. 388.
4. Trotsky, pp. 83–4.
5. Contrast the perhaps more common view of the working cultural historian to-
    day as expressed by, for example, Jeffrey Richards:

    > Cultural history today is one of the most complex and demanding branches of
    > historical endeavour. For it requires . . . not just . . . the training and tools of
    > the historian but also the analytical skills of the expert in literature and art, the
    > methodological equipment of the sociologist and the conceptual equipment of
    > the political theorist. The work of the cultural historian, as Raymond Williams
    > argued in . . . *The Long Revolution* (1975), is to elucidate the meanings and
    > values implicit and explicit in the art, literature, learning, institutions and
    > everyday behaviour within a given society.
    >
    > Broadly speaking there are two cultures: the high or elite culture and the
    > popular or mass culture. Only in rare instances do the two cultures converge
    > . . . For the most part [they] are out of synchronisation and sealed off. For the
    > historian concerned with the real spirit of an age, the collective *mentalité*, the
    > popular culture is of the greatest value; the high culture often misleads . . .

    J. Richards, 'What is the history of popular culture?' in Juliet Gardiner (ed.),
    What Is (History Today . . .? (London, 1988), p. 126.) Convincing, comprehen-
    sive and practical though these formulations sound, they leave untouched the
    sort of questions which, it seems to me, both Trotsky and Barzun – in their
    different ways – grapple with. How do we define 'the real spirit of an age'? And
    how do men and women create the spirit of an age not only as commentators
    but as active participants in the contradictory, collective practice of making
    their own history under definite circumstances? It is interesting that one piece
    of equipment Richards does not list as essential for his sort of cultural historian
    is a knowledge of the history of philosophy.

6. Trotsky, pp. 86–7.
7. Barzun, p. 390.
8. Trotsky, pp. 86–7. For a recent exposition of Trotsky's approach to cultural
    problems in the 1920s – based particularly on his *Literature and Revolution*
    (first published, Moscow, 1923; English translation, 1957; currently available
    edition, Ann Arbor, 1960) – which stresses the connection between Marxist
    cultural criticism and 'real' history, see Cliff Slaughter, *Marxism, Ideology
    and Literature* (London and Basingstoke, 1980), esp. pp. 86–113. Slaughter
    sees Trotsky's writings on cultural question in the 1920s as:

    > concerned primarily to lay the basis for a Marxist response to the cultural
    > problems raised by the Russian Revolution, and in particular to answer those

who advocated a programme of 'proletarian culture.' Here, in the turmoil of unprecedented social change, Marxist theory and practice were put to the decisive test. Unless 'Marxists' in the field of literature and literary criticism see Marxism as an abstract, general doctrine, developing independently of history and purely through scholarly research and speculation, they surely cannot separate themselves and their woork from the development of Marxism itself . . . . From the standpoint of Marxist theory, it is surely unlikely that there could be any rediscovery and development of Marxism against the Stalinist distortions, independently of the actual struggle which Marxists (and particularly Trotsky) carried out against Stalinism, including the proletarian culture myth which accompanied its early development . . . (ibid., pp. 86–7.)

9. Barzun, pp. 388. Edward A. Freeman (1823–92) succeeded Stubbs as Regius Professor of Modern History at Oxford in 1884. James Bryce said of him that he 'regarded history as almost exclusively a record of political events. He was not interested in religion, philosophy or social conditions, and thought it strange anyone should be'. (G.P. Gooch, *History and Historians in the Nineteenth Century* (2nd edn., London, 1952), p. 328.) This still useful book also gives sketches of the historical work of Sismondi (1773–1842), Guizot (1787–1874), and Blanc (1811–82) at pp. 159–62, 178–84, and 216 18 respectively. There are more modern assessments of these and other figures referred to here in *The Blackwell Dictionary of Historians*, ed. John Cannon, (Oxford, 1988).

10. K. Marx and F. Engels, *Selected Correspondence* (Moscow, n.d. – based on the Russian edition, 1953), p. 86.

11. J. Barzun, *Darwin, Marx and Wagner: critique of a heritage* (London, 1942), p. 402.

12. Barzun, p. 388. For brief assessments of Charles Beard see Gooch, *History and Historians*, p. xxii, and *The Blackwell Dictionary*, pp. 34–6.

13. J.H. Clapham, 'The Study of Economic History', in N.B. Harte (ed.), *The Study of Economic History: collected inaugural lectures 1893–1970* (London, 1971), pp. 64–5.

14. Gooch, *History and Historians*, pp. xxiv–xxv.

15. Barzun, pp. 388–89. Franz Boas (1858–1942) emigrated from Germany to the USA in 1888 and began the first teaching programme in anthropology there at Clark University in 1892, becoming himself, and through his pupils, a central figure in American anthropology through to the 1950s. Amongst the most important elements in the work of the French sociologist Emile Durkheim (1858–1917) was his stress on the importance of sociology in establishing a new basis for social coherence in the modern world. For brief assessments of these, and other non-historians referred to, see, for example *Thinkers of the Twentieth Century*, ed. Roland Turner (Chicago and London, 1987).

16. Barzun, p. 390. Oswald Spengler (1880–1936): the first volume of his *Decline of the West* in fact appeared in 1917 and was arguably not so much a product of the First World War as such as of what R.A. Pois calls 'that sense of "cultural despair" endemic in pre-First World War bourgeois circles in Germany, and, perhaps to a less extreme extent, in Western Europe in general'. (Turner (ed.), *Thinkers*, p. 725.)

17. Barzun, p. 390.

18. Barzun, pp. 391–92.

19. Barzun, p. 393.

20. Barzun, pp. 397–8.

21. E.H. Carr, *What Is History?* (Harmondsworth, 1964), p. 12. A.A. Zhdanov (1896–1948), an associate of Stalin's, who in the 1940s took the policy of state-directed 'socialist' culture to its absurd and brutal logical conclusion.

22. Barzun, p. 398.

23. Barzun, p. 399.

24. Barzun, pp. 399–400.

25. Barzun, pp. 401–02.

26. Barzun, p. 402.

27. E.g. *Modern Art and Modernism: a critical anthology*, ed. Francis Frascina *et al.* (London, 1982); and works referred to in Slaughter, *Marxism, Ideology and Literature.* For a consideration of Trotsky's relevance to the problems of Scottish culture mentioned above, see Raymond Ross, 'Trotsky among the Scots,' *Cencrastus*, 28 (Winter 1987–88), pp. 27–30.

28. Trotsky, p. 84.

29. K. Marx and F. Engels, *The German Ideology* (written 1845–46), cap. I, section 30, in Marx and Engels, *On Historical Materialism* (Moscow, 1972), p. 44.

30. Trotsky, pp. 84–5.

31. Trotsky, p. 85.

32. Trotsky, p. 86.

33. Trotsky, p. 87.

34. Trotsky, p. 88.

35. Barzun, interestingly, does not feature in Cannon's *Blackwell Dictionary of Historians* (though Trotsky does!). His entry in the 1978 edition of *The Encyclopedia Americana* (vol. III, p. 287) reads:

> American historian, educator, and author. Born in Créteil, France, on Nov. 30, 1907, he moved to the United States [in 1920] and graduated from Columbia University in 1927. That year he was made a lecturer in history at Columbia. He became a United States citizen in 1933. Appointed a professor in 1945, he was dean of the Columbia graduate faculties and provost of the university. At Columbia he helped organize a two-year course of reading and discussion of great books to advance his view that undergraduate education should involve a broad study of the liberal arts rather than specialisation. . . . In *The House of Intellect* [1959], his most controversial work, Barzun attacked the American educational system for producing pseudo-intellectuals who are 'captivated by art, overawed by science, and seduced by philanthropy . . .'
>
> For an indication of Barzun's reputation, see *From Parnassus: essays in honour of Jacques Barzun*, ed. Dora B. Weiner and William R. Keylor (London, 1977), esp. pp. xi–xxii and 337–49. A bibliography of Barzun's voluminous writings appears at pp. 353–76. The contribution most relevant to the present essay is Fritz Stern, 'Capitalism and the Cultural Historian', at pp. 209–24.

36. Trotsky, p. 90

37. Trotsky, pp. 90–1.

38. Simon Schama, *Embarrassment of Riches: an interpretation of Dutch culture in its golden age* (New York and London, 1987); *Citizens: a chronicle of the French Revolution* (New York and London, 1989).

INDEX